Touching Tibet

Niema Ash

Publisher TravellersEye
Editor Dan Hiscocks

Touching Tibet

2nd Edition

Published by TravellersEye Ltd

October 1999

Head Office:

30 St Mary's Street

Bridgnorth

Shropshire

WV16 4DW

tel: (0044) 1746 766447

fax: (0044) 1746 766665

website: www.travellerseye.com

email: books@travellerseye.com

Set in Times

ISBN: 0953057550

Printed and bound in Great Britain by Creative Print & Design Group.

1st Edition published by Rider, Random Century Group Ltd, 1992

For my daughter Ronit

Acknowledgements

With thanks to Gil Elliot for his valuable suggestions in the early days and for his support throughout; to David Wallenchinsky, Cedric Smith, Ugyan Norbu, Gyurme Dorje, Phuntsog Wangyal and Stephanie Rayner for their help; to the Tibetan specialists, Stephen Bachelor and Glenn H. Mullin for their corrections. Very special thanks to Tim Fowkes and Doune Storey for helping me remember, and for a constant supply of encouragement, and especially to Tim for his patient understanding.

Illustrations by Doune Storey

Contents

The Dalai Lama

Foreword

It has never been easy to visit Tibet, the high mountains and empty plains which surround it have deterred all but the hardiest travellers. In the past, even those who overcame such difficulties were viewed with suspicion by the local people and discouraged from continuing their journeys. Nowadays, despite great improvements in travel facilities, it remains almost impossible to visit Tibet, because the Chinese occupying forces wish to conceal their treatment of the Land and its inhabitants from outside view. As a result Tibet continues to be surprisingly unknown to the world at large, whether in terms of its spectacular landscape, its colourful history or the present plight of its people.

For a brief period travellers were allowed almost unrestricted access and a fortunate few managed to take advantage of it. Niema Ash was one of those and in ***Touching Tibet*** she tells of her adventures. No one can experience better than someone who has felt it themselves. Here the author shares her fervour not only for the awesome terrain with its striking landmarks, but also for the Tibetan people whose warm-hearted human qualities are undiminished by the hardship they have undergone. I hope that readers will enjoy the book as well as learning something about Tibet.

Introduction

Travel for me was never a peripheral leisure activity. It was a driving passion fundamental to my existence. Most of the major events of my life happened on the road.

During puberty my fantasies were not about boys and dating, but about boats, trains and planes. While my friends saved their allowances for party frocks and high heels, I saved mine for that magical ticket to ride. I craved the embrace of exotic lands. The initiation ceremony marking my coming of age was a journey into the world. At fourteen, my friend Rhoda Pomp and I set off for Brooklyn, to visit my pen pal, Horatio Silver. I had never left Montreal before. At the US border we were escorted off the bus by a customs officer who thought we were 'bobby soxers' running away to see Frank Sinatra, a practice in vogue at the time. The bus driver reprieved us. My father had slipped him a $20 bill to keep an eye on us.

We were plunged into the world at Times Square, and spent our first hour awe-struck by its marvels, before deciding to find a subway. There was one problem. We had no idea what a subway was. We asked a benevolent-looking elderly man leaning in a doorway. His eyes chilled with suspicion. 'It's a lousy hole in the ground,' he growled. In vain we searched Times Square for a suitable hole in the ground which would take us to Brooklyn, before a conscientious policeman accompanied us to a subway. The initiation was over.

My adolescence was devoted to dreams of travel abroad and the rigour of dance classes at home. At seventeen I won a summer scholarship to study dance with Martha Graham in New York. Before starting classes, Rhoda Pomp and I hitch-hiked across North America into Mexico. There, through cheekiness and outrageous fabrications, we got to meet one of my favourite artists, Diego Rivera. We had trudged through Mexico City to see one of his famous murals only to discover that the building was closed because the master himself was repairing the mural.

Our bad luck could turn out to be overwhelmingly good. I had to meet him. Having read somewhere that Diego Rivera was a friend of Henry Ford's and had painted a mural for him in Detroit, I wrote a note saying we were friends of Mr Ford's from Detroit, and that Mr Ford had told us so much about this particular mural that we had made a special trip to see it. We dispatched the note with a reluctant guard who was loath to disturb the master. Meanwhile a small crowd had gathered and we waited nervously, dreading imminent public humiliation. However, instead of exposing us as frauds, Diego Rivera stopped the crew working on the mural, and invited us in to chat.

I remember asking him how an arch-capitalist like Henry Ford got to be friends with a communist like himself. 'It's for insurance,' he shrugged. 'When the revolution comes, he wants to have a friend on our side, in case we win. And in case we lose, it's good to have a friend like Henry Ford on the other side. No? His generous face crumpled with smiles. That was over twenty years ago, before the time when young girls who hitch-hiked alone were asking for trouble. My appetite was whetted.

After the summer my scholarship was extended, and for one brief moment my love of dancing and my passion for travel conflicted. But there was no real contest. Just before my eighteenth birthday I sailed on the *Ile de France* for Europe, with money saved from waitressing and the sale of my piano, prepared to abandon dance forever. As it turned out this was not necessary - my dancing flourished. On the ship I met Basha who convinced me to go to Israel. We hitch-hiked through France, Belgium and Holland, and I continued to Switzerland and Italy alone, before sailing to Haifa. In Israel anyone with dance training was very much in demand and I was invited to teach at various kibbutzim (collective settlements). My competence grew.

It was on one of these kibbutzim that I met Shimon, a young South African, tall and slender with dark wavy hair and gentle eyes, intelligent and funny. We became friends. We had known each other for only a month when he was taken into the Israeli army. As a soldier he was a disaster, constantly falling ill. Once, when I visited him in hospital, he looked so miserable that I decided to marry him so he could get a week's leave. The day after he left hospital we were married.

Shimon had a rich powerful singing voice. I had a guitar and taught him the chords and strums I knew. It was like introducing him to God; he became a devotee and I never got my guitar back. Soon he was performing for various army units. Then someone discovered that I danced, and the army fashioned us into an entertainment duo. I began doing my own choreography, performing solo pieces, often accompanied by Shimon. We were flown in a small Piper plane to remote parts of Israel and Egypt (then occupied by Israel) with access to places forbidden to Israelis, like the Gulf of Aqaba, where the mountains of Saudi Arabia looked like Disney drawings with pastel-coloured stripes.

Shimon and I stayed married. But all the while my gypsy soul yearned for the road. As soon as he finished we decided to visit his family in South Africa and then make our way to Russia where, for

$50, we could attend an International Youth Festival devoted to music and dance. For me it was the occasion of a lifetime, an opportunity to see famous dance troupes from all over the world. I rejoiced.

We flew to Nairobi with borrowed money, to visit Shimon's sister. From there we began one of the most memorable journeys of my life, hitch-hiking from Kenya to South Africa. I preferred hitch-hiking to any other means of travel. I loved the surprise of not knowing who I would meet or where I would spend the night; each ride a capsule of adventure. But in East Africa there was no choice. Road traffic was virtually non-existent – there were no roads, only dirt tracks riddled with potholes, impassable in the rainy season. Few vehicles other than Landrovers could negotiate them. As hitch-hikers we were treated with great respect, even reverence. The driver's attitude wasn't that he was doing us a favour by giving us a lift, but that we were bestowing an honour upon him by accepting one. We were considered adventurers, in the tradition of Livingstone.

Outside Nairobi the road ceased and we became part of the jungle. We drove through herds of Zebras munching grass, Mount Kilimanjaro towering behind them, interrupted leopards stalking their prey and elephants scratching their backsides. Once we drove right up to a family of giraffe grazing in our path. They wouldn't budge, but merely paused in their meal to observe us. The driver, growing impatient, honked the horn. Startled, they took off at great speed, their bodies arching forward in long low leaps over the grass, while their necks swayed from side to side in small waves, high above. The beauty of that contrasting rhythm and movement remains one of my most treasured African trophies.

The journey was difficult, bumping slowly through areas where the tsetse fly had wiped out human life with its fatal sleeping sickness: we drove through fierce-looking nomadic tribes, seven feet tall, wrapped in blankets and beads, wandering with cows and spears alongside our car, gazing in through the windows with as much wonder as we gazed out. Not surprisingly when we reached the civilisation of Dadoma Tanganyika (now Tanzania), we treated ourselves to the luxury of Hotel Dadoma. Our bedroom had a four-poster bed, silk sheets and mosquito netting; the contrast with all the nights cramped in cars or on the floors of wooden shacks was so intoxicating that I became pregnant.

We travelled through Rhodesia (now Zimbabwe), driving along the grassy banks of the gently meandering Zambezi river, to find the earth suddenly open and the Zambezi hurl itself with a mighty roar, over the edge. These were the Victoria Falls, just as Livingstone had found them, still unmeasured, as their massive force twisted steel cables into pretzels. There were no signposts, nor any safety barriers. Each year, visitors were sucked into the falls, vanishing forever. We were robbed by monkeys who rolled down the car windows and stole our precious food. As we watched helplessly, they leapt into the trees, arms bulging with paper sacks.

By the time we got through the Kalahari Desert and reached South Africa, Shimon was wearing thin. I could have gone on. For me, travelling generated energy. However, it was time to pause; we were low on most things, especially money. The next four months were spent with Shimon's family, earning money and discovering I was pregnant. That news was a devastating blow. Babies were an alien concept. Going to Mars was more of a consideration than having one. But I was forced to stay pregnant, abortion was impossible. In despair, I decided to ignore the whole thing, hoping it would go away. It never did.

Johannesburg had little to recommend it, no natural features like sea or mountains (except for slag heaps), and no human features.

The rest of the world did not exist beyond Johannesburg, only other South Africans went there. It was like an ingrown toenail, pressing in on itself, festering. I soon became fervently anti-apartheid. A few days after our arrival Shimon and I attended a concert. It was for whites only but there was a brilliant black guitarist performing. Shimon, by now a competent guitarist, was eager to exchange guitar techniques. The man was delighted. In their enthusiasm they forgot this was not possible. A black man could not enter a white man's living room socially, nor could a white man enter a black man's shack. Unable to accept these obstacles, I made one suggestion after another. Cafes were either for whites or blacks, none were mixed. The same with parks. They would be arrested if they met on the street. The realisation that there was no place in Johannesburg where these two musicians could legally meet to play music together shocked me into political awareness.

South Africa was a good place to be leaving. We hitch-hiked to Cape Town, about 1000 miles away, to get a boat for Spain. I was invisibly pregnant although in my fifth month. It was June – winter in South Africa. We stopped in the Karroo, a dry desert-like area to visit Shimon's birthplace, a small town of Afrikaner sheep farmers. It was freezing; winds raging through the treeless plains covered us with powdery snow. We wore all the clothes we possessed and looked ridiculous. We slept in empty railway stations, on wooden benches, and once under a bridge with tramps. Finally, we indulged ourselves with a night in a hotel where we were awoken by a black servant in a starched white coat, bearing tea on a silver tray. Shimon's muddy boots were outside the door, polished to mirror perfection by 'the boy'

The ship taking us to Europe was a luxury Cunard liner with every possible comfort. Our first stop was the Canary Islands where we made an impulsive decision to leave the ship, having been told we could easily get another one. We were told wrong. After weeks of waiting we could only get third-class passage, which we had been warned against. The agent who assured us we had nothing to fear, lied. Third class consisted of two dorms in the hold of the ship, one for men, the other for women and children. They were narrow windowless rooms with two tiers of bunk beds so close together we had to shuffle sideways between them. The mattresses were lumpy and crawling with bed bugs. There was no deck. Food was unavailable. Everyone carried baskets smelling of garlic sausage. The smell of garlic, combined with the smell of engine fumes, was nauseating.

To make matters even worse, we ran into a storm the first night at sea. Everyone was sick, babies crying and spurting vomit; undigested garlic sausage splattered on the floors and walls, and me pregnant. Even though I was unable to eat I couldn't stop throwing up, my distended belly clenched in spasms of pain from the violent retching. Shimon searched for a doctor or nurse. He couldn't even find a first-aid kit, or anyone who spoke English. Poor Shimon – he was swollen with bed bug bites, green with seasickness, and terrified I would abort. In despair he sneaked me onto the tiny first class deck where at least I could breathe fresh air instead of the stench below.

At dawn next morning, I was buried in my sleeping bag; feverish, cold, nauseous and utterly miserable, all at the same time. Everything hurt. Even my teeth and gums ached, projecting thin needles of pain into my eye sockets. My head was thick with pain and it was agony to move. I was concentrating on making it through the next breath when loud, energetic male voices exploded in my head – sailors, with brushes, mops and buckets. They surrounded the bundle which had mysteriously materialised on their deck, prodding it with their mops. I forced my head out of the sleeping bag, a grey-faced vision with tangled hair and swollen eyes squinting into the sunlight. 'Por favor... por favor…signors….' I pleaded.

Desperate not to be sent back to the hold, I mimed being about to throw up, with accompanying sound effects. That did it. The sailors withdrew to a safe distance. They wanted no part of me. Each morning, from then on, I could hear them hurriedly swabbing the deck around me, resisting the impulse to see if I was still alive. For almost five days I lay on that deck, writhing in pain, my stomach contracted in a tight fist punching me from within, as the ship pitched and heaved. I thought I was dying and didn't much care. But by some miracle both the baby and I survived.

After a few days of rest in Malaga I was fully recovered and ready for the road. Shimon and I hitch-hiked through Spain where I developed an insatiable longing for Spanish food, and eating bunches of grapes (my one concession to pregnancy). Since we could only afford the occasional restaurant meal, I had no alternative but to learn to cook. I became quite good at it, cooking paella and gazpacho on a small petrol cooker with utensils which folded into each other. Not only did I become a cook in Spain; if we'd had $300 I might have become a millionaire. But that's another story.

We hurried through France, reaching England just in time to go to Russia. But Shimon became difficult. He refused to go. I was entering my eighth month of pregnancy. 'You'll end up having the baby in Russia,' he warned.

'So I'll have the baby in Russia, what's the difference?'

'What's the difference?' he said exasperated. 'The difference is that the baby will be Russian. They won't let it out.'

'Let them keep it. That would solve all our problems.'

Shimon was horrified. (Please Ronit, if you are reading this, I hope you can find it in your heart to forgive me for wanting to give you to the Russians. It was only a measure of my terrible disappointment.) 'It's my baby too, and you're not having it in Russia.' Shimon, normally amenable, was adament. My heart was broken. I was inconsolable, with an overwhelming sense of loss, mourning an experience I could never repeat. But in the end I gave in, defeated by Shimon's paternal instincts.

Having prevented me from giving birth in Russia we now had to find a place to have this baby. Montreal seemed the best choice - at least my parents were there. We arrived in Montreal penniless, the baby only weeks away. I had never been to a doctor nor done the things most expectant mothers do, but luckily I gave birth in three hours to a healthy 6IB 13oz baby girl.

I had left Montreal an adolescent; I returned an adult, with a husband, a baby and a profession. These roles put an end to my travels for the next ten years. I was pinned to Montreal by motherhood, wife-hood and poverty. In the sixties I formed my own dance group; helped Shimon run his folk club, where famous-to-be-musicians, including Bob Dylan, performed; and returned to university. In the seventies Shimon and I separated and I received a grant from the Canadian government to complete a doctorate. My ticket to ride was magically reissued. I packed one suitcase for myself and one for Ronit and we flew to London.

I liked living in London mainly because I could leave it so easily. When Ronit was fifteen we returned to the continent of her conception, hitch-hiking for nine months through North Africa from Casablanca to Tunis, through Algeria, and then deep into the Sahara. This trip was central to Ronit's development and to our relationship. We were alone in an unknown landscape which changed each day. Protecting and caring for each other made us very close. We enjoyed being together and laughed a lot. We also shared responsibilities. Because Ronit's French was better than mine, she made the arrangements with the drivers and decided which rides to accept. We never accepted any with more than one man, or with anyone even slightly off-putting. I trusted her judgement.

Our fortunes oscillated between extremes. One night we ended up in the Royal Palace of Rabat, guests of a Moroccan prince. On another, because we could find nowhere else, in a Constantine jail, sharing a cell with a talented street urchin who stole Ronit's knickers from the knapsack under her head while she slept. Our roles oscillated as well. Sometimes I was her mother, sometimes her sister, we played it by ear. Once we got a ride with a sophisticated Algerian businessman going to the oil fields in the Sahara. At one point he and I were alone and he asked me, with the utmost courtesy, if I cared to spend the night with him.

'I mean no offence,' he explained, 'but I have never been with a Canadian lady, and perhaps it will be of interest for you as well.'

'Whether I wish to or not, I cannot. I am a mother, Ronit is my daughter,' I said in my most formal voice.

'I'm sorry. Forgive me. I thought you were sisters. I meant no offence.'

I forgave him and the matter was ended.

Ronit, having a special talent for languages, learned some Arabic. That talent not only threw open many doors, but saved us spending time behind a closed one when we were almost arrested in Morocco. As often happened, her resourcefulness came to our rescue. Ronit returned to London a young woman with a new confidence. I returned to London determined to take off again. My confinement was over, I was back on the road.

Chapter One

Entering Tibet

Twenty minutes before landing, the clouds part like a heavy grey curtain heralding a drama, to reveal a spectacular scene - the Himalayas. The sky is lit by sunshine, the blue laced with delicate white clouds. The mountains are magnificent: snow-capped summits, creased with purple shadows, glinting with frozen lakes, etched with glaciers. Rugged peaks jut through the clouds, piercing the fragile webbing with a powerful thrust. It's a stunning vision, awesome, grand. Amongst these mountains lies Tibet - inaccessible.

I am totally entranced by the miracle which allows me to float above the Himalayas, delighting in the nuances of colour and texture, when suddenly the small Chinese aircraft dives through the mountains and plummets into a gorge, wrenched from the splendid panorama in the heavens. The mountain walls, hung with ice, loom steeply, tight against the plane, obliterating the sun. The floor far below is a dark desert, with sand rising into strangely sculpted dunes, creating a death valley. The valley curves and the plane leans sharply and swerves around the side of a mountain, like a racing car rounding a bend on two wheels. Hunched against the possibility of wings scrapping against rock, I suck in my breath, cold on my teeth, as we dip through the precipices into a frigid moonscape. Flying at high altitude, the mountains were superb, majestically aloof. Now, deep in their midst, they are desolate and frightening.

The landing is terrifying. It's as though the pilot is on a kamikaze mission. Abruptly we plunge deeper into the mountains. A river with a shoreline of rock appears beneath us. We are falling fast toward the river. There is nowhere to land. I'm glued rigid against the window as we drop lower and lower, sweeping through crevasses with cold blue hearts, skimming over the river, engines screaming. We are so close I can see ripples on the water. It seems certain we will hurl ourselves into the river or smash into the mountains. My body is clenched like a vice, braced for the inevitable, when suddenly, magically, a thin ribbon of runway appears at the base of the mountains. With engines roaring, we glide to a stop. The pilot receives a standing ovation.

We disembark from the modern plane with its reassuring comforts, into the disturbing landscape. A few yards from the plane the runway returns to the sand dunes, as though it never existed. There is no trace of welcome. No airport buildings, nothing to greet us except the bare mountains and several buses squatting in the sand. I take a last look at the shining plane and follow the other passengers into the sand.

Tim, Doune and myself were the only Westerners on the plane, the other passengers were Chinese. We had been travelling together in China for several weeks when we discovered Tibet was suddenly opened to individual travellers. The miracle had happened. We made an instant decision to go, and to go quickly before the Chinese authorities, who control Tibet, changed their minds. There is only one way to get to Lhasa quickly - by air from Chengdu, a town in the province of Sichuan. We took a train to Chengdu, and from there the first available plane to Lhasa, operated by CAAC, the National Chinese Airway.

I had always longed to visit Tibet, a yearning fired by the lure of the unattainable; Tibet was a forbidden kingdom, no foreigner allowed entry. Once, in Nepal, I made a pilgrimage to the border, obsessed with getting even a glimpse of Tibet. That glimpse was the most anyone could hope for. Until the twentieth century so little was known about Tibet that most maps left it blank. The mysteries of the remote mountain kingdom were kept jealously intact. For over a century no foreigner was allowed to enter the city of Lhasa's holy domain. Now I am on my way there. The trauma of the entry suddenly enhances the privilege.

Chinese buses are always packed, and in the desperate struggle to get on board, the usual courtesy shown to foreign guests vanishes. Boarding a bus is the only belligerent activity I have witnessed in China. All aggression is saved for this moment. Now the moment has arrived. The Chinese swing into action in a frenzied outbreak of pushing and shoving, which causes the gentle, soft-spoken Doune to shout, 'Animals! You're behaving like animals!' The Chinese take no notice.

Tim is more convincing. After two months in India, he has refined the skill of 'push and shove' into an art. Tim is a master shover. Being a powerful six foot two helps; his featherweight competitors barely reach his shoulder. Releasing a martial arts scream which stuns the opposition, he claims the entrance and the choice seats. Doune and I recede from the fray and after the others have squeezed on the bus, we enter, like ladies. Everyone is finally seated and the bus about to pull away when Doune begins to look around frantically. 'Where are the bags? They haven't put the bags on the bus.'

'I'm sure they'll meet us in Lhasa.' Tim says reassuringly. 'Nobody else seems worried.'

We have to assume that somehow our baggage will appear in Lhasa. In any case there is no one to consult. The aircraft staff didn't bother leaving the plane. I can't blame them. This isn't exactly an ideal place for 'R & R'.

The Lhasa bus is old and worn, but more comfortable than it looks. We settle into the thinly padded purple seats. I am secretly pleased. Purple is my favourite colour. Almost everything I have with me is a shade of purple. A good omen. It's nine am, a lovely June morning, warm and sunny. We begin to relax. About half a mile from the landing strip we see several wooden huts with a stream of people leaving them, carrying luggage, heading for our plane and Chengdu. Later we learn that they have spent the night there. Anyone leaving Lhasa by plane must spend the night by the runway. We soon discover why. The road from the airport to Lhasa is totally unpredictable, only partially paved, with roadworks in progress and inevitable long waits. With exceptional luck the trip should take about two and half hours, but can easily take seven or eight. Our luck is average and the trip takes five hours on a dusty road strewn with rocks, holes and ditches. The landscape is parched and inhospitable, with a few stark villages set among the barren mountains. There is nothing green. The only colour comes from prayer flags on the roofs of huts, torn bits of rags impaled on twigs. What a bitter place to live.

Bumping along in the hot bus, I muse on my obsession with Tibet. Did it begin years ago when I first saw a picture of the Potala Palace? That image became permanently etched in my imagination, the symbol of my travel dreams. I was not alone - I had never met a traveller whose eyes did not light up at the mention of Tibet. Yet I had never met anyone who had actually been there. I knew nothing about Tibet, its history or culture, and my travel information was limited to a few sentences hastily uttered during a chance encounter. The last day I was in Chengdu, I was lunching alone in the hotel dining room. Several Americans were at the next table and I overheard one of them saying he had just returned from Tibet. I was hungry for information.

'I'd like to help you, but I must run,' he said. 'I have to meet this Swedish chick in the bar,' he added, with a gratuitous wink. However, he did manage to say, 'You can't get permission to go anywhere outside of Lhasa, and Lhasa gets boring after three days, absolutely no nightlife. And, oh yes, don't forget to take surgical masks, it can get very dusty.' (This last bit of advice was to prove invaluable.) Then he mumbled something about the Number One Chinese Guesthouse being the best place to stay. It sounded clean and sterile, without soul, and I decided to avoid it. He started to leave, then suddenly turned back as though he had forgotten something especially important. 'If you want to blow your mind, go to the sky burial.'

'The what?' but he'd already rushed off.

I try to console myself for my ignorance. Perhaps it's an advantage that I know so little about Tibet. I can see it with a freshness untainted by expectations. A lurch jolts me out of my speculations as the bus stops abruptly. Roadworks. We line the roadside and watch the workers smashing rocks with sledgehammers. After more than an hour I grow restless and wander away toward the mountains. In just minutes the road, bus and passengers are swallowed by the landscape. I find myself alone in a valley of twisted rocks - tombstones in an alien cemetery. The silence is like eternity. I creep carefully among the boulders, conscious of their hostility, feeling soft and vulnerable as they graze my skin. I am the only living thing trapped in a soundless universe unchanged since creation.

I shudder as though someone has walked over my grave. Hurriedly, as if pursued by ghosts, I retrace my steps, startled by the voices of the passengers squatting by the roadside. I enter the bus tentative and silent.

As we approach Lhasa we begin to see foliage, meadows, trees, flowers. I drink in the moisture, nourished by the green life. Then, in the distance, I see golden domes shining in the barren hills: the Potala, with its miracle of smooth rounded shapes rising in the blue sky, glowing like a vision. After the harsh mountain peaks tearing at the heavens like broken claws, the domes are a welcoming embrace, a circle of comfort. Then suddenly, the full force of the Potala Palace. As though aware of the impact, the bus slows down.

Brilliantly etched in sunshine, a powerful structure of white, red and gold dominates the mountains. The image is so intense that for a moment my eyes shut tight as though encountering a dazzling light. But as I succumb to the sense of wonder, an unexpected surge of joy sweeps through me. It is more than the excitement of finally seeing something I've imagined for so long. It is an exhilaration, an elation, beyond the scope of reason.

I am not a religious person. I subscribe to no church. I have never been on a spiritual quest. Yet I am aware that I am entering an unexplored spiritual realm. I feel like the Wandering Jew first glimpsing the Wailing Wall, or the Arab pilgrim finally entering Mecca. Instinctively I know that the Tibetans have some special secret to survive the unsparing Himalayas and create from bare rock this Potala Palace. I know too that I will have to experience both extremes to understand that secret, to fathom any of the mysteries of this mythic mountain kingdom. I have no idea how I will do this, but the possibility excites me. Travellers make lucky things happen. I hold the image of the Potala carefully, closing my eyes to preserve it, as the bus moves on into the Forbidden City.

Chapter Two

In Lhasa

I say nothing to Tim and Doune. Not yet. In any case there is no time. Within minutes my spiritual reflections come to an abrupt end. The magic, the mystery vanish as we are unceremoniously ejected outside the CAAC office and plunged into the uninspired ordeal of baggage arrangements.

The CAAC office is a large bare room with people milling about. There are no facilities of any kind. I watch enviously as fellow passengers disappear into waiting arms. No one expects us. Our bags are nowhere in evidence. We search inside and outside for some clue to their whereabouts. 'Perhaps the bags are on one of the other buses,' Doune suggests, always hopeful. We wait until the last bus arrives, the last passenger disappears, but there is still no sign of our bags. Our twenty word vocabulary, as yet at the 'neehow' (hello) stage, gets us nowhere. Finally, Chinese phrase book in hand, I approach a man wearing a tarnished badge, who looks vaguely official. He smiles and I am encouraged. I find the perfect phrase under 'travel by air', sub-section, 'airports'. It reads, 'Where are my bags?' I point enthusiastically to the Chinese version. The man shrugs his shoulders, still smiling. Tim takes the book and thumps his finger in staccato beats under 'Where are my bags?', indicating he means business. The man looks bewildered. Suddenly we realise he is Tibetan and doesn't read Chinese. He has, however, understood that Tim is in earnest, and hurries off obligingly in search of assistance.

He returns with a young efficient-looking Chinese lady. Assisted by the phrase book, I make another attempt. 'Where are my bags?' I point, trying to convey a sense of urgency. She nods with crisp understanding. Thumbing through my book, her eyes light up as she points to a word. Relieved, I peer at the word. It translates as 'tomorrow'.

My face squeezes into a perplexed grimace as I mutter 'tomorrow' to Tim and Doune who are anxiously following the procedure. 'She can't mean "tomorrow",' Doune moans.

'That's exactly what she means.'

'Give it another go,' Doune urges.

I repeat the process from the beginning and again the answer comes up 'tomorrow'.

Conceding defeat, I hand the book to Doune. 'You try, maybe your Chinese is better than mine.'

With infinite patience, perfected by her travels in the East, Doune (assisted by Tim, who is far less patient) begins the tedious process of search-and-point in an attempt to extract more information. The Chinese lady is coolly polite. She's had enough of us by now, and is anxious to end the interview.

I collapse on the floor, suddenly worn out. My psyche has been fragmented like a kaleidoscope, shaken by the day's turmoil of emotions and events; and my body is shattered by the altitude. Lhasa is on a high plateau, 12,000 feet above sea level. The air is extremely thin and, for the newly arrived, exhaustion comes easily.

Finally Doune relays the news. 'Our bags are not here. We have to come back tomorrow to get them,' she sighs.

'I don't believe it,' I say, believing it at once.

She thanks the Chinese lady and the Tibetan man, for whom

the charade has been riveting, even if incomprehensible.

'Thanks for what?' I ask wearily. 'Why didn't anyone tell us? What will we do without our bags? Doesn't it get cold at night? We have nothing to wear. What about toothbrushes? Soap? Look at us, we're covered in dust.' Increasingly forlorn, I recite the hopeless litany, knowing there are no responses.

Tim and Doune join me on the floor, disheartened. We are feeling lost and more than a little faded - drained by excitement, altitude, fatigue and now no bags. We've been awake since four am. It's one of the less exotic travel adventures. There follows some moments of replenishing silence during which the disjointed fragments of my brain slowly knit. 'Never mind our bags,' I say, with renewed optimism, 'we'll get them tomorrow. It's better that way. At this point I couldn't carry a handkerchief. The amazing thing is that we've made it to Lhasa. We're actually here.' For a moment, overcome by exhaustion and frustration, I had forgotten to give thanks for being in Tibet.

'You're absolutely right,' Doune agrees. 'We're in Lhasa and that's what really matters. I'm over the moon.' But in truth it's difficult to be over the moon, or even under it, while breathing thin air.

The ever-practical Tim is already studying a map drawn for him by a traveller he met, who suggested we stay in a Tibetan guesthouse called the Banak Shol. 'I've got it together,' he announces. 'No point hanging around, let's get out of here.'

Standing up feels like a day's work. The Banak Shol is in the old part of Lhasa, a long walk from the CAAC building, which is in the new Chinese section. We make our way, too tired to talk, intent only upon getting there. As I struggle to keep pace with Tim and Doune, their legs much longer than mine, I make a point of looking only straight ahead, not wanting to spoil my first impressions with an unreceptive mood.

We arrive dusty, hot and faint from lack of oxygen, but the sight of the Banak Shol revives us. Like the embrace of an old friend, it bestows an immediate welcome. Unlike hotels in China which are often vast and formal, built by the Russians with Western conveniences, this guesthouse is small and primitive, and although there is nothing Western or modern about it, it has a familiar comforting feel. A boy of about fourteen, squatting by the open doorway, greets us with a friendly smile. 'Room?' He enquires. We nod enthusiastically.

'You speak English?' I ask, delighted by even the possibility of verbal exchange.

'A leetle,' he says.

He shakes hands with each of us and the matter is settled.

There are no forms to fill, no hassle with tourist currency, none of the usual Chinese formality. Gratefully we follow him upstairs to our rooms. 'This is definitely where the Tibetans stay,' Tim observes, obviously pleased. I admire his ability to communicate. I can hardly breathe, let alone speak, my heart thumping wildly as I climb the two flights of stairs. We walk along a balcony which runs the length of the building. And in spite of my thumping heart, the sight of the mountains, sparkling with patches of snow, brings a flash of pleasure. I make a mental note to take a more leisurely delight in them once we are settled.

All the rooms are off the balcony. A door leads to an entrance room with three bedrooms leading off it. The rooms are small, with blue and yellow plywood walls, colourful quilts and two narrow beds, painted red. A chipped wooden table, a chair and a washstand containing a flowered enamel basin, complete the furnishings. There are about eight of these units, each with three rooms and entrance. There are no amenities whatsoever. The loo is a slit in the floor of an outdoor shack at the top of the stairs and there is no running water.

Through mime and a few English words, the boy explains that we each get one thermos bottle of hot water daily for all washing and drinking needs. But right now it feels like the Hilton. We make a decision to splurge and take an entire unit, all three rooms. The idea of privacy is appealing, as we have been sharing rooms for some weeks, ever since we began travelling together. Besides it's not exactly a fortune at $2.50 a night each.

Clutching a thermos of water, I retire to the luxury of my own room, grateful to be alone and quiet. The first thing I do is pour some water into the basin, watch it cool and sink my face, hands and arms into the liquid, feeling my parched skin suck in the moisture. Over and over, slowly, carefully, like some healing ritual, I repeat the process, until gradually I begin to revive. My dehydrated skin tingles as it dries quickly in the pure clean air. As I stretch out on the bed, the strands of muscles wound into knots begin to uncoil. The tension drains from my body in diminishing waves. The events of the day, tumbling through my brain, pause. I become stilled by a satisfying sense of achievement. Today I made it to Lhasa. It wasn't easy, but in the end everything worked out; somehow it always does. And now, excited yet quiescent, in the aftermath of exertion, contentment eases my body and mind into perfect tranquillity. Drifting into Tibet, I close my eyes for a short respite. The day is not over, the journey just beginning.

Chapter Three

Tim, Doune and Niema - Freak Show in China

Three weeks earlier, Tim, Doune and I were strangers. We became acquainted in the Hong Kong check-in queue at Bangkok airport, and shared a seat on the plane. We also shared a taxi since we were all going to Chungking Mansions, known as Junkie Mansions by travellers forced to stay there because reasonably priced accommodation was scarce in Hong Kong. It was soon evident that we had much in common. We all lived in London (although I was originally from Canada) and had been travelling in Asia for several months. We were all heading for China, about which we knew very little, and were planning to spend about three months there. We all had low but not desperate budgets. Most importantly, we all recognised that we had a special rapport, and decided to join forces in one of those frequent if temporary 'coming togethers' - the overland traveller's equivalent of the ship-board romance, usually minus the romance.

That decision was unusual for me. If travelling was my favourite thing in life, being on my own was my favourite way of travelling. The experience was very different from travelling with a partner. I was more exposed, more vulnerable, but also more aware; my senses finely tuned, absorbing the full impact of experience without the cushion of a companion. Being with someone else was like travelling with blinkers. You didn't have to look right or left, but only straight ahead, or toward each other. Alone I was dependent on the people I met, forced to engage.

There were more risks - but I enjoyed risks - and more rewards. Like the time I waited on a small road in the mountains of Thailand, hoping for a bus to take me to the Hill Tribes information Centre. A little pick-up truck stopped with a Thai driver who spoke some English and several Chinese men and women. 'You are too much alone standing on the road,' the driver said. 'Better for you to come with us.' He offered me a ride to a Chinese refugee village deep in the mountains, totally out of my way. I had to make an instant decision. I accepted.

The experience was one of the most rewarding I had in Thailand. By the time we got to the village, struggling up recently widened roads where only donkeys had climbed a month earlier, it was late afternoon. Transport to and from the village was limited, the Chinese needing official passes to enter and leave. Nothing was leaving that day or the next. For two days I became the guest of the Thai military who were in control. I attended classes in the Thai language, ate and slept with the villagers, and admired the opium poppies presented to me by grinning soldiers. I was part of village life, with a privileged glimpse into how the refugees lived and the military operated - a fascinating two days.

On my own, I made more contact and learned more about the local people, who trusted me because, being female and alone, I was no threat. I also learned more about myself, developing resources I never knew I had. I felt most alive, vibrating with a sense of adventure, like an explorer uncovering new territory.

Being a woman on my own in South-East Asia presented no special hazards. Unlike North Africa, especially Morocco, where the atmosphere was charged with sexuality, or Mediterranean countries (like Italy) where men were always trying to rub up against you, the Asians - mainly Buddhists - were polite and respectful. There were no lecherous eyes, no lurid invitations, not even an obscene gesture.

With the exception of India, and Muslim countries like Malaysia and Java, there was hardly a trace of sexual innuendo. I was free to make my own choices.

However, although partial to the freedom and adventure of travelling alone, I wasn't oblivious to the virtues of an alliance with fellow travellers. The advantages were undeniable: sharing experiences, dividing the tedium of being one's own travel agent, not having to enter places alone, to say nothing of the comfort derived from knowing someone is there who cares if you live or die. Besides it was cheaper. The disadvantages were equally undeniable: compromises, disagreements, having to submit to someone else's rhythms, to name but a few.

However, my liaison with Tim and Doune was a union made in heaven. China was too difficult to navigate alone. In the infancy of its tourism, it had little experience with foreign tourists and less with individual travellers. It didn't even know if it wanted them. Confusion and inconsistency prevailed. In London, when applying for a visa, it was not uncommon to be told that one could only visit China as part of an organised group. Yet in Hong Kong there was no such restriction. Tourists travelling in tidy pre-packaged tours, bringing in big bucks, were definitely desirable. Travellers, over whom there was little control, who challenged the rules, who appeared in places for which permits were not granted, and who resisted paying inflated tourist prices, were at best a nuisance. China was not set up to accommodate them.

It was hard to find anyone who spoke anything but Chinese. Information was difficult to obtain and the invaluable travellers' grapevine was undeveloped. Desperate for information and advice, travellers meeting for the first time became instant bosom buddies, whereas in most countries they would have passed each other unnoticed. The resulting conversations were more like interviews than discussions. 'Where did you stay?' 'How did you get there?' 'How much was it?' Essentially one was on one's own, with only the help of a recent Lonely Planet guidebook, *China, a Travel Survival Kit* (affectionately known as 'The Bible'), which every traveller clutched, even though it was already outdated. Although this made travel in China exciting, it also meant that it was fraught with frustrations, hard to bear alone.

One major frustration was caused by the inevitable 'mayo'. 'Mayo', the big word in China, was a combination of all the negatives the traveller dreaded. 'Don't have, don't know, don't want to know, even if we did have we don't have, go away.' It was used extensively by officials in ticket offices, hotel receptions, and other places where the traveller's need not to hear it was greatest. It had a short sharp finality which left the traveller, weighed down with backpack, miserable and hopeless. That is until he learned the magic response to 'mayo' - 'yo'. 'You do have, if you don't have you'd better get, because if you don't I'm going to stay right here until you do. I'll even sleep in the lobby, think of the impression on the other guests'. A firm 'yo', accompanied by a smile - losing one's temper was fatal - and the unbuckling of one's rucksack, to show one meant business, worked wonders. The Chinese have a passion for neatness and order, coupled with a deep-seated respect for guests, especially foreign guests. They detest scenes. A determined 'yo' created havoc, challenging tradition and the foundations of their thinking. They were thrown by someone who defied authority, who wilfully refused to obey, especially when that someone was a foreign guest. The 'mayo-yo' battle could be a protracted one, but if fought relentlessly yet tactfully, a room or a ticket somehow became available. However, it was a battle I could not fight on my own. Reinforcements were essential.

Another major frustration resulted from the tricky money

situation. The official currency in China was called Remembi, or RMB, people's money. Foreigners, however, had a special currency all their own called FEC, Foreign Exchange Certificates. This currency, not available to the local Chinese, allowed foreigners to shop in special tourist places, like the Friendship Stores. Of course the Chinese wanted FEC in order to shop in Friendship Stores and acquire scarce luxury items.

Although the tourist FEC and the Chinese RMB were theoretically equal in value, the Chinese were willing to give more RMB for FEC. A black market resulted, enthusiastically supported by travellers, who could increase the value of their money by fifty to seventy percent. The problem was how to dispose of the RMB once procured, since tourists were supposed to pay in FEC. Using RMB instead or FEC became a way of life.

Tim had a special talent in this field. He always carried a wallet containing only RMB. When someone, for example, a taxi driver, pointed to a sign saying , 'FOREIGNERS MUST PAY IN FEC', Tim would insist, 'Mayo FEC' and open his wallet displaying only RMB. Being polite and kindly, like most Chinese, and not wanting to create a scene, the driver eventually acquiesced and accepted the RMB. The trick was to ignore the sign 'FOREIGNERS MUST PAY IN FEC'. It helped to flash a fake student card obtained in Junkie Mansions, certifying that 'The bearer is a Student in Taiwan, Studying Chinese.' Since the Chinese considered Taiwan a renegade province but still part of China, this entitled someone studying there to the same privileges that the Chinese enjoyed, including paying Chinese prices, often half those foreigners paid, and of course paying in RMB. But, since many employees who worked for institutions like railway stations and hotels were becoming wise to the devious methods of travellers, this was no mean achievement. Skills in the art of bluff and in 'out-mayoing' the

Chinese were best pooled.

Aside from the effort exerted in spending RMB, there was the paranoia produced by procuring them. In Guangzhou (formerly Canton), where the majority of travellers entered China, the main streets were lined with 'change money' ladies. Every few yards a female would furtively approach the foreigner, surreptitiously chanting 'change money, change money', and attempt to lure him down some back street. I saw several of these 'change money' ladies pulled away by police, arms twisted behind their backs. The police, however, did not interfere with foreign guests, who had a special status backed by officialdom and could do pretty much as they liked so long as they didn't kill. Despite this, doing black market deals in dubious alleyways, was unsettling. The required dedication, mathematical skill, bargaining ability, and the fear of police interference, resulted in a host of anxieties which were best shared.

In this atmosphere of uncertainty, where one invented the rules as one went along (because even the Chinese didn't know them), it was a blessing to have Tim and Doune for support. Besides, a single room was the same price as a double, and a triple hardly more.

Visually we were a trio of stunning impact. For the Chinese, isolated for so long, any Westerner is the object of intense curiosity and unabashed stares. But on to the spectacle provided by the ordinary Westerner, with his kettle-spout nose, strange attire and high-tech equipment which bleeped, buzzed, flashed and even played tunes, we superimposed extraordinary dimensions. Our act was unique. First of all there was the phenomenon of our height. In China I was a good size, whereas in the West I was several sizes too small. Just over five feet, I was described as 'petite' by kind friends. In my own view I barely made it as a normal member of the human race; anyone shorter was deformed. However, whereas I measured up to Chinese standards,

Tim and Doune did not. Doune was an outrageous five foot eight and Tim loomed six foot two, like some Swiftian giant.

As though the preposterousness of our heights wasn't enough to engulf us in a sea of mesmerised eyes, fixed in unblinking wonder, there were the dual phenomena of non-human hair and eyes. Except for the elderly, women in China all had straight black hair, usually long, and men were clean-shaven with straight short black hair. Both Doune and I had curly hair, like sheep, and Tim sprouted hair from his cheeks and chin, like a monkey. My hair had the sensitivity to be long and dark, and my eyes to be brown, but Tim's hair was an indecent sand colour, his eyes cat green. Doune was a worse transgression, with hair not only short and curly but the colour of honey, and eyes the colour of sky or sea. Most Chinese had never imagined such variety in human appearance, let alone encountered it. We were the cause of major bicycle accidents. When we walked out together, the Lilliputian and the Giants, flagrant in our gross abnormalities, it was as though the freak show had come to town. We could have made a fortune selling tickets.

Chapter Four

The Banak Shol - Medieval Guesthouse

As I stretch out on my narrow Banak Shol bed, slipping into a delicious sleep, my well-being suddenly dissolves. I am wrenched into anxiety by a heart thumping rapid, erratic, boom-boom-booms, executing double somersaults, trapped like a wild thing, crazy to escape. Instantly I am wide awake. I take my pulse. It's one hundred and twenty. Normally it's around seventy. I remember Steve, a young American doctor I met in Burma who had been working with mountain climbers in the Nepalese Everest base camp, about the same altitude as Lhasa. Steve confided to me that Hillary himself had once come to his post suffering from altitude sickness.

'Hillary!' I said, surprised, ' But he's climbed to the top of Everest. Surely he must be used to high altitudes.'

'That's something the body never grows accustomed to, it has to make a new adjustment each time,' Steve said. 'Hillary may have been used to high altitudes but his body wasn't and he came down with all the plebeian symptoms, nausea, dizziness, headache, the works.'

If Hillary succumbed to altitude sickness, what chance do I have? I will my heart to beat slower. It refuses. I try not to think about Mr Nolan, an American I met who worked for his embassy in Beijing, but our discussion over coffee returns to haunt me. I compulsively review every detail.

'Do you have any special problems with American tourists in China?' I asked, hitting on a neutral topic.

Without hesitation he drawled, 'Yup, elderly folk dying in Tibet.'

'Dying?' My voice was edged with hysteria. 'Dying of what?'

'They arrive in Lhasa, step out of the plane and some of those buggers drop dead right then and there. Their hearts pack in.'

'Right on the runway?'

He paused to savour my distress. 'Sometimes they wait until they climb the steps of a monastery. But last week we had one old biddy who began bleeding from the ears as soon as she stepped off the plane and haemorrhaged to death right on the runway.' He gazed deep into his cup. 'Getting the bodies back home is a real pain in the butt.' He sipped his coffee with great concentration, reflecting on transportation difficulties, while I gulped mine, anxious to leave before I heard any more.

Although Tibet had only just been opened to individual travellers, it had already been opened to tour companies. Groups of tourists were flown into Lhasa and housed in a specially built hotel miles from town. They were whisked from palace to monastery in an attempt to minimise their contact with Tibet and especially with Tibetans. Their tight schedules precluded acclimatisation to the drastic change in altitude. The price for this guided marathon was so exorbitant that only the rich and retired, mainly elderly Americans could afford to pay it. They were not in the best physical condition, not used to exertion and often already suffering from some form of heart problem. It was no wonder their hearts couldn't cope.

I lie on my bed, prying Mr Nolan loose from my brain (hand on heart, in an effort to smooth the bumps), tormented by Steve, Hillary, blood-stained runways and Shelley, who wrote, 'Caesar's bust is on the shelf, and I don't feel too well myself.' I forbid myself to think of

Caesar or the elderly Americans, and especially of the lady bleeding from the ears. Besides, my heart is strong and healthy. Nobody in my family ever had a heart problem. With this tiny consolation I finally fall asleep.

When I awake about an hour later, I am no longer aware of the effort my heart is making on my behalf. But having appeased my heart, I now have to gratify my stomach. I am hungry. We last ate light-years ago, in that happy encapsulated time in the heavens, before we met the Himalayas, indulging in great wads of oxygen and awful sanitised sweets. My room is next to Tim's and I tap lightly on the wall in case he's asleep.

'I'm up,' he says immediately as though waiting for my signal.

'Me too.' Doune's voice is as clear as Tim's. We are really sharing one room with flimsy partitions.

'I'm hungry,' I say.

'I'm hungry too,' Tim replies.

'Me too and three,' Doune chimes in.

'Let's find some food,' Tim suggests.

'Brilliant,' Doune agrees.

I come to a slow sitting, then standing position, not wanting to suddenly drop dead.

'The restaurant, or whatever it is,' Tim corrects himself, careful not to raise false expectations, 'is downstairs, through the back.' Somehow Tim always knows these things.

I open my door and stagger into Doune. 'Remember we have to take it easy until we get used to the altitude,' Doune cautions, lending me support.

'How can I forget? I've got altitude sickness on the ears,' I mutter.

'It's just a matter of resting and not drinking booze. We'll be all right,' Tim says, as he leads us down a narrow dirty flight of stairs at the other end of the balcony. It's almost seven pm, but still light, and mercifully not cold as we're only wearing T-shirts.

We pass through a small yard (stepping over some dubious puddles), enter a door, and cross the threshold into a medieval kitchen. Near the entrance several Tibetan men, wearing broad-brimmed hats and sheepskin jackets, are drinking tea and chatting around a long wooden table. Conditioned in China, we attempt to slip by unobtrusively, shoulders narrowed against the anticipated barrage of curiosity. They smile and nod as we pass, their talking uninterrupted. Our entrance is totally unsensational. Nobody is dumbfounded, nobody falls over in his seat, nobody even stares. We sit on a bench by an empty table, blissfully ignored, in the middle of a scene which has the energy and profusion of a Brueghel painting, Tibetan-style.

The room we are in is large and windowless with damp stone walls and a door at either end, dim after the daylight, and smoky. The ceiling is braced by great wooden beams black with soot. Near our table is a brick oven and a wooden board, beside which two Tibetan girls - black braided hair tied with bright ribbons - sit kneading dough, pounding it into round flat loaves while singing. Another girl takes hot loaves from the oven, piles them into a straw basket and pops uncooked ones into the oven. They smile at us and continue working.

In one corner a man is pouring small steaming glasses of tea from a large sooty kettle. Near him is a massive blackened stove with round holes for woks, and a shelf beside it holds wooden bowls filled with food, jars of spices, and wreaths of garlic. A woman wearing a less than spotless apron is stirring something in a wok. Scattered around the room are chopping blocks where old men and girls wearing dirty aprons and boots with pointed curled-up toes, are peeling potatoes and chopping vegetables. On one block chunks of cooked meat are steaming, on another a man is dismembering a yak, hacking at its joints, its silky black hair lying on the floor with other bits of rubbish.

Cut into the stone floor, a gully runs through the centre of the kitchen. While we are watching, a woman strains a noodle pot into it, the murky liquid raising a cloud of steam, a man spits with a direct hit, and several people dump assorted slops. A dog wanders in and heads for the gully, checking for scraps. He looks well fed. Against one wall a large tank with a spout provides the washing facilities. A woman stands scrubbing glasses and bowls with a toothless brush, the grey water flowing into the gully and spilling over on to the floor. She wears rubber boots and layers of shabby black clothing. The smell of baking bread and frying garlic mingles with the burning wood and cigarette smoke.

The table is sticky with soggy noodles and spilled tea. I clean it as best I can, while we assess the chances of getting fed. No one approaches. We're treated with the casual familiarity of regulars at the local cafe and are reluctant to shatter that illusion. Our problem is solved by the arrival of two Westerners who head straight for our table. 'This is Texas Dave and I'm Gina,' a plumpish short girl with dark eyes says, as she plonks herself beside me. She has straight black hair with a fringe, Eskimo-style, and a pleasant round face. We introduce ourselves.

Tim stands up to shake hands. Texas Dave towers over Tim, a lean sinewy six foot seven inches. He looks like he's been on the road a long time and enjoying it. His face is a leathery brown, lined with sunshine, wind and a stubbly beard. His eyes are bright blue. He wears a cowboy hat, boots and a sheepskin waistcoat. He's right out of a Spaghetti Western - the good guy.

'Just get here?' he asks.

'A few hours ago,' Doune replies. He nods sympathetically.

'We were just wondering how we go about getting ourselves fed,' Tim says.

'OK.' Texas Dave takes matters in hand. 'What you do is walk right up there.' He points to a table with white porcelain bowls piled upside down. 'Get yourselves one of those babies, head for the stove and fill it up with whatever grabs you. There's meat, vegetables, eggs, you'll see when you get there. That lady chef will cook it up for you Tibetan-style.'

'What does it cost?' I ask, from force of habit.

'Oh she charges according to her mood. She looks in a fine mood at the moment.'

I glance over just in time to see her embracing a small boy as she wipes his nose with her grubby apron. My involuntary grimace doesn't escape Texas Dave. 'All in a day's work,' he says, 'takes a bit of getting used to. This place is as clean as a baby's ass compared to most.' The simile does nothing to reassure me. 'The Tibetans aren't big on hygiene, but the food is primo,' he smacks his lips.

'Do you have your own chopsticks and mugs?' Gina asks. 'They're a must here.'

Tim dips into his bag, which is almost part of his body, and produces three pairs of chopsticks and three white mugs with lids, like those the Chinese carry. 'The Bible' had advised buying chopsticks, as the wooden ones served in Chinese restaurants are a source of hepatitis. It also advised carrying mugs - hot water for making tea being available in hotel rooms and trains throughout China. We are never without either.

'Good.' Gina nods approval.

Texas Dave does a short investigative round of the chopping blocks to sample the menu of the day and returns to report. 'There's some nice-looking yak meat, just cooked up fresh, and some good-looking vegetables.'

'Tim's a vegetarian and I'm not ready for yak meat,' I say. 'Are you?' I ask, turning to Doune. 'Too dodgy. Vegetables and eggs will do me fine.' Doune stands up, leading the way.

We each get a bowl. I dry mine carefully with a precious tissue from a small pack I save for special occasions. We fill our bowls with chopped vegetables, beansprouts, green onions, tinned mushrooms, cooked potatoes, nuts, eggs and beancurd. The cook puts some branches in the stove, waits until they catch fire, pours oil into a wok and sets it in one of the blazing holes. She throws Tim's vegetables into the hot oil and scrambles his eggs over them, sprinkling pinches of herbs and spices into the mixture, waiting for him to signal enough. She stirs and tosses, then flips the result into his bowl. She repeats the process for Doune and me. We each take a fresh round of bread, still hot, from the basket. I sniff mine lovingly. It's been a long time since I've smelled freshly baked bread. In China, even stale bread is a rarity. Gina has brought mugs of hot tea. In spite of filthy aprons, sooty walls and dirty tables, the food that emerges is mouth watering.

'Delicious,' Doune pronounces, tasting our first Tibetan meal, 'and real chai with milk and sugar! I've been suffering withdrawal symptoms for this. I couldn't bear another cup of jasmine tea. I love it here already,' she says, caressing the mug.

Tim is even more delighted. As a strict vegetarian he was appalled by Chinese cooking, which uses bits of meat and fish in all its dishes. He ended up eating mostly rice strewn with limp soggy green vegetables. I remember him sighing plaintively, in a moment of despair - faced by yet another bowl of sticky white rice for his dinner, 'I'd give fifty pounds for a baked potato.' He meant it.

'How's the grub?' Texas Dave asks, returning from the stove balancing two bowls heaped with food.

'Best meal I've had in Asia. No green slimy stuff, and real potatoes.' Tim says, overwhelmed by his good fortune.

'Brilliant. Absolutely brilliant,' Doune adds.

'I love Chinese food, but I didn't love it in China. This looks great,' I say.

'Knew you'd like it.' He smiles, pleased, as though he had prepared it himself.

Texas Dave and Gina are mines of information and we dig relentlessly. If we knew little about the workings of China, we know nothing about those of Tibet, and the 'Tibetan Bible' hasn't yet been written. Texas Dave and Gina are patient and generous, having sat where we sit only three weeks earlier. Besides giving us information they offer towels and soap until ours arrive. The kitchen is their living room and soon they seem settled in for the evening. 'Man, this is where the action is. Hang out here and you get to know it all.' Texas Dave says, sipping his third cup of tea and considering beer.

While we talk, a number of Tibetans and several Westerners come in to eat. Texas Dave greets them all by name.

'He certainly is the man in Lhasa,' I whisper to Doune. 'Thank goodness he found us.'

Another American joins us. 'Hey Dave.'

'Hey George. Man it's good to see you,' Texas Dave says, slapping George on the back. 'Thought you were leaving today.'

'Couldn't get out. No places to Golmud, the trucks were full. No problem, I'll try again tomorrow.'

'Did Karl and Ingrid get away?' Gina asks.

'They sure did. Luxury style. Brand-new truck, seats in the cab. Fifty RMB each.'

I am all ears. 'Golmud', 'truck', 'RMB' - exciting words. I make instant calculations. I thought Golmud wasn't open to foreigners

- the police refusing passes to travel there - obviously there's something I don't know. Texas Dave introduces us to George and I plunge right in. 'Did I hear you say you were going to Golmud?' I ask, with the instincts of a squirrel storing bits of sustenance against the lean times ahead.

'You did,' George replies.

'But how is that possible?' Isn't Golmud closed?'

'Officially it's closed; unofficially, who knows? The Chinese haven't gotten around to enforcing their laws.'

'And you're able to get there by truck?'

'That's unofficial too,' George says.

'The drivers aren't supposed to take foreigners,' Texas Dave explains, 'but they do. Fifty RMB (about $10) is a lot of money for them, probably about a month's wages. The trip takes three days, sometimes longer, the road is the shits, it hardly exists, and its a good seven hundred miles, maybe more.'

'How do you go about arranging it?'

'You don't, it just happens,' George says, enjoying his enigmatic replies.

Texas Dave, sympathetic to my hunger for exact details, fills in. 'You get up very early in the morning, before it gets light, and hang around the truck stops, there are two main ones in town. Eventually somebody takes you. If not that day then the next or the day after that. So far everyone who's tried has got away. I plan leaving that way myself. They've cancelled the planes to Xian, so it's either back to Chengdu by plane or a truck to Golmud. There's no other way to make it to China.'

'They've cancelled the planes to Xian?' Doune asks, travellers' anxiety in her voice. 'But that's how we were planning on getting back to China. We want to see the terracotta soldiers in Xian and we certainly don't want to waste time and money going back to Chengdu.'

'How long are they cancelled for?' I ask, equally perturbed by this sudden hitch in our plans.

'Who knows?' George says, 'Maybe forever. The Chinese aren't exactly eager beavers when it comes to giving information. Right now it's impossible to fly to Xian. It's either back to Chengdu or onward to Golmud.'

'Hey, give me a break,' Tim says, 'we only just got here.'

'Sorry. Just thinking ahead.'

But I've already decided to travel through Tibet to China by truck, illegal or not.

We pay for the food in RMB. It works out at less than fifty cents each. 'They don't know what FEC is in Tibet and don't tell them. We're keeping it a secret,' Texas Dave says.

'They'll find out soon enough,' George adds.

We leave Texas Dave and George celebrating their reunion with beers. Gina escorts us up the rickety stairs, lit only by a thin crescent of moon. I cradle my heart in preparation for the climb and ascend with the care of a ninety-year-old mounting a ladder. Still, I must rest after every few steps. My heart is on overtime, and my legs feel like jellied eels, they refuse to support me. 'I'll never take breathing for granted again,' I pant.

'Not to worry. It will only last a few days, everybody goes through it,' Gina consoles me.

I reach our balcony faint and dizzy my mouth agape like a beached fish. Tim and Doune are sitting on the bench doubled over with breathlessness. 'The first day is often the worst,' Gina says and goes to the room she shares with Texas Dave. She returns with soap, a towel and candles, which she lights for us, the electricity having failed.

'You'll feel better after a wash.' Thermos bottles filled with hot water wait outside each of our doors. My basin is still filled with the water I hadn't emptied earlier.

'Where do we pour the dirty water?' I ask Gina. 'Is there a sink somewhere?'

'No sink. You pour it over the balcony. Look downstairs first to check no one is underneath.'

'Are you sure?' Doune asks.

'That's how it's done. Not to worry. You'll get used to it. No one minds. It's Tibet.'

Her mission completed, Gina leaves with an enviable vitality to rejoin Texas Dave and George, while I fight imminent collapse. Struggling against impending illness, and a weariness so profound I can't summon the energy to change the water, I wash in slow motion, disturbed by strange flickering shapes, wondering if I will survive undressing. Still wet and half-dressed, I drag myself into bed, my head roaring with Tibet and aching with exhaustion. But as I blow out the candle and sink into darkness something wonderful happens. As though I had swallowed some marvellous substance, I experience a sudden onrush of elation, a wild ecstasy. Today I have seen the Potala.

Chapter Five

Old Lhasa

The Taxi

My elation narrowly survives a fitful sleep shattered by implacable wails and terrible howls as wild dogs tear each other to bits outside my window. I awake feeling fragile and reduce all effort to a minimum. Tim and Doune have suffered the same fate. After a too early breakfast of tea and last night's bread, eaten on the balcony while meditating on the magnificence of mountains folded with new snow, and a rest to recuperate from the effort of meditation, we head for the CAAC office to collect our bags.

Texas Dave told us Lhasa boasted one taxi, and drained of energy by the conspiracy of altitude and dogs, we treat ourselves to it. The taxi's prestige is enhanced by having its own office, a short walk from our guesthouse. The street is wide and filled with an assortment of trucks, bicycles, donkey carts and people carrying sacks and baskets. The pavements are lined with street vendors selling tinned fish, tinned fruit, sunflower seeds, boiled sweets, bicycle parts, insoles for shoes, and clothing, all arranged on plastic sheets directly on the pavement, or on tables. Vendors squat beside their wares chatting with each other as few customers are about. It's dazzlingly bright, and air is clear warm, and very thin.

The taxi office is a wooden shack containing a table and a broken sofa with springs poking through the dirty upholstery. Outside the office the taxi sits proudly. It's a bright blue clapped-out once-regal vintage Warszawa limousine with splendid haunches, badly dented, and a wood-framed windscreen, badly cracked. Its bald tyres bulge with swellings pressing through from bloated inner tubes, like boils about to burst, and its leather seats are slashed and stained. But to us it's a Rolls Royce. We wait until the driver finishes his breakfast of noodle soup and then tinkers interminably under the hood using a variety of rusty tools, rubber hoses and bits of metal. It seems he's rebuilding the engine, but he's only trying to get it started. Finally he does. Jubilantly he dons his chauffeur's cap and with a triumphant blast of exhaust fumes we take off, bumping to the CAAC office at ten miles an hour, the odds low on us actually getting there. By some miracle, we do, and by some greater miracle our bags are on the floor, buried under a pile of luggage.

I search my pockets for the baggage tickets before realising with horror that I've left them at the Banok Shol. This is a minor tragedy. In China nothing is possible without the appropriate bits of paper. We met a girl in Kunming who was refused a train ticket because she had misplaced her reservation slip, even though the tourist office had her reservation listed. She was forced to wait a week before another seat became available.

'Now we won't be able to get our bags .... Damn ... I've never done that before,' I plead my own defence to deaf ears. 'There's nobody about. Let's just take the bags,' Tim says, not too respectful of Chinese bureaucracy at the best of times.

'It's too dodgy. What if someone comes? They'll think we're stealing them. We can't prove they're ours. You know what the Chinese are like about doing things by the book,' Doune says, reluctant to provoke Chinese officialdom.

'I'll go back and get the miserable tickets. It's all my fault anyway.' But the thought of going back is depressing.

'Let's just take the damn bags before someone comes,' Tim persists. I agree.

'Be careful, I don't have the energy for a scene,' Doune finally gives in outvoted.

Tim stalks the pile cautiously, closing in for the kill, while Doune and I stand guard. Suddenly several Tibetan men enter, wearing caps and badges, pushing carts loaded with luggage. Too late. Tim has already freed one of the bags. Doune moans quietly and looks miserable, her fears realised.

'Don't just stop now. Just help me, let's hurry up,' Tim instructs nervously. Suspending all moral judgement, oblivious of the consequences, we wrestle our bags from the heap as the men create a new heap, unloading directly beside us. As we slip by them like thieves, our bags hung with tickets and pasted with unresolved baggage checks, we expect a three-point alarm to go off, instead they smile at us and wave. After all, as Gina says, 'No one minds. It's Tibet.'

Our chauffeur is waiting. We leap into the car, relieved. 'Banok Shol, James,' I command, flushed with success. James steers his way with professional pride through the heavy vehicles, jeeps, bicycles, animals and people. Everyone peers through the windows curious to see the privileged passengers reclining in the soft leather, to smile their blessings and to partake in the event. When we stop to allow a donkey cart to pass, an old women gives us an enormous toothless grin, and from somewhere inside layers of clothing produces a tiny infant, stark naked, for us to admire. She swells with pride as I praise the baby's thick black hair and is still smiling as we pull away, the baby no longer visible. We're the only motor vehicle on the road, and feeling rather grand, I wave with queenly aloofness to the admiring Tibetans as we limp back to the Banok Shol.

The Barkor Bazaar

The next afternoon, revived by a long rest and a briefing by Texas Dave and Pascal (a Swiss traveller who has been in Tibet for over two months), we attempt Old Lhasa and the Bakor Bazaar. Leaving our wide road we head through an alleyway into the original part of town. Lhasa is really two cities. The new clean Chinese one is larger and neatly laid out, with broad paved roads and uninspiring buildings like those in most Chinese cities. The Tibetan city is ancient and dirty with a maze of narrow cobbled streets and a medieval atmosphere. Two storey stone houses painted white, with flat roofs, ramshackle and crumbling, line the dusty streets. The windows are divided into small panels and the doorways are low, with painted frames, often chipped and in need of repair. Above the windows are friezes with flowers and leaves painted in blues, yellows, reds and greens. Plants and flowers fill miniature balconies projecting from the upper windows. The houses are built directly on the street. We can see into a courtyard at the back of one house, with a well in its centre and ceramic urns leaning against it. Several Tibetans are seated on the ground with bowls in their laps, eating and tossing bits of food to the resident goats without breaking the rhythm of their chopsticks.

We wind our way through the narrow dirty alleyways, emerging into an open market – Barkor Bazaar. We are in the vegetable section with tiny stalls pressed together, heaped with cucumbers, green onions, white radishes and garlic. Nearby, several men and women sit in a ring, baskets of boiled eggs between their knees. Two of the women nurse babies. Next to them is a small dairy section with jars of yoghurt and pieces of white cheese. A women sells round flat loaves of bread from a large straw basket while mending a torn jacket. Beside her, sacks of barley flour stuck with wooden scoops, bulge like fat bellies. A man has fallen asleep against one of the sacks while grinding flour, his cap fallen into his lap, his brown fingers sunk in the white flour, still clutching the grinder.

One entire street is devoted to yak butter. Slabs of yellow butter, reeking with a rancid odour, that permeates everything and sticks in the nostrils, are moulded into squares, cubes, circles and even stars. The smell of burning juniper branches emanates from a dome-shaped monument, hung with prayer flags, mingles with the yak butter. Another section, appropriately called Yak Alley, is devoted to meat. Lumps of yak hang from hooks or sit on bloodied tables among severed heads gazing with mournful eyes. Children play under the tables.

Everything is available in the market: pots, dishes, silver bowls, containers for yak butter candles, clothes (both Chinese and Tibetan), carpets, bolts of material, plus a wide assortment of oddities, including snuff from India, old seventy-eight rpm records from the Soviet Union, dusty condoms from America, lipsticks and hair rollers from anywhere. We look for jewellery and handicrafts. There is not as much as I expected, most of it having found its way to Nepal. Exporting antiques is now prohibited and it's supposedly illegal to sell old Tibetan handicrafts and jewellery. These are offered surreptitiously, or sold by the people wearing them. We do see some coral and turquoise on several stalls, hidden amongst the bits and pieces. I buy five turquoise beads for $2 and Doune buys a coral, turquoise and silver necklace for $5, transactions of doubtful legality.

At one stall featuring a bewildering selection of clothing, including a striped bikini bottom, one surgical stocking, a pair of orange fishnet tights and a monogrammed pyjama top, I watch a young Tibetan invent a game. He examines a mystifying article of clothing, curiously fingering its lacy flesh coloured waistband and dangling elastic appendages, before determining what use he can put it to. Holding it like a slingshot and positioning himself for attack, he takes careful aim. Then, pulling one of the elastic strips by the metal bit at the end, he stretches it to its limit and releases it with a snap. He repeats this with the other strips, leaping from the concealed crouch to surprise attack, without a trace of self-consciousness. When he finally lays down his improvised slingshot, I recognise it as an old fashioned sanitary belt, such as my grandmother might have worn.

The atmosphere in the Barkor is friendly and accepting. Tibetans smile easily. Like the Chinese, they are curious about us, but their curiosity is tempered by a sense of humour. We are not regarded as freaks to gape at, but as wonderful fantasy creatures from an unknown star, whose reality they want to confirm. They have no desire to distance us on a stage. They want us close, to touch our differences, to feel the stuff we're made of, and they aren't shy or diffident about doing so.

Several young men touch Tim as we squeeze past them, prodding his arms, his legs, even his bum. Their smiles and eye contact eliminate overtones of insult or aggression, so that Tim is unsure how to react. The children are cheekier. Dressed in rags, with dirty snot-caked faces, matted hair and impish smiles, they tug at our arms, pinch our legs and handle our clothes. Avoiding Tim, they concentrate on Doune and me. Unlike Chinese children, who never beg, they extend open palms and ask for money and the inevitable pens. It's not serious begging, however, more like a teasing game they play before running off.

I am looking at a piece of beautifully embroidered Tibetan cloth at a stall selling hand woven materials, wondering what I could do with it, when an old women comes up to me. Without the slightest hesitation she takes hold of my Burmese shawl and fingers it with an expert's admiration, nodding compliments and muttering praise. Then she points to the apron she is wearing, tied over a patched and torn long sleeved cloak. Its embroidered strips are faded to a unified non-colour, except for one new strip, which stands out vividly. She holds it up proudly for my inspection. I admire the intricate stitches and fine workmanship, and pointing to her and miming the act of sewing, ask if she did the work herself. Through gestures and facial expressions she explains that the embroidery is the work of a daughter or perhaps a grand daughter; in any case, someone smaller than herself and belonging to her. Covering her eyes and wrinkling her face in a grimace, she laments the fact that her eyes are no longer equal to the task. Then she sighs plaintively, raises one hand and tilts her head back, in a gesture signifying the acceptance of her fate. I nod in sympathy and she smiles, pleased with our conversation. As I leave the stall she takes my hand. Hers feels cool and rough, her fingers strong and reassuring. We walk along holding hands until she turns off into an alleyway, with a small parting smile. I can hear her Tibetan boots, several sizes too large, flapping on the cobblestones after she has disappeared.

As we stroll through the tangle of streets, we notice several young women seated in a small opening between two shops, combing each other's hair. One girl carefully rubs a lump of yak butter into her long black tresses. This done, a second girl – a baby tied to her back with a red cloth – braids the gleaming strands into long plaits and twists the plaits around her head, tying them with ribbons of purple and green silk. The baby grabs at the colourful strands and the girls squeal with delight. A third girl, her head trembling with masses of dreadlocks, is polishing large beads, rubbing them between her palms and handing them to another girl who, with enormous dedication, weaves them into the dreadlocks, interspersing them with turquoise and coral. She looks freshly combed, her shiny plaits extended with purple and white strands of silk, falling below her waist.

All four girls wear similar embroidered sashes with bright wool tassels over dusty faded jackets, and similar earrings and bracelets, but just as no hairdos are the same, no pair of shoes is alike. The yak butter girl wears black Chinese slippers like cloth ballet pumps with ankle straps; the girl carrying the baby, a scuffed pair of tennis shoes; the dreadlock girl, Tibetan boots with pointed curled-up toes and embroidered cloth tops; and the girl attending her has kicked off her red wool slippers with their thick straw soles, to go barefoot. They giggle and smile brightly when they see us watching them. For a moment they stop their work while one girl touches my hair, admiring the curls, and another, even more impressed by the colour, admires Doune's. But they soon return to their hairdressing, taking great pleasure in its meticulous rituals.

The street scenes in old Lhasa strengthen my impression that Tibetans are more spontaneous, extroverted and physical than the Chinese, with open faces expressing changing emotion, and none of the Chinese inscrutability. They are certainly more colourful, both in behaviour and in dress, and far dirtier. The few Chinese who have ventured here are unmistakable, not only because of their lighter skin, flatter faces and different-shaped eyes, but especially because of their clothes and a tightness in their bearing. Dressed alike in clean blue jackets and trousers, with Mao-style caps, they seem prim and self-contained, out of place in the dishevelled market streets.

Lhasa, as the religious and commercial as well as the political capital of Tibet, is a melting pot, attracting people from the furthest reaches of the country. Its streets are alive with a pageant of Tibetan styles and appearances. I'm surprised by how tall Tibetans are, some men as tall as Tim or taller, and by the colourful boldness of their dress. Like the women, men are also covered in jewellery: earrings, bracelets, necklaces, even hairpieces. Some have blankets draped over one shoulder and tied with a coloured sash, others are shabby in baggy trousers and grimy jackets. Their headgear is splendid with variety: wide-brimmed hats, straw hats, fur hats, hats like fedoras, hats like temples with a wing on either side, coloured tassels and pieces of silver braided into their hair, and black or red headbands stretched tight against their foreheads. With blankets, wide hats, high cheekbones and brown skin, some look like South American Indians. Others – their dreadlocks studded with turquoise, and wearing long earrings, chunky necklaces and rings – wouldn't raise an eyebrow in a West Indian suburb of London.

Conspicuous on the streets is a group of tall men from eastern Tibet called Khampas. They have strands of red silk twisted through their hair, their bodies are taught like arrows, and they carry jewelled daggers and knives hanging from leather belts fastened with silver buckles. From a distance they look fierce and threatening (we have been told that knife fighting is not unusual). We pass a group of these men conversing in the road, the impression of violence tempered with warm smiles.

One man, complete with dangling jewelled dagger, grins broadly at Tim, and signals him to come over. Tim does. The man pulls from somewhere in his clothing, a remarkable necklace, a mixture of turquoise and coral, strung with pieces of silver and old coins. He offers it to Tim for the equivalent of $15. Whether through fear, or trust, or simply recognising a superb deal, Tim agrees to buy the necklace without bargaining (unheard of for him). The man removes the necklace and slips it into Tim's pocket while his fellow tribesman shield the transaction from view. Later, Texas Dave tells us that some Tibetans come to Lhasa on a religious pilgrimage, run out of money and are forced to sell their jewellery and sometimes their clothes. When Tim tells him what he paid, Texas Dave says 'It's a steal', and I feel a twinge of regret for something more than the necklace.

The streets of the Barkor, vivid with prayer flags, colourful dress and the medley of assorted wares, are seething with Tibetans buying, selling, begging for alms in wooden bowls, whirling prayer wheels and attending to routine chores. We pass a dentist plying his craft on the pavement. A Tibetan man is tilted backwards, diminished in an oversized stuffed chair, grand with armrest, footrest and a hand crank which adjusts the angle of the occupant. The dentist drills the man's tooth while furiously pumping a foot pedal, demonstrating enviable powers of co-ordination. The drill whines as it grinds into the tooth. The patient clutching the armrest squeezes his eyes shut, but opens them again to smile between bouts of drilling. A small group gathered to witness, return his smile. I take a photo.

'I want to get a jacket made with that lovely brocaded Tibetan silk,' Doune interrupts the sound of drilling. 'I saw some brocaded material in one of the stalls and Texas Dave told me where I can get sheepskins for the lining. He said a tailor will sew it for pennies.' We head for the sheepskin vendor.

On the way there, a Tibetan woman confronts me with urgency. She is more finely dressed than most, in a long black heavy skirt, an apron embroidered in panels and tied with a sash, a matching black jacket, and a white wide brimmed hat. My sunglasses are sticking out of my back pocket. She points to the case and, pulling it out of the pocket, slaps my hand. Her eyes are snapping as she admonishes me in no uncertain Tibetan terms, waving the glasses at me. I am taken aback, flustered. I have never seen the women in my life – how could I or my glasses have offended her? Replacing the case, she creeps around me and whips it from my pocket, waving it at me yet again, with a renewed burst of reprimand. Then, unzipping Tim's camera bag, she stuffs the case in, zips the bag shut and nods curtly.

I make a desperate effort to understand but fail miserably and look helplessly at Tim. 'She's trying to tell you not to keep your glasses in your pocket, that it's easy for someone to rip them off. She wants you to put them into my camera bag.' Tim's Tibetan is suddenly fluent.

'Tim's right,' Doune says, 'she's warning us to be careful.'

Meanwhile a chorus of women has gathered to reinforce the message with wagging heads and mutterings. Relieved, I shake the woman's hand and pat Tim's bag, demonstrating my gratitude for her advice and protection. She nods sagely and smiles, her eyes suddenly kind, then wiping her slap from my hand, continues on her way. The chorus disperses.

We locate the sheepskin stall with piles of skins heaped on a table. Doune rifles through the skins and finds several she likes. She narrows her choice down to two and holds them up for my approval. 'Take that one,' I suggest. 'It looks less like a sheep.' She agrees, and discarding one skin, indicates her interest in the other, laying it down ready for the bargaining. Tim assists. Bargaining is his speciality. The stallholder writes a price on his palm. Tim throws his hands up in disbelief, crosses the figure out and reduces it by two thirds. A process of 'write and cross out' covers the man's hand in tiny blue numbers. He begins to write on his wrist. Finally they come to an agreement. A crowd has gathered for the entertainment. Doune pays. The man proffers both skins, and Doune, somewhat confused, takes the one she wants and wanders down the street, pleased with her purchase.

We have gone only a short distance when an old woman comes up to Doune, takes the skin, points to the stall and holds up two fingers. Even Tim looks blank. Through inventive hand and body movements, as though she is acting out parts of a charade, we gradually come to understand that although Doune has paid for two skins, she has only received one. In a huff, Tim and Doune hurry back to the stall to claim the second sheepskin, prepared for a scene. The man gives it to them without a murmur. They return to the woman who is waiting on the sidelines, triumphantly waving both skins. Doune shakes her hands gratefully, first one then the other. The women embraces Doune, her face crumpled with smiles, her eyes bright with pleasure.

As we wave goodbye, I say, 'We have to watch these Tibetans, they may not be as honest as the Chinese, but isn't it great how the old ladies are looking after our interests?'

'Someone has to, we're not doing too well on our own.' Tim mutters disgruntled.

Doune, who was pleased with her one skin, is now twice as pleased.

Outside the Jokhang

The crowd thickens and we find ourselves in a stream of people all moving in the same direction. We are approaching the Jokhang, in the heart of old Lhasa, and can see its gold roofs rising in spires and domes, gleaming against the blue sky. Pascal told us that the Jokhang is the holiest temple in Tibet and Tibetans from the remotest part of the country make arduous pilgrimages to it, crossing mountains and rivers, pressing through mud and snow, in order to gain spiritual merit and express their religious faith. The throng of people circling clockwise around the temple sweeps us along. Some are walking with slow measured paces, others are crawling, with leather strips and bits of cardboard protecting their hands and knees, mumbling prayers, spinning prayer wheels, gaining more merit the more circles they complete. We come to the entrance of the Jokhang. In the courtyard people are prostrating themselves before the temple, some with legs bound together, dogs lying at their sides, goats tethered to stones. We watch in silence as they put their hands together in prayer, fall to their knees, gradually lower their bodies on to their hands and slide to the ground, arms stretched out in front. They remain still, faces pressed into the worn flagstones, quietly praying. Then, reversing the procedure, they rest on their hands, rise to their knees and slowly stand up in a kind of arduous religious push-up. One old woman stumbles as she rises, her body stiff with age, her hands crippled with arthritis. Over and over and over she prostrates, muttering prayers and mantras, struggling with her swollen, twisted joints.

Some worshippers mark the place where their heads touch the ground and begin the next prostration from that point, inching forward towards the entrance of the temple. Their eyes see nothing, turned inwards in rapt devotion, their faces lit with a mystical intensity. I am deeply moved and disturbed. I have never been so close to such intense religious communication, such naked elation, but the mixture of pain and ecstasy is difficult to watch. I feel uneasy; what I am witnessing is too private to be shared.

One of the first things that struck me in Lhasa was this prostration. It's bizarre to see people stretched out in the dust or lying on roads in pools of mud, the jeeps and bicycles carefully circumventing their prostrated bodies. The first time I saw an old man lying in the street in this manner, in filthy tattered clothes, I thought he was some poor beggar, hurt or sick. He was in fact a pilgrim, prostrating towards the Jokhang, slowly, painfully, his bones rigid with age, his face reflecting a passionate zeal, his eyes blind to the traffic. Pascal told us that until 1950 the only wheels in Tibet were prayer wheels. Lhasa had no wheeled vehicles for fear that their wheels would penetrate the earth and release evil spirits, so lying in the road presented no problems. Nowadays Tibet is a strange mixture of the medieval and the modern, its ancient religion and traditions so profoundly entrenched as to survive even the motorcar intact.

I am unable to enter the temple. Watching the prostrations is enough for one day. I feel overwhelmed by the unfamiliar. I must close my eyes and reflect. Also, I want to know more about the Jokhang before I enter it. Tim looks pale, his eyes sunk in dark circles. Doune is twisting the beads of her new necklace, her eyes remote. We leave the Jokhang and in silence make our way back to the Banak Shol, my head whirling like a prayer wheel.

Chapter Six

New Lhasa – Pascal, Ian and Jaye

I am up early. No one else is on the balcony. I have the mountains all to myself. I sip my tea leaning on the railing, watching the mist curl away from the peaks as the sun splashes them with pink, lavender and gold. I experience a deep contentment, an extraordinary serenity. It feels as though I've been here a long time and I want to remain longer. Much of travelling is riddled with the desire to get to the next place and the anxieties inherent in getting there. But sometimes the body, the spirit and the place are in perfect harmony and an exquisite stillness results. This is such a time. I am free from the compulsion to move on. I want to be exactly where I am.

People gradually emerge from their rooms with basins of water, toothbrushes, mugs of tea. They gather in small knots, greeting the new day. The balcony is our washroom, breakfast room and parlour. We wash, eat and socialise with the changing patterns of cloud, sun and stars, rising and falling over the mountains.

Our floor is occupied by Westerners, an intelligent lively group of travellers, more serious and seasoned than I have met elsewhere. All have been in China and enjoy exchanging stories of boat trips through spectacular gorges; bicycle rides in countryside resembling Chinese paintings, with limestone pinnacles pointing to the sky, one with a moon-shaped hole cut through its summit; visits with peasants who welcome you into their homes; a temple city where one can live in

Confucius' mansion and meditate by his graveside; any number of wild and wonderful tales which far outweigh the less poetic encounters and bureaucratic hassles.

I think China attracts the hard-core travellers' elite. To travel there one must not only have money – China is more expensive than other Asian countries – but commitment and endurance. The uncommitted fall by the wayside. We met people who were leaving after a few days, unable to cope. China is not exactly a holiday. There is no beach culture as in Thailand and Sri Lanka, and - except for wild marijuana – no drugs. There are no spaced-out dharma freaks, subsisting on pennies begged from other Westerners, as in India; no opium pipes shared with hill tribe people, as in Thailand; no Thai stick indulgences, no ganja milkshakes. One must be interested in experiencing China, rather than in lying back on a beach or getting stoned on a mountain-top. Travellers who survive China are generally more adventurous and resilient. I enjoyed meeting them, but the energetic pace of travel and the vastness of the country made this difficult. However, in Tibet the pace is leisurely; travellers are concentrated in the few available places and are therefore more accessible. In the Banak Shol there is a warm intimate atmosphere, a feeling of kinship, of family.

Pascal joins me. He has a tranquil presence which doesn't disturb my sense of peace. I was immediately interested in him when we met, attracted by his sensitive face and enigmatic manner. Like Texas Dave, he has been on the road for over ten years. But whereas Texas Dave's financial arrangements are up front (he has money invested in America and lives off the interest), Pascal's means of support is mysterious. There are hints of gambling, smuggling, and involvement with the underworld, which belie his soft-spoken gentle manner and make me want to know more. Besides, he's my chief source of information on Tibet and has loaned me several books about the country.

He invites me to his room for coffee. I pause in the doorway, surprised. 'This is lovely, Pascal....your room is beautiful.'

'I spend much time in hotels and must make my room something of myself to feel good in it.'

I understand the urge to convert the anonymity of a hotel room into something personal and friendly, having the same impulse myself. Pascal's efforts have had impressive results. He has removed one of the beds, making the room look more spacious. Reproductions of Tibetan tangkas cover the walls like exotic wallpaper. His table, draped with a woven cloth, holds a silver incense burner. The bare light bulb is hidden behind a Chinese Lantern and there's a Tibetan rug beside his bed. It's amazing how these touches have transformed a rather shabby room into some inner temple chamber, mysterious and inviting. He lights a stick of incense and begins to prepare the coffee. Unlike the rest of us who, at best, travel with Chinese Nescafe which we mix with thermos flask water, Pascal has finely ground aromatic coffee and brews it in an Arabic coffee pot, over a tiny cooker. He serves it in pale blue porcelain cups. It's delicious.

Pascal speaks a smattering of Chinese and limited Tibetan. That is, he *says* it's limited; to me it sounds fluent when I hear him chatting with the girls who bring the water and sweep the floor. He tells me he is arranging a trip to Nagarze, a small town approached through a high mountain pass south of Lhasa.

'Would you like to join me?' he asks casually.

'How can you manage that?' I ask, excited by the possibility, 'Our permits are only valid for Lhasa.'

'I have some friends,' is all he says.

'I'd love to go!' I leap at the opportunity, thrilled not only by the prospect of entering forbidden territory but by the chance to see a rare close-up of village life. 'Is there room for Tim and Doune?'

'We will make room. I will arrange it and tell you.'

I ask no further questions, confident I can rely on him. What luck. This is exactly what we had hoped for. I can't wait to tell Doune and Tim.

Tim is feeling ill. Both he and Doune smoke and suffer from shortness of breath and fast pulse rates. Tim also has a headache and chest pains. But nothing will interfere with Nagarze. 'I'm going, sick or not,' he vows.

I'm feeling surprisingly well. I still tire easily and my pulse is a little fast, but aside from these minor discomforts, the high altitude has lost its grip. However, my body has always been a good friend, the perfect travelling companion. When there is nothing to eat, it doesn't demand food. When there is no liquid, it doesn't get thirsty. It manages on either a little or a lot of sleep, depending on what's available. It rarely gets ill. In return, I don't smoke, hardly drink and take vitamin supplements, especially 'c', supposedly a natural antibiotic. It seems to work.

A little before noon I am sitting on the balcony rewarding my co-operative body with a rest and an English polo mint, engrossed in one of Pascal's books about Tibet, when all at once I find myself lifted into the air, as arms encircle my waist in a powerful hug. It's Ian. Jaye is grinning beside him. Ian and Jaye are an Australian couple we met in China at a hotel in Kunming, who took a year off their jobs to travel. They too, like us, were heading for Chengdu to get the plane to Lhasa. By coincidence we shared the same hard class sleeper to Chengdu.

It was our first train journey in China and most impressive. The sleeping compartment had two tiers of three berths each, with a table in between by the window. There was no door. The berths led on to a windowed corridor with two small foldaway seats by each window, where we could read, drink tea, smoke or just change the view. A mattress, sheets, pillow and even a towel, were provided. Everything was well-ordered. The loos were clean. The train left on time. The management was impeccable. Each car had its own conductor. Ours was a tiny efficient lady who ran a tight show. During the twenty five hour journey, which took a night and most of the next day, she washed the floor several times, swept it twice as often and hung our towels on a rail by the corridor window, making certain each time she passed that no one towel hung higher or lower than its neighbour. Throughout the day she brought thermos flasks of hot water for tea. In the evening she lined up our shoes neatly under the berths.

There was no sixth person in our compartment – the ticket office didn't dare condemn a Chinese soul to the hell of five foreigners. We had a great time. We laughed a lot, played games, ate, read, exchanged travel notes (Ian had an enviable collection of maps and timetables), and enjoyed the superb scenery, when we weren't submerged in a tunnel. Long noisy tunnels dug into the mountains ran for almost half the journey. They were a colossal engineering feat, but made much of the trip reminiscent of the London Underground.

At one point I broke out my stash of Stone-Forest Green. I remember when Tim first spotted the marijuana growing wild in the Stone Forest, several hours outside Kunming. He did a double-take and pointed to the plants with a Cheshire cat grin.

'Is that what I think it is?' I asked, inspecting the leaves in disbelief.

'It sure is.'

'Do you think the Chinese know what it is?'

'I wonder…. It's a mind-blowing thought,' he said, executing a heavy pirouette, then added, 'but I know who does know exactly what it is – those Lonely Planet guys who wrote the China Bible. I couldn't figure out what they were on about when they said. "The Stone Forest has some mind bending weeds". Clever buggers.'

'We must pick some,' I urged.

'Not a good idea.'

'But how can you get busted for picking a weed that grows wild? Besides, at the American Embassy Mr Nolan told me there are no Westerners in Chinese prisons.'

'And we want to keep it that way.'

'Come on. What can they bust me for? I'm not dealing or growing or importing, I'm just picking. How can you resist grass from the stoned forest? I'll just pick a handful.'

I picked two handfuls, dried the leaves hidden in my bureau drawer and crumbled them into a thimbleful of grass. In the intimacy of our hard class sleeper, Tim rolled several thin joints, American-style. We were more turned on by the idea than the grass.

We left Chengdu before Ian and Jaye and weren't sure when we would meet up with them again. Now they are here and I get Tim and Doune, who are delighted to see them. It' s a warm day, although not sunny and we decide to take showers after Ian and Jaye have rested. We all need them. Ian and Jaye are hot and dusty; Tim, Doune and I have had only C and A's (crotch and armpits) since our arrival. I have researched the shower situation and there are two possibilities. The Number One Chinese Guesthouse, where many travellers stay, has clean shower rooms with hot water that stays hot. The Tibetan Public Bath House is less savoury and the water only intermittently hot. We decide on the Number One. For some things it pays to choose Chinese.

Doune and I head for the Chinese section of Lhasa to visit the

Friendship Store, having arranged to meet the others later on. It's windy out and the wind spins dust in our faces. Most Chinese are wearing gauze face masks. We don ours. I dislike breathing through the mask, being sensitive to any sensation of smothering, but it helps, and I reluctantly keep it on. We come to a traffic circle, in the middle of which a policeman is directing traffic from a high podium. He wears long white gloves, a white jacket and trousers and a white helmet, all spotless. He moves with aloof staccato formality, like a well-groomed robot, incongruous in the muddle of people (masked and unmasked), donkeys, dogs, bicycles, carts, jeeps, trucks and swirling dust.

The Friendship Store is much like those in China but shabbier, and the locals are permitted to shop on two of its floors. There are three floors selling a poor selection of mainly Chinese goods. The ground floor has tinned and packaged food and I buy some Russian mackerel in tomato sauce, some instant noodles and tinned Chinese peaches as there is no fresh fruit in Lhasa. We point to what we want, and the Chinese girl serving us takes it from the shelf, calculating our bill on her abacus.

Doune wants to buy sugar. We find 'sugar' in the vocabulary section of our phrase book and point to the Chinese counterpart. Despite the simplicity of our request, we are shunted from one counter to another. Finally someone presents Doune with a tray of sweets. Doune shakes her head. The girl looks perplexed and consults someone else. After a huddled discussion someone offers a jar of jam. Doune shakes her head again. Confusion. By now most of the salespeople in the section have gathered round us. Noticing a mug and thermos bottle on the counter, Doune gets an idea. She mimes pouring tea from the thermos into the mug and stirring it. Although the Chinese don't sugar their tea, some astute saleslady, familiar with Western peculiarities, understands, and rushes off to get a bag of sugar. When Doune nods and claps her hands, everyone smiles and chatters excitedly, relieved. The foreigners have been appeased. All is well. 'I wonder what the book translates sugar as,' Doune says. 'Apparently nothing simple like "sugar",' I reply. Later we discover that the translation was 'sweet'. Not surprising that the girls were confused.

We avoid the middle floor which sells mostly modern Chinese clothing and arrive, panting, on the third floor. This is a smaller room catering for foreigners only, with a strange assortment of goods intended to please them: Chinese silk pyjamas, furry toys, coca-cola, T-shirts printed with panda bears and the Potala, foreign cigarettes and chocolate and Tibetan postcards arranged in sets, each set in a folder. They include photos of the Jokhang, several of the Potala and some of Lhasa. The best thing about them, apart from their cheapness, is a brief English explanation. The idea of beginning a card with 'Greetings from the rooftop of the world' appeals to me. I buy many sets.

The effort of conducting these transactions is exhausting and we head for the nearby Number One Guesthouse to wait for the others, hoping to get some lunch before they arrive. The Number One is completely Chinese, with no trace of Tibet in its architecture or atmosphere. When we enter the large bare dining-room, exactly like those in China, with its big round tables filled with Chinese workers eating, we are given to understand that lunch is over. We are back in China where meals are served at specific times only and damn the deviant. We sit at an empty table, nibbling left-over peanuts, and watch the men eating noisily, employing the Chinese suck and spit method, sucking bits of flesh and spitting the bones on the floor. They eat quickly with intense concentration and leave as soon as they finish. The waitress and waiter clear up instantly. What a different atmosphere to our laid-back Banak Shol. No wonder the Tibetans and Chinese have problems relating; their focus, pace and lifestyles are whole cultures removed. And the two cities they have created in Lhasa are histories apart.

Jaye and Ian arrive and then Tim. We are all thirsty. Ian, being a bit of a performer, manages to mime a gigantic thirst, which inspires a sympathetic waitress to bring us warm Chinese coca-colas. After we finish them Ian notices a refrigerator behind a counter at the far end of the dining-room. We order another round and through mime and charm, Ian explains that we want to put our cokes in the fridge and drink them after our showers. Surprisingly, the girl not only understands, but agrees (she must fancy Ian). Ian writes our names on the bottles and watches as the waiter helps her arrange them in the refrigerator.

The showers are in another building. When we try to buy tickets we are refused. A Western guest says it's because the water is heated by solar power and there hasn't been enough sunshine. Whatever the reason, we are terribly disappointed. 'I must wash my hair, it's crawling,' I complain. 'We can always go to the public showers,' Tim says. 'I guess it's better than nothing.' Reluctantly we cross the street to the Public Bath House. It hasn't received good press and we soon discover why. The Bath House has two sections, one for men, another for women, the latter mysteriously more expensive.

In the ladies' there are two small areas with shower stalls and an entrance room containing rows of benches. Tibetan women in various stages of undress pack every inch of available space. The benches are jammed with soap, towels, clothing and women combing each other's hair. The place is filthy, globules of spittle splatter the floor and hang from the walls. The room is thick with steam. As though the thin air isn't enough, our lungs now have to contend with heavy steam. Struggling to breathe, we undress on the spot, standing barefoot on the slimy floor, one behind the other in the narrow aisle, naked except for a towel, clutching our belongings, waiting our turn. Nasty drops spit from the ceiling. Vulnerable and exposed, I shudder as I am suddenly reminded of a queue waiting for a shower in a concentration camp. I shake my head hard to dislodge the image.

Only five of the twelve showers work, and the women take forever. It's a social event, a day out. They come with laundry and families. The atmosphere is lively, if oppressive. Babies scream as they're washed, girls giggle, women gossip. They enter the shower in twos and threes, laughter and squeals coming from behind the closed doors. When I finally get to it, the shower stall is cramped, with a bench so filthy I am loath to put my clothes on it. The walls are rotting with mould, the floor covered with scum, and the drain stuffed with hair and muck. I shower without bending, arms tight against my body, dreading to touch anything. But the water stays hot and miraculously I exit with a scrubbed glowing body, wonderfully clean.

We meet Tim and Ian in the Number One dining-room. Their shower experience was less horrific and much quicker. Having dehydrated in the Bath House, we are all looking forward to our cold drinks. The same waiter is behind the counter where the refrigerator and our precious cokes reside. Ian explains, his limited vocabulary supplemented by sober mime, that we want them. Total lack of comprehension. Ian presses on. Finally the waiter leaves and returns with a man who speaks some English. He seems to know the situation because the first thing he says is, 'Mayo coca-cola.'

'But I know they're in the fridge. Please get them for us,' Ian says politely.

The man shakes his head. 'Lady not here,' he says by way of explanation.

'But you can get them for us.'

'Not my work.'

'Listen, we've paid for them, we want to drink them, we're very thirsty.' Ian is getting slightly irritated.

'Wait for lady come.'

'When will lady come?'

'Tonight.'

'Tonight? We want them now, not tonight.'

'Mayo coca-cola. Wait for lady come,' is his final verdict. He shrugs his shoulders and begins to leave the room.

Suddenly Ian leaps over the counter, opens the fridge door and removes the cokes. The man is horrified. He attempts to reclaim the bottles. Ian shows him our names, but he is adamant. 'Wait for lady come.'

Very calmly Ian takes out his Swiss knife, withdraws its opener, opens a bottle, and begins to drink. Blood rushes to the man's face and he stalks out of the room in angry protest. We have ruined the order in his existence.

'Why are the Chinese so helpful and kind when you meet them on the street and so unhelpful and rigid when you meet them in some official capacity?' I ask.

'Bureaucracy. It all comes down to bureaucracy,' Ian replies. 'The individual is diminished by the system. Only the rules matter.' We gulp our cokes, wishing it had been otherwise.

That evening, in honour of Jaye and Ian's arrival, I decide to make dinner. Tim and Doune are delighted. I also invite Pascal. 'Don't expect much,' I warn him.

'I don't understand how I can expect anything,' he says.

The idea of a dinner party is exciting and I take a long time with the preparations. I examine my plastic larder which contains a small bottle of olive oil, bought in Hong Kong and saved for special occasions, and my stash of tiny plastic bags filled with oregano, basil, dried parsley, dill, paprika and ground chilli. I have bought some boiled eggs in the market, and now mash them with olive oil, dried parsley and paprika, adding diced onions and sweet white radish. Next, I make a fish salad by mixing the Russian tinned mackerel in its tomato sauce and adding chilli and chipped cucumber. For the main course I mix tinned tomatoes and boiling water from the thermos, adding Italian herbs, fresh garlic and chopped onions. Then I empty instant noodles into the mixture, creating Chinese-style spaghetti. I get fresh bread downstairs.

Flushed with success, I prepare tinned peaches and yoghurt, with a trickle of apricot jam, for dessert. I remove one of the beds to make more space and replace it with chairs scrounged from various rooms. As a final touch I cover the table with my Burmese lavender shawl, set it with plates and cutlery borrowed from the kitchen and light two purple candles. Doune has created napkins from an old kerchief and folds them into elegant peaks. Tim sets up his walkman with speakers. Pascal arrives bearing two bottles of French red wine, a minor miracle.

We dine by candlelight to the music of UB 40, Bob Marley and J.J Cale. The food is pronounced delicious. A cordon bleu chef couldn't receive more compliments. The alcohol ban is relaxed under special dispensation and we all get beautifully mellow. Wine at high altitudes is very effective. After eating, in keeping with the dinner club atmosphere, we dance in the entrance room, my newly washed hair flying like a girl in a shampoo ad, instead of sticking to itself in greasy clumps. Texas Dave, Gina and several others join us. Beer appears. I get very turned on to 'Red Red Wine', my Sunsilk-ad hair, and Pascal.

The dancing continues. It turns out to be quite a party. But by midnight even Texas Dave is exhausted.

Pascal kisses me goodnight, softly, slowly. I want more but don't have the energy to make any moves. Apparently neither does he. 'Remember the sky burial tomorrow. I'm going by bicycle so I'll meet you there. Sleep well,' is all he says. By the time I open my eyes he's gone. Through a euphoric haze I recall that tomorrow is the day I've been dreading. But my body and mind are too wonderfully relaxed to register any anxiety at Pascal's parting words. I fall asleep, remembering only his kiss.

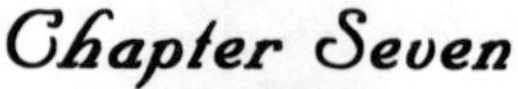

Chapter Seven

The Sky Burial

Six am, I awake before the alarm, filled with apprehension about attending the sky burial. I had resisted making the decision to go. 'It's like being in Pamplona and not attending a bull fight,' Texas Dave said. As a matter of fact, I had been in Pamplona and hadn't attended a bull fight. But Pascal finally convinced me this was different – a unique ancient ritual at the heart of Tibetan culture and belief. Experiencing such an event was the essence of travelling and to miss it would be like travelling with blinkers. I might as well be on a tourist bus, sheltered and shielded not only from Tibet but from myself.

It's just beginning to get light and it's chilly. Tim, Doune and I gulp a hurried cup of Chinese tea. We've been given directions to the burial site. It's about an hour's walk. We are to turn left at a rubbish dump, and at that point should see a fire on a hill. That's our goal. We head into the countryside. It's early morning and the road is dotted with peasants going into Lhasa on foot or in small donkey carts. They carry sacks of grain, hay, vegetables and other goods for market. Traffic is sparse; several trucks filled with workers, some army vehicles carrying soldiers. We are in a valley, green with barley, surrounded by stark, barren mountains. Then the rubbish dump. We pick our way through rusty cans, metal bits, rotting clothing and other unsavouries.

We can see a fire burning on a hill and climb to a small rocky plateau. This is the burial site: a stubbly patch of ground on top of a rocky hill at the base of bare mountains, looking like wrinkled old elephant's hide. Below are the tin roofs of Chinese barrack-like buildings, glinting in the rising sun. Five Tibetan men and a boy of about ten are seated around the fire drinking tea, talking and joking. They wear ordinary work clothes – worn jackets, peaked caps, rough cotton trousers. They smile and motion us to sit. Nearby is the 'altar', a large flat rock with bowl-like depressions. It is separated from where the Tibetans sit by a shallow gully, strewn with bits of discarded clothing and hunks of hair.

Pascal arrives and joins us; it's the second time he's been. We sit by the edge of the gully facing the altar rock. Pascal gestures towards the mountains. I look up. Neat rows of silent birds are perched on ledges – vultures. Their colours blend so perfectly with the mountains that at first they are hard to distinguish. Ravens swoop in and out of the gully and gather nervously in black patches on the altar rock. A white square bundle, tied with a rope, sits among the ravens. A small dog struggles up the rock and chases them. The rising sun slowly turns the drab greys and dull browns of the mountains to patches of pale gold and dusty pinks. I become pleasantly warm.

About fifteen Westerners trickle in. No Chinese are present. There have been some unpleasant incidents with the Chinese. In the past some have jeered at the burial procedure, proclaiming it barbaric. Now Tibetans stone them whenever they appear. Westerners still seem welcome, although this surprises me because they too have created incidents. Despite of the fact that Tibetans strictly forbid photographs, some Westerners are desperate to capture the sky burial on film. Several days ago one such desperate Australian hid himself, his telescopic lenses and his elaborate camera equipment, high in the hills, determined to take the prize photos. His frenzied preparations frightened the birds away, an intensely evil omen. He was discovered and bombarded with rocks. Next day the Westerners who attended were stoned. Yesterday several filtered back and were allowed to remain. Today we are greeted with smiles. Tibetans are wonderfully tolerant and forgiving. Still, I feel certain that our days at the burial site are numbered.

A little after eight am. The sun touches the altar rock. This is the signal for the burial to begin. One of the Tibetan men dons a grubby white coat and a white surgical-type cap. He is the man in charge. He says something to us in Tibetan. Pascal translates: 'While they work, no pictures.' The man in charge, two of the Tibetan men and the boy, climb on to the rock. The other two Tibetans, relatives of the deceased, remain by the fire. The man in white is thin and wiry with flashing black eyes and black hair sticking out from under the cap, wild-looking. He unties the bundle. A woman, naked except for an unbuttoned faded red blouse, tumbles out. She looks pregnant, youngish, with long black hair. (Later we learn that her body was carried a long distance on someone's back, since there are only a few places in Tibet where sky burials are performed.)

The man in charge drags her body over the rock and lays it face down in the centre. He begins without ceremony by pulling off the woman's blouse and flinging it into the gully. He yanks a large knife from his belt and with surgical precision cuts a slit down her spine. Starting from the shoulder blade he strips the flesh away down the left side of her back, using swastika-patterned cuts. (For Tibetans the swastika is the symbol of eternity.) This done, he neatly hacks off her left arm with his knife. The severed arm is tossed to the young boy who, squatting on his haunches, pounds it to a pulp with something which looks like the back of an axe, using one of the depressions in the rock as a container. It's hard work for a boy and he grunts and groans as he works. The man in charge continues to hack the left side of the body, panting loudly, like someone chopping wood. The two men, also squatting, are thrown flesh and bones which they too pound in the bowl-like depressions. The sounds of panting and puffing combine with the squishing sound of flesh being pulverised and bones being smashed. Tsampa, a mixture of barley flour, tea and yak butter, is added to the flesh and bones to make a paste. Everything happens quickly. The men work with a practised skill, pausing only to sharpen their axes, or for a short cigarette break. So engrossed am I by their expertise, I almost forget what they are doing.

The woman's right side is begun, the flesh sliced efficiently from the ribs. The man's white coat becomes splattered with blood as he severs the limbs, detaching them from the rest of the body with a bloodied white cloth. By now the rock looks like a butcher's shop, bloody with tattered flesh and strewn limbs, and the woman like a butchered carcass. I turn away many times, unable to watch, then turn back, unable not to watch. Some vultures fly off the mountains and begin circling the alter rock, gliding over our heads. The butcher continues working. He flips over what remains of the body, a torso with no back or limbs. He chops hard with one resounding blow, through the chest cavity, and reaching inside pulls out the heart. Holding it up, he shouts something to the two Tibetans by the fire. They nod. He chops the heart to bits. Then the stomach is slit open and the organs removed. These are cut up and kept separate, not pounded.

The work is easier now. While they work, the men talk, laugh and joke, but do not break their work rhythm. The Westerners are silent. Lastly the head is separated from the neck with one neat blow. The severed head is held up. I remember John the Baptist; only this man is no Salome and the seven veils are bloodied rags. The butcher holds the head by the hair and deftly scalps it. Then, tying the long black hair into a knot, he flings it into the gully. Next he picks up a large flat stone and, holding it overhead, mutters a short prayer and smashes the skull, twice.

One of the seated Tibetans brings tea on to the rock for the workers. The vultures circle closer. An old monk dressed in crimson and saffron robes appears close to us. Facing the rock, he says a prayer with his hands held together, and prostrates before the rock. A Chinese man carrying a briefcase, dressed in navy blue trousers and a sparkling white shirt, appears from nowhere. He climbs the rock and hands the man in charge a cigarette. They discuss something. Apparently a small group of well-dressed official-looking Chinese have been given permission to attend. At a signal from their leader, they hasten to the edge of the plateau and sit with us.

At this point the man in charge faces the mountains and turning to the vultures, calls: 'Shoo…..Tzshoo….' At the signal, about a dozen vultures (the vanguard) leave their mountain perch and swoop on to the rock. The rest remain, not breaking rank. He throws bits of flesh as they gather around him. They are huge beautiful birds with white necks and legs, and speckled tan and white bodies. Their wings flutter and spread to reveal white undersides and dark brown tips. Some are so close that we can see their bright blue eyes. The vultures wait with restraint as the work continues. The boy bundles the chopped organs into a cloth. Several vultures, unable to maintain discipline, try to steal bits of flesh from the boy. The man in charge angrily chases them off the rock with kicks and abusive shouts, as though punishing them for bad behaviour. When he is finished, the boy carries the bundle off the rock. The two men leave with him. Then the man in charge, facing the mountain ledges, raises his arms to the vultures and addresses them in a shrill singsong voice: 'Tria… soya…..tria'

Suddenly hundreds of vultures fill the sky, hover in a quivering cloud above our heads, their wings beating a nervous fluttering sound, and descend on the rock, completely covering it. As the vultures vie for space, the ravens cling to the edges. The birds are served with the preparation of flesh, bones and tsampa. The tsampa has been added to make the mixture more palatable, for it is a bad omen if anything is left uneaten. The vultures eat greedily, fighting over scraps of flesh, slipping off the rock, pushing each other in their haste to consume. The ravens join the feast cautiously; uninvited guests, they must be content to scramble at the outer edges, snapping up any morsels the vultures accidentally drop.

At this point several Westerners attempt to photograph the vultures. The man in charge becomes incensed. Leaping off the rock, he rushes at two German girls, brandishing his knife and shouting. He points the knife at the heart of one of the girls. Livid with rage, he grabs both their cameras and rips the film from them, tearing it to shreds and flinging it in the fire. He's like a rabid madman and shouts at us to leave. I begin to go, disturbed and frightened. Those who have brought cameras quickly hide them. Several people leave immediately. The rest are suddenly signalled to stay by the other Tibetans.

The birds finish eating but do not leave the rock. They flutter about, timid and nervous, in staccato hops. I wonder why they linger. The answer comes quickly. The bundle of organs is returned to the rock. They have been waiting for these choice morsels – dessert. Voraciously they devour every last bit. Finally the feast is over. The vultures take to the sky bearing the deceased with them, upwards to the heavens. The rock is empty. An hour ago there was a body on the rock, now there is nothing. The Chinese and then the Westerners begin to leave. The man in charge sits with the other Tibetans around the fire in animated discussion, his black eyes flashing. Tea is served. There is no sign of mourning, no tears, no wailing, no prayers.

Attending a sky burial for a Tibetan must be the equivalent of going to the morgue for a Westerner. Family members are present only to ensure that everything is done as it should be.

Two men climb the rock to check that all has been eaten and to clean it for the next burial. They joke and laugh as they work. I sit, too stunned to move. This has been the strangest, the most bizarre thing I have ever witnessed. Powerful images rage through my brain. What amazes me is that despite the horrific nature of what I have seen, I feel no revulsion. One reason must be the inevitable distancing of oneself from the intensity and nearness of the experience. But more important is a feeling that the sky burial fits in with the isolation and strangeness of the setting. Somehow, in that alien environment, it all makes sense. I am the last one to leave.

Chapter Eight

Tashi

The others are waiting for me at the bottom of the hill. Tim, Doune and I planned on visiting Sera Monastery, not far from the burial site. Pascal suggests we go instead to a tea house in Lhasa where he is to meet Tashi, a Tibetan friend who is soon returning to India where he lives, his parents having left Tibet in 1959, when the Dalai Lama and thousands of Tibetans fled the Chinese. I am glad to postpone Sera. My head is seething with the sky burial, reluctant for more input. Tim and Doune opt for Sera.

'You'll be glad to meet Tashi,' Pascal says, 'He's a very special person, very magical.'

'I could do with a bit of magic, I'm all magicked out.'

'Then Tashi is the man.'

Pascal gets his bicycle which is propped against a rock. 'We're taking a short way through the mountains. Do you want to ride with me on the bicycle?' He asks.

'If you don't mind doing all the work.'

'I don't mind. You can't be too heavy. In any case we must walk much of the way, but it is very beautiful.'

I climb onto the seat of his bicycle and we take off along the dirt road, wobbling and bumping as Pascal steers between stones and gravel ridges. To steady myself I hold his waist. His body feels firm, solid, reassuring under his thin cotton T-shirt. As he struggles with the terrain, the shirt rides up and my fingers spread slowly, embracing the contour of his muscles, memorising the moist, vibrant life, filling my senses with it, blotting out that other body on the rock.

The makeshift road becomes a narrow path, too difficult for cycling. We walk, Pascal pushing the bicycle, my head blistering with images leaping at me from every rock. I feel fearful, troubled, resisting some unnamed threat.

'Are you thinking about the sky burial?' Pascal asks hesitantly, not wanting to intrude. But I am grateful for the intrusion.

'Why do you suppose they let us watch it, especially since we are so insensitive, so rude with our cameras. It's such an intensely private ceremony, you'd think they'd want to keep it to themselves, not share it with a bunch of gaping foreigners.'

'For them it's not private. It's their most common way of burying the dead. For a Tibetan, once a person is dead his body is not important. Only his soul is important, and the sky burial protects his soul. It makes sure that it is taken to heaven by the birds. Tibetans are not afraid of death because they believe if they have gained merit in this life they will be born to a higher form in the next life. My friend Tashi will explain it to you, it's part of the Buddhist philosophy.'

We continue walking, me still struggling with the sky burial and now the Buddhist philosophy.

Pascal interrupts my thoughts. 'In the West we allow our bodies to be eaten by worms. But of course we do not see the worms doing it. For me, I would prefer to be eaten by birds and to rise into the sky, it has more poetry.'

'I guess it does,' I say without conviction, unhappy with both options.

We walk in silence. But I am still convinced that there is something wrong, something voyeuristic, about Westerners attending the sky burial. Our Western culture doesn't equip us to deal with it. For us it can only be horrific, with nothing religious or secular to temper the horror, no context in which to place it. To see a body mutilated, chopped to bits and fed to vultures can only signify brutality, the ultimate disrespect for the ultimate personal disaster. Even animals, like the South American Guanaco, stand vigil by their dead calves to prevent scavenger birds, like vultures, from eating them.

We hold that the body is sacred in death. We adorn it, paint it, beautify it so that our last vision of the deceased is a pleasing tranquil one, as though by prettifying death it becomes less terrifying. 'He looks just like he's asleep, not a bit changed. May he rest in peace.' That last vision shapes our memory for all time; we want it to be uplifting, whole, untampered with. I remember when my father died suddenly, the doctors wanted to perform an autopsy to determine the cause of death. The thought was unbearable to me. 'Don't touch my father,' I warned, fierce with anguish, 'don't cut him. I don't want my father cut up. Please leave him in peace.' I was part of a cultural bias to bury the body intact. Even the medical profession respects the bias. I was told that when a body is dissected for medical reasons, all parts are carefully assembled before burial. Some religions even forbid burying the body with an organ missing.

And what about our reverence for cemeteries, for graves and grave-stones. Burying a loved one in a special place where he can be visited, communed with, paid respect to, is vital. We chisel his name so deeply that several lifetimes cannot obliterate it: 'In Loving Memory'. We compose careful epitaphs, sometimes coy: 'We were not there to say goodbye, to hold your hand and see you die'; sometimes profound, like the one W.B. Yeats wrote for himself: 'Cast a cold eye on life, on death. Horseman pass by'; or humorous like W.C.Fields', 'I'd rather be in Philadelphia'; or even commanding like Marx's 'Workers of the world unite'.

The dead want to be remembered and the living make pilgrimages to graveyards to remember. To have a body vanish, disappear into thin air, is horrendous, often more terrible than death itself. Why else do we go to such extremes to reclaim a dead body, rescuing it from disasters, often at great risk to the living, carrying it home over many miles? Why else would the British police still be trying to persuade the murderers of two children, buried on the Yorkshire moors over twenty years ago, to reveal the whereabouts of the bodies 'as an act of compassion to the families involved'? The body, even in death, especially in death, is wanted, needed.

I remember visiting a small fishing village in the Aran Islands off the West Coast of Ireland. A fishing boat had capsized weeks earlier but the women still waited with the desperate hope that the sea would return their dead. Each day they sat on the shore, looked over the rocks and prayed. 'Dear God, return him to me so that he can have a clean burial and a deep grave. Return him to me so that I may know where he lies buried and can watch over his grave.' The burial would make the death bearable; without it neither the women nor their men would know peace. The man, even in death, is his body. Without it he is doomed to some unlocatable desolation, and the woman, with nothing tangible to mourn, is doomed with him. I realise how important my father's grave is to me. I cross the ocean to visit it, perform small rituals beside it, and tend to it with the care and love I wish I had given him before he died so suddenly.

Thoughts about death, especially my father's death, are painful. I break the silence to dispel them.

'Pascal, don't you find it strange that Tibetans have kept foreigners out of their country for centuries, but when they are finally allowed in, nothing is prohibited, nothing seems sacred? We can wander in anywhere, enter into the most personal rituals, see anything: monks eating, people prostrating, holy temples, sacred sites, even the sky burial.'

'The Tibetan people never kept the foreigners out; it was the Tibetan authorities, especially the lamas and monks, they wanted to keep their culture pure, not contaminated by foreigners. They wanted to keep themselves isolated because they were worried that their traditional life, their customs and their religion, would crumble if it was exposed to influences from the outside world. They were isolated by nature anyway – Tibet is surrounded by the highest mountains in the world – but they increased their natural isolation by keeping foreigners out of Tibet. They were even more frightened than the Chinese of the foreign devil's poison. But the Tibetans themselves, the Tibetan people, are very welcoming and very tolerant. It is part of their culture and religion to welcome everyone, to respect all beliefs. You know there are minorities living in Lhasa who have been here for a very long time without any problems. The Muslims built their mosque right in the heart of Lhasa, and they practise their religion freely. What I find most wonderful about Tibetans is that they don't try to convert anyone to their way of thinking. They respect everyone.'

'But Pascal, maybe the lamas and monks were right. Lhasa was probably the last forbidden city, perhaps we should have left it that way, left one ancient civilisation alone and left ourselves one mystery.'

After a long while Pascal says, 'Perhaps'.

The grip of searing images and disquieting thoughts gradually eases as I become aware of the sun, warm between my shoulder blades. It's a perfect day, a perfect place, the essence of a landscape, a climate, I have no experience with. A valley of stones, the mountains stark on either side, cut with deep shadows and sudden patches of light, the sky a bright hard blue. I'm in a place that as yet has no memories for me, but as I contemplate the harsh landscape, the boulders trembling in balance, I can almost remember something. I feel the stirring of an uneasy excitement.

The path widens and Pascal helps me mount the bicycle. 'You must be exhausted,' I say, feeling the strain in his body as he forces his way through the hills, 'even I'm feeling tired and you're doing all the work.'

'I don't mind. I'm used to the altitude, you're not.' With me clutching Pascal we cycle back into Lhasa and head for the tea house.

I look forward to the Lhasa tea house. In China, tea houses were my favourite places. We had found three in Kunming. The first while wandering through the back alleys, directly on the pavement of a narrow street. Men with thin pointed white beards and wispy whiskers, looking like fragile sages, sat by long wooden tables, as ancient as themselves, their backs against the tea shop wall, observing. They sucked on narrow amber glasses while puffing on pipes with small silver bowls and curved stems from which hung delicate chains strung with jade. Continuously filled from a steaming kettle fragrant with jasmine, no glass was ever empty. They invited us to sit with them and we accepted eagerly, welcoming the opportunity for social contact with the Chinese. We had bought a flat round bread with sesame seeds, for us a rare treat, and Doune offered them some. Politely, they refused. Tim tried cigarettes. They accepted, but carefully, without haste, and with slow nods of appreciation.

Their curiosity about us was patient, gentle, tempered by centuries of civilisation. Our phrase book was passed from hand to hand. They were all able to read and quickly grasped the idea of pointing to the English equivalent of a Chinese phrase or word. Limited to simple phrase book questions, they asked where we came from, what work we did (Tim's answer of 'carpenter' delighted them), where we had been in China, if China pleased us. Our answers were shared among them and pondered with thoughtful nods. Children on their school lunch break, carrying empty white mugs, to be filled at a communal kitchen with rice, vegetables, and perhaps fish, gathered around us, sparkling clean with shiny black hair. 'Hello', 'Goodbye', 'A, B, C, D', they chanted, anxious to practise their English. The men, pleased by this display of erudition, smiled proudly, their mouths pursed with pride, but after a few minutes signalled them to leave, careful that we were not disturbed. The children ran off laughing and waving, with parting cries of 'A, B, C, D'. When we started to leave, the men held us a while longer with a final glass of tea, pressed upon us with small rueful smiles. The quiet dignity of their welcome and their restrained but obvious pleasure in our company was deeply touching.

Another day in Kunming we found a tea house oasis in a small open square. Men and women sat under pagodas, drinking tea, their heads moving like pendulums to the rhythm of Chinese music coming from a speaker in a tree, and dozing peacefully in the shade, having rocked themselves to sleep.

We discovered a third tea house in a disused temple with elaborately carved and painted pagodas set in a sparse garden. In one pagoda young men played billiards. In another, men and a sprinkling of women sat around tables in animated groups, sipping tea, playing mahjong and smoking bongs, sheltered from the sun and the crowded streets jangling with bicycle bells. Delicate old ladies, with tiny feet bound from childhood (a practice no longer allowed), tripped with small steps among tables, filling tea glasses. Their smiles and nods as they filled ours conveyed the empathy of an understood shared existence.

But my favourite Chinese tea house was in Chengdu (although I hear the ones in Shanghai are even better, set in elaborate gardens with streams bright with goldfish and waterlilies). We stumbled upon it while strolling through Remin Park, the 'People's Park' which every Chinese city has. Its bamboo tables and chairs were set among flowers and shaded by trees. As in the other tea houses, we were the only Westerners but in contrast to the singling out in the streets, we were accepted and quietly welcomed. This tea house seemed more family-style, with mothers cradling babies and the inevitable old men balancing toddlers on their knees. One elderly man with a thin pale face and skin like fine porcelain, shuffled from table to table, keeping the tea glasses brimming.

On a nearby chair a man was leaning back in enviable bliss, having his ears cleaned with something resembling a thin single-pronged tuning fork which quivered when flicked, and being massaged with a carved stone the masseur wore around his neck. We watched as the masseur stroked the stone, feeding it energy, then rubbed its smooth surface over the man's face, caressing his forehead, eyes and cheekbones with the slow curves of Chinese script. My body oozed with pleasure. Unable to resist, I signalled the masseur to do me as well. He froze in distress, his face pained. He had probably never touched a foreigner before, let alone a female one, and was only too willing to forego the experience.

Trembling like his tuning fork, he darted frantic looks at his fellow tea drinkers, appealing for assistance. None materialised. And I was merciless, beckoning persistently, until, under the silent pressure of losing face, he stoically advanced, rubbing his stone for comfort. But then, with the determination of a professional, he proceeded confidently with his work, safe within the confines of its familiarity, busy with its small rituals. Tim took a photo. I was ecstatic as the delicate vibrations shivered in my ears and the cool stone, manipulated with divine secrets, flushed away the knots and kinks concealed in my foreign body and alien psyche, leaving me as blissful as any ordinary Chinese customer – all for a flat fee of twenty cents. When I tried to tip him, he returned the money in confused embarrassment. Hadn't I caused him enough grief already?

The Lhasa tea house is disappointing. It's a Muslim tea house close to the Jokhang Temple, a bare room with a dirty, uneven stone floor, and tables and chairs scattered at random. Several Tibetan Muslims wearing small pillbox hats sit poring over papers and slurping tea. The owner, distinguished by a dirty white apron tied over a round belly, greets Pascal with a huge smile and a flood of enthusiastic Tibetan, then rushes out to bring tea, his gestures large, like an Italian opera singer. The tea is served Muslim-style, in covered cups, with lids like pointed roofs, and crystals of rock sugar in a saucer. It is neither the Chinese green (without milk or sugar), nor the Tibetan black (milky and sweet, or greasy with yak butter), but made from lotus seeds, drunk without milk and sweetened with rock sugar. Delicious. It redeems the tea house.

Tashi comes after our first cup and is welcomed with even more enthusiasm and still larger gestures. His area of the table is wiped clean and tea brought before he is even seated. I am immediately drawn to Tashi. He is in his late twenties, tall and lean with straight black hair falling over his ears, high cheekbones, black eyes and an extraordinary beauty. He wears a white shirt, the sleeves pushed up, dark cotton trousers, sandals and one long exquisite silver and turquoise earring. Pascal and Tashi embrace with affection, a great fondness between them, then Pascal reaches in his bag and produces two medical books in English, (Tashi is studying traditional Tibetan and also Western medicine in India) and a book I gave him about the Canadian doctor Norman Bethune, who worked in China. 'For you Tashi, a present for going away.'

Intense delight spreads over Tashi's face, flooding it with magic. 'Thank you my friend.'

My eyes do not leave his face. It is like gazing into a deep, still pool, tranquil, calming, yet tinged with excitement.

Pascal introduces us, and as Tashi reaches for my hand, a bridge springs up joining our eyes. 'Niema?' he says, surprised. 'That's a Tibetan name.'

I am even more surprised. 'Really? What does it mean?'

'The sun.' How strange. Whenever possible I sign my name followed by a smiling sun.

For a moment we are silent, our hands joined, our eyes linked, each remembering something. Then he says, 'I had a younger brother called Niema'.

Dimly, I register the 'had'. 'Really?' again. 'Is it a boy's name?'

'Sometimes. It can be either.'

'When I was young I wanted very much to be a boy.' Then I add lightly, 'Perhaps I was a Tibetan once, or maybe I am yet to become one.'

Tashi searches for something in my face, then says, 'Yes. It is possible.' I wait for him to continue but he smiles and sits down, his interest turning to the books and the tea, while mine is riveted on him.

When Tashi has flipped through the books, unable to postpone the pleasure, and the ceremonial sugaring and stirring is over and we settle into the sipping, he asks, 'Where have you been this morning?'

'We are coming from the sky burial,' Pascal says.

'Ah, the Jhator….that's the best way to be buried. I will be buried that way. When I die I want to go up to the heavens with the birds.' He smiles serenely as though anticipating some great joy.

'The idea of vultures gobbling up your body doesn't bother you?' I ask, mention of the sky burial evoking a fresh flood of images now permanently embedded in my consciousness and still surface vivid.

He turns toward me with a wonderful serenity. 'I wish my body to be eaten by vultures. You see in Tibet there are no cemeteries because for a Tibetan the body is of no use when the soul has departed. It is good to feed it to the birds. It is an act of altruism, of compassion, and compassion is the heart of the Buddhist belief. The word "Jhator" in its exact translation means giving alms to the birds.'

I cling to every word, fascinated, not wanting to interrupt, but the pragmatist in me has its way. 'Someone at the Banak Shol told me that the sky burial exists because it is the easiest and cheapest way of disposing the dead.'

'It is true, we cannot waste soil for burial or wood for burning, but the consideration of economics is not the reason for the Jhator, the main reason is altruism. You know, even high lamas, who by our custom have the right to be cremated and their ashes shaped into small figures and venerated in a chorten in their own monastery, ask instead that their bodies be fed to the vultures as an act of charity and compassion.'

He sips his tea and I wait, eager for more of Tashi, of Buddhism, of Tibet. Instead he orders more tea. Fearful that the conversation will slip away, I ask, 'Why do vultures deserve acts of charity?'

'You see, because the Buddhist believes in reincarnation, he has a love for every living being, a universal compassion for all creatures. Birds must eat too. And for us, vultures are very special birds. They do no living creature any harm, they eat only what is already dead, they never kill. They are sacred birds.'

'Sacred birds?' The idea comes like a surprise thump. 'That's so different from how we think of them. In the West we have an instinctive fear, a dread, of vultures. The circling of vultures is an image of doom.'

'They are birds which bring bad news,' Pascal adds.

I nod in agreement. 'Exactly. Vultures are involved with the ugly side of life, greed, mutilation, death. To eat a human body is unthinkable for us, it's a terrible violation, loathsome, vile. To call someone a vulture is the ultimate insult. I was actually shocked to see how beautiful vultures are. I've always thought of them as ugly, repulsive, as though their morbid calling would spill over into the way they looked.'

'Not only beautiful,' Tashi says, 'but well-behaved, well-disciplined. They follow civilised rules of behaviour.'

Again I am forced to interrupt, recalling the pulling and tearing. 'Their table manners leave much to be desired, they devoured that girl's body with a speed hard to believe.'

'Perhaps there has been no Jhator for some days and they were very hungry. On some days several people are buried at one time, but on other days there is no one to be buried. The vultures have come to depend on humans for their food, just as humans have come to depend upon animals and birds for theirs.'

Tashi is right. I remember Texas Dave saying he had gone to the sky burial two days running but nothing had happened. 'Nobody showed,' he laughed, 'hope you have better luck.' I hadn't found it funny at the time but now I make allowances for the vultures. 'I guess if I was ravenous, I'd grab too,' I concede.

'As a rule vultures are very orderly,' Tashi continues. 'I am sure that even though they were hungry, they waited patiently for their leaders before they ate.'

'Yes, that's right they did. I wondered about that. Did the man conducting the burial call to the leaders? Does he know who they are?'

'Yes, he called to them. He must know the leaders because he works through them, and they must know his calls and work with him. The man and the birds must co-operate together. The vultures know this as well.'

'My opinion of vultures obviously needs a complete overhaul, especially now that I've not only met a vulture fan, but the very vultures themselves.'

Tashi smiles and I sip my tea with the feeling that I'm in for considerably more overhauling, yet knowing that this too is what travelling is about, the imprinting of disturbing images and emotions, and the formulation of questions which may require a lifetime to answer. Determined to get some of the answers now, I say, 'Tashi, there are so many things I'd like to know about the sky burial, so much I don't understand, it's so totally overwhelming.'

'I am glad to explain, if Pascal does not object, because he has already asked the questions.'

'Of course I do not object.' Pascal says with a magnanimous wave of the hand. 'For me it is always interesting to hear more.'

'Are you sure?' I ask, with the false politeness I picked up in England, because had he objected I would have clobbered him.

'It was I who promised that Tashi would explain.'

So, with Pascal's blessing, I devote myself to Tashi and the Jhator. 'Tell me Tashi, why don't relatives of the dead person come to the sky burial? Is there no funeral service for the family of the dead?'

'It is because the main burial rites are performed before the

Jhator takes place. You see when a person dies, his body is blessed, then covered with a white cloth and put in a quiet place where he remains for at least three days while special burial rites are performed for him. We believe that even though he is physically dead, his mental consciousness (if you like, his soul, or spirit) is still in his body and therefore he is not really dead, but only in the process of dying, in a meditative state, between ending this life and beginning another one. He can remain in this state from a week to a month if he has reached a high level of spiritual development. In India, I have known dead people to remain in this condition for over two weeks, even in the hot season. They are like ordinary dead bodies, they do not breathe, their hearts do not beat, but because they are not really dead, they have no bad smell. While the person stays in this dream-like trance, monks and lamas surround him with beautiful thoughts and chant recitations from a sacred book to assist him to receive his death, for to be reborn well, one must die well. They also say prayers for the release of his soul from his body. His family and his relatives and friends make special contributions like incense, tsampa and white silk scarves, which are a symbol of purity, hoping to secure a better rebirth for him.'

'If he is not really dead when he dies, how do you know when he is really dead? My great horror is being buried alive. I have a recurring nightmare about it. I'm submerged in a deep hole, helpless, as earth and rocks tumble over me, muffling the sound of my cries. I'm gasping, fighting to breathe, terrified, until overcome by the avalanche I am sealed forever in the earth, still alive.'

I hadn't intended revealing this nightmare, I never do, yet I feel compelled to continue. 'I once read a story about a man who was thought dead because he was unable to move, but he was not dead, his mind was alive, he could hear and understand. He was about to be buried but at the last moment he managed to shed a tear ….. It was terrifying… How can you be sure you're not cutting up someone still alive?'

As I disclose my obsession with being buried alive, I am conscious of a shadow crossing Tashi's face, darkening its features, shrouding them in pain. But almost before I am aware of it, the shadow passes and he answers my question as though it was never there. 'Because we are certain when a person is dead. You see, a fluid, usually a whitish fluid, comes from the dead man's nose and his head leans to one side. When this happens it is the sign that his soul has left his body and his body is ready for the Jhator. He cannot be buried before this occurs.'

'And then is he buried straight away? Is there some special procedure?'

'Once the signs have been received that he is really dead, his family consults lamas and astrologers and they advise them of the most favourable day for the Jhator. Then his body is wrapped in a sheet and the head of the family carries it to the entrance of the house and there he makes three circles. This circling, and then further prayers to ensure a good rebirth for the departed soul, is the family's final farewell to their loved one, after which the body is handed over to special lamas. Then monks and family representatives take the body to the Jhator; the family members themselves do not go. The farewell has been said to the soul, to the spirit, the body is of no interest.'

More tea is brought and I fear the owner's intrusion, but he slips away with a sensitivity I could not have predicted. My attention is so focused on him that Tashi continues without pausing for tea. 'As you saw this morning, incense and cypress wood are burned at the Jhator and prayers are chanted by the monks. They also sprinkle tsampa on the fire, this tsampa causes a heavy smoke which the vultures know, even if they are very far away. From then on, as you saw, everything is in the hands of the special lamas who are in charge of the ceremony; they tell the monks when to pray and they call to the birds when the time is right. At the end of the Jhator the family representatives serve them food, tea and chang.'

'And is that the end of it?' I ask. 'Is there no ceremony, or celebration, or mourning afterwards, like the Irish wake, or the seven days of mourning the Jewish people call Shiva?'

'No, that is not the end of it. Buddhists believe that there is a 49-day period called Bardo, between death and rebirth, when the soul has left the old body but as not yet found a new one. On every seventh day of these forty nine days, monks and lamas say special prayers, recite mystic chants and perform ceremonial rituals to guide the dead person's soul through the Bardo, until he has reached his new incarnation. The family mourns for one year, they avoid celebrations and wear no jewellery or other ornamentation, and their friends are quiet and respectful in their presence.'

'Is that what happens to all Tibetans when they die? Do all Tibetans get buried by the Jhator?' I ask, my head jammed with fragments of religion, tradition, facts and images, yet eager for more, as though the amassing of enough detail will somehow complete the picture, make it comprehensible. Besides, meeting a Tibetan like Tashi, who is not only knowledgeable and sensitive but who speaks excellent English is a rare event, unlikely to be repeated.

'Oh no, although the Jhator is the most common form of burial and most Tibetans are buried in this manner, it is not the only one. There is also ground burial, water burial and cremation, and when a high religious person dies he is buried in a special way, his body is rubbed with precious ointments and spices and then it is embalmed in a stupa, a religious monument, like a small temple. Have you been to the Potala Palace?'

'No. Not yet.'

'When you visit there you will see the stupas where seven Dalai Lamas are buried. They are wonderful stupas, shaped like bells, about thirty feet high, with solid gold plating and decorated with precious gems.'

'I'm really looking forward to seeing the Potala, it's very special for me….but the other forms of burial you mentioned, are there also only certain people who are cremated or buried in water?'

'Yes. Great lamas and high officials are cremated unless they have expressed a wish for Jhator. People who die from smallpox or leprosy or any other contagious disease are buried in the earth, and generally it is small children, babies, who are buried in water. But there are exceptions. Sometimes, for some reason, a person is not buried according to custom but by some other means, like the lamas who request the Jhator. One exception of special interest is the baby brother of the Dalai Lama who died when he was only two years old. The lamas and astrologers advised that he should be preserved rather than be given the customary water burial for young children, so that he would be reborn in the same house. They advised that a small mark be made on the baby's body so that when he was reborn he could be recognised. When the Dalai Lamas' mother next gave birth, it was to a baby boy, her last child, and he had the same mark on his body. The proof was there, the baby who had died was now reborn in a new body to begin a new life.'

The story must be new to Pascal for we both listen with the intensity of children mesmerised by magic. Neither of us wish to doubt it. It is too perfect.

After a long silence, I say, 'Will your Jhator take place in India, or will you return to Tibet?'

'I will return to Tibet when I finish my study of medicine and healing. I am a Tibetan and I want to live and work and die among my own people. You see, my parents brought me to India when they escaped from the Chinese, but most of my family remain in Tibet and I come to visit often. I grew up in India but I was raised there in a Tibetan village, as a Tibetan. My family is close to the Dalai Lama, they are very much involved with Tibet, and although they may never return here themselves, they wish me to return. There are many young Tibetans living in India who are considering the same possibility, although most Tibetans exiled in India will not return to Tibet until the return of the Dalai Lama himself.

Tashi pauses and feels his tea cup. It's cold. 'I will order some more tea.'

'Please do,' I say contritely, 'I've talked you as dry as a desert. I'm sorry.' Actually I'm feeling a little deserty myself, and somewhat dizzy, whirling in an eddy of fragmented impressions. The intense concentration, the shifts of involvement from Tashi to what he was saying, have left me light-headed and depleted. Pascal has already excused himself. I suspect he too needed a break. It's time for me to go.

'Thank you Tashi, but I won't stay for more tea. It's been a real privilege talking with a Tibetan, especially one who explains things so well. I am very grateful. Tibet is strange for me, so filled with mystery, so difficult to understand. There are many questions to ask, so much I want to know. Thank you for being so patient and forgive me for getting carried away.'

'No, forgiveness is not necessary and please do not thank me. It is a privilege for me as well. Pascal is acquainted with my cousin Lobsang, and Lobsang's brother is a high lama in the Sera monastery, I will arrange for you to visit him. The Lama speaks a little English, Pascal speaks a little Tibetan; between them you can find some answers.'

I have made my parting speech but I make no move to leave. I am pulled towards Tashi, compelled to stay. Pascal was right, his presence is magical and I cling to it. I want more of him and his Tibet. But somehow I manage to tear myself away from both. Having monopolised Tashi's attention, I graciously decide to allow Pascal some time alone with his friend. 'I am going to return to the Banak Shol to rest. Please tell Pascal I'll see him there, the Jhator has exhausted me,' I say, gathering myself for departure. Besides it's true.

But as I begin to get up, something extraordinary happens, something I am totally unprepared for. As Tashi rises from the table, our eyes lock and I am overcome by a terrible poignancy, an acute sense of loss, of bereavement. I hear myself saying. 'Have we known each other for long?' His eyes hold me motionless. 'Yes.' An unbearable swell of love rushes at me, so intense, so naked, that I have no way of dealing with it. I feel panicky, unable to move, unable to breathe. I am impaled, bound by an unknown force. Suddenly, I feel my face wet with tears. 'Go now, with love.' Tashi's voice spreads over me like a balm, healing, giving me breath. The wild grief is over. His eyes release me, his kiss gentle on my forehead. 'Do not fear the strangeness of Tibet, allow yourself to be embraced.'

I leave the tea house in slow motion, balancing on the knife-edge of an elusive perception.

Chapter Nine

Outside the Potala

For the next two days I keep a low emotional profile. Needing familiarity and containment, I stay close to the Banak Shol, mainly in my room or on the balcony. I spend time reading about Tibet, sending my 'greetings from the rooftop of the world', and writing in my journal, trying to recollect in detail what passed between Tashi and I, for perhaps in the process of committing it to paper, I will come to understand something. I know I will see Tashi again. The knowledge is calming and comforting, and I am patient by nature.

In a way I can't explain, without any conscious effort, I find myself entering a meditative state, sometimes lasting hours, my mind and body still, poised on the edge of a trance, yet fully conscious. I have never meditated. The closest I got was attending an introduction to transcendental meditation at the Swiss Cottage Library in London. I was impressed by what I heard, but never followed it up, never took the course, never learned the techniques, the mantras, the way of crossing one's legs and holding one's fingers in a particular posture. But now I find myself doing just that, sitting crosslegged on my bed and chanting the Tibetan mantra contained inside prayer wheels and printed on prayer flags, flown into the universe by the wind horse, 'Om Mani Padme Hum' ('Hail to the jewel in the heart of the lotus'), the condensed expression of the path to enlightenment. I slip into it easily, naturally. The meditation sharpens my senses, and gives me both repose and energy. It restores me. With senses heightened, I seem to blend into the mountains, the patches of snow, the sky, absorbed into the landscape, enveloped by an unknown ethos I am nevertheless in harmony with.

Sometimes when travelling one comes to a place attuned to one's being. For me Lhasa is that place. Despite the fact that I speak no Tibetan, despite the vast cultural, social and religious gulf between myself and the Tibetans, I feel an affinity, a blood understanding, which I don't have, for example, with the Germans in Hamburg. Although I've seen little of Tibet, it's as though I've been here several lifetimes. I feel good here, aware of a subliminal bond with the landscape and the people. I'm not sure what is happening and I certainly can't explain it, but I like it, and suspending my disbelief, I allow myself not only the physical landscape of Tibet, but the spiritual landscape as well.

I have developed some small rituals, my own forms of communion. Some part of each day I stand on the roof of the Banak Shol gazing over the green plain on which Lhasa is built and the barren hills surrounding it. On one side the hills are considered holy, perhaps because of the ancient monasteries nestling in their slopes. On the other side, near the Kyichu river, a hill smoulders with incense and juniper burning as offerings – the higher the place the luckier the burning – and I watch the smoke curl upwards, ridden by the wind horse, dispersing prayers for peace and happiness for all sentient beings, into the cosmos. But most of all I contemplate the Potala. Seeing it over and over does not diminish the original impact. Instead it grows more magnificent, its already overwhelming scale further magnified by the sun's rays piercing thin air at high altitude. With the constantly changing conditions of light and sky, there is always a new way of seeing it. Sometimes clouds obliterate the mountains and the Potala rises like a mirage hovering above the city, separated from everything but itself, superbly detached. At other times, as though lit by flames, it appears like an enchanted palace in a childhood fantasy. Lhasa is becoming increasingly familiar, but the Potala remains mysteriously remote, growing out of a solitary hill, like a living thing, so that palace and hill have become one in a fusion of nature, God and man. Looking at it from a distanced rooftop compounds its remoteness, not only geographically but imaginatively as well. It seems a place to be wondered at rather than entered.

Towards the evening of my second day of quiet, Doune and I are on the Banak Shol balcony and I suggest a walk to the Potala. Doune is enthusiastic. 'Brilliant. We can't get in but we can walk around and have a good look up close.' No one else is about. Tim is collecting a pair of Tibetan boots made for him in a little workshop recommended by Texas Dave. Pascal has made few appearances in the past two days. Ian and Jaye have borrowed our bicycles and are off cycling to Norbulingka, the Dalai Lama's summer palace. Bicycles are a precious commodity. Tim managed to procure them for us. He and Doune never did get to Sera Monastery after the sky burial; instead they went bicycle hunting. There are only three bicycles for rent in Lhasa – Pascal had one and two English people had the others. Tim discovered they were leaving Lhasa the day of the sky burial, so he and Doune skipped Sera, returned to Lhasa, and appropriated them. I can't ride either one, my legs don't reach the pavement, but Tim takes me on the back. It's illegal, but so far no one has stopped us. The police find it amusing.

The road to the Potala is quiet, the daytime activity over, the vendors gone except for a few selling sunflower seeds and boiled sweets. Groups of young Tibetans stand near the entrance to the cinema which is close to the Banak Shol, cracking sunflower seeds between their teeth, chatting, waiting for the doors to open. It's a long walk to the Potala but the late afternoon is pleasant, the temperature perfect, the light pure, the air crystal, and the wild flowers radiant. The Potala towers above the city, and as I watch it approach, lit by sunlight, rising out of hills, surrounded by mountains with snowy tips glowing like ember, I experience a delicious mellowness.

Doune smiles at me for no apparent reason and my mellowness embraces her. She seems especially dear to me at this moment, a friend with whom I have shared a lifetime. I am moved to share something of myself with her, to ask her things, tell her things, and I say, faltering….'It's so good being here…..Travelling is incredible…..so many possibilities…..meeting people…..like meeting you…….like being here….right now……isn't it wonderful?'

'It's the first time I've been to Asia, the first time I've travelled on my own….I'd never been away from home for more than a few weeks ….. it is wonderful, fascinating.'

I move to easier ground. 'How is travelling on your own? Do you find it hard?'

'No. Not really. I had my doubts before leaving, but now I wouldn't have it any other way. I love the freedom of no commitments to anyone and doing exactly as I please. I have no one to suit but myself. For one entire year what I do with my time is totally and utterly up to me.'

'I know exactly what you mean. But it's certainly a big step to venture out all by yourself, especially on your first big trip. How come you did it?'

'I couldn't find anyone to travel with and I knew if I didn't take the opportunity to travel now, I might never have it again. I always wanted to travel to the East, especially India. I've had a yen for India as far back as I can remember. I talked about going there long enough. Then one day I just did it. I sublet my flat, packed in my job, put together my bits and pieces and took off. I was actually doing what I'd always wanted to do, finally. I must admit I didn't find it easy. Even though I was looking forward to the trip, I was also dreading it, dreading leaving my predictable, secure lifestyle and venturing into the unknown. For the first time in my life I would be completely dependent on my own initiative and resources. It frightened me, but I needed some time and some space on my own. My boyfriend, Graham, wants us to live together and I have to decide if I want to make that commitment. I thought travelling would give me the perspective to find out more about myself and what I want.'

'And did you make it?......the commitment?'

'I haven't had the time. Frankly, I'm too busy enjoying myself, too involved with what's going on right now ... with the experience of travelling itself ... enjoying each day, each minute ... all the different adventures ... It's been wonderful meeting you and Tim. I don't know how I would have managed on my own in China.'

'Me too. I'm really glad we met ... But you must have met other people on the road, other travellers?'

'Only briefly. I sort of kept myself to myself ... maybe I didn't know how to go about it. I guess I didn't really make the effort. I didn't seem to have the time or the opportunity or the desire to make any connections until we met at the airport in Bangkok. But you probably initiated that ... Canadians are much more friendly ... or maybe it was just shyness, or my English upbringing, I don't know.' She pauses, her brow drawn, considering some awkward question. 'There's something I'm curious about ... You do so much travelling, how do you manage financially?'

'With great difficulty ... It's a question of priorities – travelling is my priority. I don't own anything; no flat, no car, no machines ...

I hardly buy clothes, I rarely go to restaurants, even though I love to. I see plays and films mainly when someone takes me. Every penny I earn, in whatever way I can earn it, goes on travelling … Sometimes I get a little help from my friends … I have some great friends. But it doesn't come easy … In London I'm the poorest person I know. Don't get me wrong, I'm not complaining … all I have to do is think about India and the people starving on the pavements. Simply by being Western and white I'm privileged, rich. I learnt that the first time I went to Asia, in Bali. Someone there warned me to be careful with my travel bag because there had been a spate of robberies. "There's nothing in there worth stealing," I said.. Smiling at what must have seemed incredible naivety, he said, "What you have in your bag most people here won't have in a lifetime." That gave me something to think about … But really it's a matter of choices, and my choice is always travelling … Travel is my passion. But getting back to meeting people … Weren't you ever tempted to become involved with some male traveller, even temporarily?' I ask, curious about the experiences of another woman travelling on her own.

'I didn't really want to get involved with a man. I wasn't interested in that sort of thing, that's not what I'd come away for … don't forget I was trying to sort out my situation with Graham … and I certainly wasn't interested in one-night stands.'

'What about men hassling you? Did you ever get into hassles, with guys bothering you, lust-ridden types, horny locals? You know what I mean.'

'No. Not really … Except for a few ogling Indians and the odd unpleasant reprimand and scornful look from Malaysians … part of the Muslim disapproval of Western women, I suppose, especially women on their own, even though I made a point of covering up as much as I could. I tried to be especially careful to avoid anything that could offend, that could lead to unpleasantness. I was always anticipating … which is a shame, because I probably missed out on some interesting experiences. In Buddhist countries it was different. I was never bothered, and of course in China and Tibet I've never once felt threatened. I must admit I watched the way I travelled, I didn't take chances. I never hitch-hiked or accepted offers of lifts. Maybe I was just lucky … What about you? You did a lot of hitch-hiking, did you ever run into problems?'

'It's funny. I've hitched all over Africa, Asia, even countries like Morocco and Algeria but the only place I've ever had trouble was in Europe, in Germany.'

'What sort of trouble?'

'It's a long story …'

'Go on … I really want to hear it.'

'My daughter Ronit and I were hitch-hiking back to London from Greece. She was sixteen then. In Yugoslavia we got picked up by a lovely young German called Willie, a doctor, going all the way to Munich. He was more Mediterranean than German; warm, friendly, he even had black eyes and hair. Willie had come across a sick dog in Greece and when he picked it up to take it for help, it began foaming at the mouth. He was very worried that it might have given him rabies … it hadn't bitten him, but he had a cut on his hand and it's possible to get rabies through cuts. When we stopped in Austria that night he had to phone Greece to find out if the dog had rabies (it was being tested). The phone call was a real ordeal, but finally he got the news … the dog didn't have rabies. He was delirious with relief. He wanted to celebrate big. Ronit and I were all for celebrating and for the next few days we danced polkas in Austrian hotels and had some marvellous dinners. I even drank beer, which I normally dislike.'

'Willie took us all over Bavaria, to small inns, pretty villages …

we sat in beer gardens … had picnics … it was great. We both fell in love with him and were on cloud nine. But we came back to earth with a bang. Ronit remembered she had to be back in London to register for the courses she wanted. The registration date was two days away and we were in Bavaria. Willie obligingly drove us to Munich. Then we did something we never do. We hitch-hiked at night. We knew it was a bad idea but if we didn't get to London on time, Ronit's school year would be ruined.'

'About one am, somewhere on the autobahn in Germany, a big lorry stopped. That's something else we never did. We never took lifts with lorries, but we broke this rule too. The lorry had one of those enormous cabs, miles from the ground, and a sleeper in which someone was sleeping, the second driver, I suppose. He must have been exhausted because he didn't move a muscle. We climbed into the cab, pushing and pulling each other. I sat next to the driver. I always did that, kind of motherly protection.'

'The driver was a young guy, blue eyes, short blond hair, tall and thin, very Aryan-looking. If I were to allow myself, I could easily imagine him in storm trooper boots and a black leather holster … so I didn't allow myself … but I must admit I was more than a little uptight. I felt so isolated high up in that cab, so vulnerable. He couldn't speak any English and I couldn't speak any German, so after I told him where we were going, communication was over. We drove several hours in silence, me sneaking glances at him, trying to suss him out … but gradually I began to relax. He seemed to be concentrating on the road and he didn't try anything funny.'

'By the time we got to the Belgian junction, Ronit was fast asleep, and I was half asleep. He pulled up alongside the road. I woke Ronit and we were getting ready for the awkward descent … Ronit had already thrown one of our knapsacks onto the road. Suddenly, out of the clear blue, he grabbed me, put his hand down my blouse and began kissing me in an awful frenzied way. I struggled to free myself but he only clasped me tighter, squeezing my breasts hard, fumbling in my crotch, crushing my lips, hurting me. He was crazed. By the light on the road I could see that his features were twisted with cold lust, engorged, ugly. I knew he was going to rape me. My main thought was for Ronit. I had to spare her this horror, but I was helpless. In desperation I broke out into German … I didn't know I could speak it. "Ich bin mutter," I panted, pushing at him, "das ist mein kind… my child … mein kind … ich bin mutter." This impressed him to the extent that he indicated Ronit was to get out (I guess so she wouldn't have to witness her mother's rape … his concession to motherhood). He muttered something in German and I understood the words, "Mach schnell". He might have been saying that he'd make it fast so Ronit wouldn't have to wait too long, or perhaps he was telling her to hurry up and get the hell out of there. "Mach schnell," he rasped, forcing me backwards onto the seat, pulling at my clothes, his knee hard in my crotch.'

'Ronit grabbed his arm, "Das is mein mutter, ich bin kind … bitte schön … is mein mutter." Her voice was plaintive, pleading. For a moment he paused in his assault and in that moment my German became fluent. "Du bist gut man. Du hast mama. Ich bin mama, das is mein kind … du bist kind, du has mama." I knew I was getting through to him. By some miracle I was saying the right things, something was in conflict with his lust, some small flicker of humanity. I pressed my advantage. "Du bist gut man … bitte schön, nichts machen … is mein kind." He released his tight grip and I could feel his confusion.'

'To my surprise I felt a rush of compassion for him. He was good looking, young, healthy. What would make him want to force himself on a mother in front of her daughter? What could have gone through his head in those long hours of driving, what sick thoughts, ugly calculations? I know it sounds stupid but somewhere in amongst my fear and disgust, I felt pity. I took his hand and looked at him right in the eyes, "Du bist gut man, gut man," I said patting his hand, I even kissed him quickly on the cheek. He looked bewildered, the lust was gone, he was limp. "Quick let's get out," I said urgently, under my breath, "before he changes his mind." Ronit and I leapt out of that cab with the agility of two gazelles. He said nothing, he didn't try to stop us. He just sat there, dishevelled, lifeless, as we slammed the door. The other man never woke up, thank goodness for small mercies. Finally he drove away. I felt drained, wrung-out, but incredibly grateful that somehow I had been able to reach him and had actually talked him out of raping me. Funny thing is I didn't feel anger or hate, only a terrible sadness for this pathetic creature who had demeaned himself in this hideous way.'

'Ronit and I stayed by the side of the road, shivering, wrapped in our sleeping bags, recovering from shock. I felt sick, rubbing at the imagined saliva on my face, trying to cleanse it. Ronit put her arm around me, "Mummy, I'm so frightened … that was so scary. Let's not hitch-hike any more." She never did again.'

'What a horrific story. Lucky for both of you it ended the way it did. And you … did that end your hitch-hiking too?'

'No … it didn't … but I never hitch-hiked at night again and never in Germany.'

After a pause Doune says, 'What amazes me is that you travel so much and nothing seems to put you off … Do you still find it as fascinating as you did at the beginning?'

'It gets better. Once you realise you can actually manage on your own and that things somehow work out, you relax into it and it actually gets better.'

'I can understand that. I was a bag of nerves to begin with, anxious about little things, worried about getting tickets, places to stay, about making myself understood … but as I got used to doing things by myself, I began enjoying the trip more and more … I've been travelling for seven months now and I must admit, I do get a little tired being on the move all the time, and I do get lonely sometimes, but now I know I can do it. I know I can cope. It's a great feeling. I know that I'll always be interested in travelling but maybe next time I'll take one country at a time, and perhaps travel for shorter periods. I think once this trip is over and I get back to England I'll be ready for a break.'

'That's it. I'm never ready for a break. I want my life to be a continuous adventure. I hate routine. When Ronit was small I had to make her sandwiches for school. I hated it. Not actually making the sandwiches, that didn't bother me, but the fact that I had to make them every single day. I can't stand the idea of devoting my life to routines, doing the same thing in the same way, getting on and off buses, in and out of tubes, travelling the same old routes, old places, old habits. It drains my energy, blinds me to the excitement of experience, one day blurring into the next with no vivid moments, high emotions, intense loves, or discoveries. For me it's a kind of death.

'When I travel it's the opposite. I feel alive, full of energy . I love getting up in the morning. I wake up feeling good, looking forward to what comes next with a sense that the best is still to come. Each day is new, different, challenging. There is so much out there. I want to experience it rather than just look at it. I can't remember a place I was anxious to get out of, except maybe Jakarta. I always feel there's more to see, more to do, or just getting into the rhythm of being there.

For me travelling isn't linear, a progression from place to place, it spirals and circles and winds, full of flashbacks, mingling other times, other places. I find that the same place revisited is different, not only because it has changed, but because I have, the difference depending on what I bring from previous journeys. And I love the simplicity, the freedom of travelling with a few essentials, rather than living with the clutter of accumulation'.

I have never before articulated these ideas and my intensity surprises me. I feel troubled, as though I have suddenly launched into a speech nobody asked to hear, but I'm on the crest of a wave and I can't seem to stop. 'Travel is my great fulfilment. After a trip I seem to know better than before who I am. It's as though I've had a psychic bath, been washed clean. I'm renewed, alert, my head full of excursions, my visions and feelings expanded. I have the sense that … ' Abruptly we both stop. Doune and I look up simultaneously, as though drawn by a magnet.

The late afternoon horizon has split in two, one side black and threatening, the other blue and tranquil. Between the light and the darkness the Potala glows like a mystical apparition, poised between day and night, imagined and real, forever and now. We stand motionless on the road, mute. My passionate diatribe on the virtues of travel seems banal. What words can express the magnitude of this moment?

The Potala is the most magnificent structure I have ever seen. Unlike the Taj Mahal with its graceful polished symmetry, its delicate curved marble, and its perfect proportions, the Potala emits an awesome primitive power, a wild elemental force. In the last rays of sunshine the crumbling dwellings huddled beneath it are disappearing into the evening shadows, but the Potala is radiant, a great red-golden inspiration preserving a formidable distance between God and man.

As we slowly circle the Potala, I gaze at its fortress walls and the hundreds of small windows embedded in the white and crimson stone, like blind eyes, concealing a secret world. I imagine the strange rituals and practices, the mysterious lives of God-kings, saints and holy lamas which have filled its hidden passageways and thousand rooms throughout the centuries. As the sun drops in to the mountains, the Potala no longer blazes but is strangely luminous. A vision between waking and dreaming, it induces in me a mingling of my time with those centuries, and it's as though I know something of that life, that time, can see shadows of light, hear echoes of sound. Suddenly Tashi comes to mind, his finely chiselled features, his high cheekbones, his eyes conveying some memory, and a particular anguish, a particular ecstasy, eludes me. I find myself sitting on a rock, Doune beside me. Dreaming our separate dreams we watch the Potala recede into the night, the secrets intact.

By the time we emerge onto the main road it's dark. A jeep pulls up alongside us and two youngish Chinese men offer us a lift. Despite my recently reiterated vows not to hitch-hike at night, both Doune and I climb into the jeep without a trace of hesitation. There are some matters upon which the Chinese can be trusted implicitly. Chinese honour is not to be taken lightly. Respect for women, especially foreign women, is total. The punishment for rape is death. The men go out of their way to take us right to the door of the Banak Shol and help us out of the jeep with polite formality. Wanting desperately to communicate some intangible, I shake each man's hand and then impulsively kiss them on both cheeks. No reaction. But as the jeep pulls away, I swear I can detect a smile.

Chapter Ten

Celebrating the Buddha's Birthday

The Jokhang

The following day is the Buddha's birthday with celebrations throughout Lhasa, dancing, music, parades. In the evening the manager of the Banak Shol is having a party for his guests. Texas Dave has been asked to invite friends staying at the Snowlands, the other Tibetan guesthouse, closer to the Jokhang, with larger rooms boasting more elaborate Tibetan décor, but with loos rumoured to be smelly in the extreme. I am ready for celebrating, feeling refreshed and energetic, and Tim, Doune and I head towards old Lhasa and the Jokhang.

As soon as we enter the Barkor I sense the excitement. The streets are filled with the scent of incense and juniper, and crowded with pilgrims, dogs, goats and the odd donkey, circling the Jokhang, everyone moving clockwise, the direction for circling all sacred places. The usual easy mixture of business and religion – people interrupting their devotional rounds to bargain for something – is absent. Today all is religion. In amongst the shuffling and prostrating pilgrims and residents of Lhasa, are rows of beggars seated on the cobbled street, holding wooden begging bowls in their laps, twirling prayer wheels, fingering rosaries with one hundred and eight beads (the holy number), and chanting incantations with such fervour it's as though their lives depend upon it. Perhaps they do. Food and money are being dispersed in such abundance that it seems more like the beggar's birthday than the Buddha's.

Begging in Tibet is an honourable profession. A beggar could be a wise man seeking enlightenment or a pilgrim come from a distant corner of the land. Even the Buddha himself had begged. Until not so long ago, prisoners were allowed to leave the prisons on the Buddha's birthday and beg for alms, chained together. Giving to beggars accumulates merit for the giver and on the Buddha's birthday, all deeds, good and bad are rewarded a thousand fold, so it's an auspicious day for beggar and donor alike. Some prosperous-looking Tibetans carry entire sacks of barley flour from which each beggar receives a scoop. The beggars are amassing so much food I can't help thinking it must be what they live on until the next celebration. Their eyes remain glued to their wheels and beads, seemingly oblivious of the food which mounts so high in their bowls that special accomplice beggars must patrol the narrow spaces between them, packing the offerings into sacks hidden at their backs.

The prayer flags seem to have exploded overnight into a riot of colour. Prayer flag sellers fill every inch of space, their wares dangling from arms or tables, or lying on the cobblestones. In some places the prayer flags strung over the street are so numerous they form a canopy. Prayer flags fly from every rooftop, fluttering an orgy of prayers into the brilliant blue heavens.

We squeeze past groups of monks praying on the street, blessing prayer beads held out to them, reciting from prayer books, their recitations and chanting punctuated by the beating of drums and the sounding of ritual bells and cymbals. Some monks hold small drums hung with leather thongs and as their hands twist the drums back and forth, the thongs beat a rapid tattoo of sound on the tightly stretched skin. The mixture of droning voices, drum beats and ringing bells lends an air of solemnity to the atmosphere of celebration.

Although the Potala dominates Lhasa, the Jokhang is its spiritual and geographical centre. Old Lhasa is built around the Jokhang. Like a spider it sits, large and commanding, in the centre of a web of roads reaching out in all directions, a magnet drawing pilgrims from the remotest corners of Tibet, persisting for months, even years to reach it, often dying in the attempt. Long before we arrive we are able to see its golden rooftops sloping elegantly above the flat-topped houses, built low because no building can be over two storeys high, as rivalling the Jokhang or the Potala is considered blasphemous. The gleaming peaks, mandalas, wheels of life and exquisitely shaped Buddhist symbols shine like spiritual beacons in the pure clean air.

From what I have so far managed to learn, the Jokhang, the first Buddhist place of worship in Tibet, and its most sacred temple, was built by King Songtsen Gampo in the seventh century for his Nepalese queen. Actually he had five queens including three Tibetan ones, but his Nepalese queen and his Chinese queen were the most influential. Both were Buddhist and between them converted him to Buddhism. It was King Songtsen Gampo, the first of the religious kings, who brought Buddhism to Tibet. He originally built the Jokhang to house the statue of the Akshobya Buddha, a gift from his Nepalese wife, but then his Chinese queen outdid the Nepalese lady by giving him the 'Jowo', the treasured statue of 'the' Buddha, Siddhartha Gautama, known in Tibet as Shakyamuni.

Siddhartha Gautama was the founder of Buddhism and the individual held in the greatest esteem by Buddhists throughout the world. Actually he was the son of an Indian king who lived in about 500 BC. What must be of profound significance to Tibetans is the fact that he abandoned his wealth and royal position to become a beggar and seek enlightenment. The prestigious statue of him has a splendid history, and reading about it has made me even more excited about seeing the original. The statue was a gift from the King of Bengal to the second emperor of the T'ang Dynasty, who happened to be the Chinese queen's father. He gave it to his daughter as part of her dowry when she married the Tibetan king, Songtsen Gampo. She brought the statue with her to Tibet, carrying it all the way in a palanquin. King Songtsen Gampo was so impressed by the gift that he had a special chapel built for it. However, the Jowo was later moved into the place of the Nepalese queen's gift, and from then on the temple which housed it was called 'Jokhang', the shrine of 'Jowo'.

'Jowo' means 'precious one' and this statue of Shakyamuni as a youth of about twelve, before he was enlightened and became the Buddha, is indeed precious, venerated and exalted by the Tibetans who believe it to be one of only three statues made during the Buddha's lifetime and blessed by the Buddha himself. It is their most sacred image, their supreme treasure, and their prostrations are always towards the Jowo.

I'm also most eager to see the inside of the Jokhang. It too has a long history and has seen many changes. It had been damaged and repaired several times, enlarged and refurbished. Major additions were made by leading religious figures – Tsongkapa in the fifteenth century and the Fifth Dalai Lama in the seventeenth century; its architecture gradually becoming a blend of influences from India, Nepal, China and Tibet. But apart from the Jowo itself, there are few statues which date back to its origin. The Jokhang's three storeys are filled with chapels containing over two hundred and fifty statues of Buddhist deities, Tibetan kings and queens as well as Indian holy men, many of them made to replace those which were destroyed.

We pass through the outer courtyard, stepping carefully to avoid treading on dozing animals and prostrating people, and reach the main entrance, the massive wooden doors swung open. On the left of the entrance are two giant prayer wheels which the Tibetans spin as they enter and exit. Huge and ferocious Guardian King statues flank the entrance. We slip by them and enter an enormous inner courtyard, the centre of which is open to the sky. A passageway extends around the sides, bordered by double rows of red lacquered pillars with gold trim and curved projections at their tops, like elaborately carved wings, supporting a beamed roof. On one side banners covered with Tibetan symbols hang from an ornate balcony, intricately carved and painted with murals showing thousands of Buddhas who are still to appear and also depicting stories drawn from the life of the Buddha, Shakyamuni.

The courtyard is filled with people, though not as crowded as I had feared, probably because of the other festive events. The first thing that strikes me is how alive and busy the atmosphere is. If I had expected some decorous order, some ritualised procedure, some reverent ceremony, I was wrong. The courtyard is a medley of activity, everyone occupied with his or her particular form of devotional duty. Facing us at the far end are monks, dressed in dark orange robes, sitting in rows, chanting. Before them is an altar blazing with butter lamps, separating the monks from the profusion of activity. Behind the altar is a door leading to the main part of the Jokhang containing the chapels which house the statues, murals and carvings.

We wander around the courtyard, swept along by its energy. On one side several young monks are busy setting up small brass vessels, inserting wicks into the melted yak butter, making them ready for burning as offerings, while others are moulding little pyramids from a mixture of yak butter, barley, flour and tea, and fashioning paper-thin discs of yak butter. They are not too busy to smile and invite us to observe their work. Several large yak butter lamps burn in ceramic vats and pilgrims pour melted butter into them from a wide assortment of containers, jars, brass bowls, even Chinese thermos flasks, which they carry carefully, along with beautiful old leather pouches containing tsampa. Behind the rows of butter lamps are golden bowls with offerings of grain, tsampa and coins, left by pilgrims. The smell of incense and butter lamps mingles with, by now, a pleasant familiarity.

We watch the young monks making butter sculptures and listen to the chanting for some time before Doune decides to join the long queue waiting to enter the chapels. Tim and I sit on the shining stone floor, polished by centuries of prostrating bodies, beside a pillar hung with hats, removed in respect for the Buddha, and watch the scene. It's a strange mixture of the ordinary and the extraordinary, the sacred and the mundane. Babies riding contentedly, tied to comforting backs, protected from evil spirits by little black marks on their foreheads; mothers wiping squirming noses, fathers gathering children who have strayed; groups of people chatting casually as they sit on the floor resting against pillars; juxtaposed with bodies bent solemnly in various stages of prostration, mantras chanted by a mesmerising chorus of deep harmonious male voices, prayer wheels whirring over muttered incantation, and burning butter lamps illuminating strange practices and esoteric images with a fragile golden light.

Although it's very warm, everyone is wearing winter clothing because as yet there has been no official declaration that the winter season is over. The day when summer clothing is permitted is determined by various omens and not by weather conditions.

Several feet from where we sit an old man is prostrating in a heavy chuba (a long cloak worn by both men and women). By now more comfortable with the practice, I observe him closely. With joined hands he touches first the crown of his head and his forehead, then his throat and lastly his heart, symbolising the surrender of his body, speech and mind to the Buddha and his teaching. A young woman, possibility his daughter, approaches. Waiting for him to rise, she produces a string from somewhere in her clothing and ties the bottom of his chuba around his waist, I assume because of the heat. The man takes no notice. Abstracted from all earthly things, his palms pressed together, his eyelids shut tight, his sacred mutterings continue uninterrupted.

Two small boys, perhaps brothers, with shaven heads (a precaution against lice), sidle over and sit beside us. They sneak fascinated glances at Tim's camera. Tim shows it to them and they finger it gingerly as though expecting it to explode. Tim allows them to look through the zoom lens. They laugh in delight, looking again and again, their eyes wide with disbelief, and then pose to have their photo taken, embracing each other with smiles. Their father arrives carrying another child and indicates shyly that he too would like his photo taken with the baby. Tim obliges. A passing monk, wearing a surgical mask and carrying a steaming kettle, pauses to watch. Tim photographs him as well.

Things are not as precious here as in other places of worship. There is not the hushed rarefied atmosphere, the self-conscious praying, the distanced altars, the tourists, wandering with cameras, admiring stained-glassed windows and carved stone archways, inspecting tablets inscribed with historical information and 'in memory ofs'. There is no trace of a museum atmosphere: no fragile walking on eggs. It's all go, clutter, disarray, a sense of life, involvement, unselfconscious devotion, an integral part of everyday life, of a living religion and not a Sunday speciality. It's a new experience to be in the middle of a religion and not on its fringes. In countries like India we were either excluded or made to feel like spectators. The only other temple where I experienced any sort of inclusion was the Shwe Dagon in Burma, but that was massive and impersonal; the Jokhang is intimate, friendly.

Not two minutes after Tim has expressed surprise that there

are no other Westerners present, the long lean figure of Texas Dave ambles into the courtyard, hat in hand in deference to the Buddha. He circles the courtyard like a defrocked cowboy, towering over a dishevelled herd. Tim takes a photo. He sees us, waves and strides over, the clicking of his boot heels on the smooth worn flagstones resounding over the shuffle of felt boots. 'Howdy folks.'

He looks happy to see us, a familiar focus in a strange collage. He tells us he's just come from the Dragon King Pool behind the Potala, which has a tiny island with a temple built on it. Special celebrations for the Buddha's birthday are being held there: singing, music and sacred dancing. Tibetans decked out in their finest are rowing around the temple in yak-hide boats, and picnicking in the park surrounding the lake.

'I have a head full of chang (the home brew)', he moans, 'couldn't rightly refuse a birthday toast, and every last citizen of Tibet offered me one ... Tim, the grub was just up your alley, only vegetarian delicacies, Tibetans don't eat meat on holy days, and they don't take no for an answer.'

I am sorry to have missed out and gaze upwards, resting my eyes on the balcony above, contemplating my loss.

Following my eyes to the balcony, Texas Dave interrupts his account of the festivities. 'The private quarters of the Dalai Lama. That's where he used to stay during Monlam, the great prayer festival and pick up pointers from the monks chewing the fat down here, debating their philosophy ... thousands of them used to pray and debate here. Some monks live there now, not many, about sixty or seventy. They say there used to be hundreds. You can get up there today, special dispensation for the Buddha's birthday. It's worth seeing. Highly recommended.'

Then he asks, 'Have you paid your homage to the Buddha yet,

Jowo Rinpoche, the dude who began it all, the big "J"?'

'Not yet, we're just about to,' I answer.

'I've come to pay my respects, it's the least I can do for such a grand old dude on his birthday.' He offers his hand and pulls me to my feet. Tim is already standing. We make our way to join the queue, me feeling like a small thin volume, pressed between two giant bookends. I lose Tim and Texas Dave somewhere in the entrance to the great hall. The last thing Texas Dave says is, 'Don't forget the party tonight, we gotta do right by the Big J.'

Before entering the main part of the Jokhang I pass through a dark corridor with a chapel on either side. In the chapel on the left are five male and female beings looking irate and fiercesome, while on the right are three looking kindly and benevolent. All five fiercesome ones had to be subjugated by King Songtsen Gampo before he could complete the temple. Now they watch over the Jokhang, giving it their eternal protection. I leave the protectors and enter the main hall.

At first I can hardly see. There are no windows, the only light comes from flickering butter lamps. But as my eyes grow accustomed to the darkness I find that the half-light adds a special quality, opulent and mysterious. The great hall is magnificent with alcoves and small dark chapels cut into thick stone walls. Murals and paintings cover the walls. Richly coloured brocades and satins decorate the pillars and are draped over carvings, clothing the figures of deities who watch solemnly over everything. I weave slowly in and out of the chapels heavy with the scent of butter lamps and incense, surrounded by the soft murmuring of pilgrims whirling prayer wheels and making offerings, imbued with a sense of the ancient wonder of the temple. A line of shadowy figures lit by a yellow glow silently circles the many beings who, although mute and inanimate, convey powerful portents, and whose blessings can be invoked, beings from the past with the ability to shape the present and future, and who, therefore, must be heeded, appeased, loved, feared and paid homage to.

The chapels are of different sizes, some alcoves, some tiny chambers, others almost rooms. Before every altar are small piles of tsampa and offerings of coins, banknotes and white khata scarves denoting respect. The chapels contain a multitude of figures, stupas, thrones, religious objects and a variety of golden Buddhas all manifesting a mystic inner peace, an eternal calm, the accumulation of which creates an aura of great serenity. Incense smoke weaves bluish veils around the golden images.

One chapel is that of Chenrezig, the patron deity of all Tibet with one thousand arms and eleven heads. When Songtsen Gampo and his two wives died, they were supposedly absorbed into the statue.

The chapel before the one containing the Jowo has special significance because it is here that the pilgrim prays for all 'karmic hindrances to seeing the Jowo to be cleared' so that he can receive the Jowo more fully.

Between this chapel and that of the Jowo sits king Songtsen Gampo with his two queens: his Nepalese queen, Trisun, on his right; his Chinese queen, Wen Cheng, on his left. This revered trio watch over their temple and all the people who have endured incredible sacrifices to make the holy pilgrimage on this special day.

With a sense of awe I climb the steps leading to the Jowo chapel. It is truly splendid. Occupying the very centre of the great hall, it is the largest and the most impressive shrine, with an elaborately carved and painted ceiling, venerated figures lining the walls (including those of the seventh and thirteenth Dalai Lamas), and gold and silver ornaments sparkling everywhere. The usual meshed wire curtain, which protects the Jowo, has been removed for this occasion. Surrounding the entrance, protected by the four Guardian Kings, is a special quiet. The gold Buddha, twice the size of a man, is enthroned in the centre of the chapel, glowing softly in the light of the large butter lamps placed at his feet. He shines from his shadowy surroundings with a golden radiance. Bedecked in brocades and covered in jewellery and precious gems, he projects a massive unbelievable splendour.

A mother in front of me, her face radiant with the fulfilment of a great dream, lifts a tiny baby from her back, wrapped in a soft purple blanket with a satin square in its centre. She ensures that the infant pays homage to the Buddha by touching the Jowo through a small door made for that purpose, and then moves back so the baby can receive the Jowo's full impact. The baby stares at the golden Buddha with exquisite wonder. It is an expression I've seen on the faces of Western children enraptured by the magic of a fairy tale. Only in Tibet growing older does not diminish the wonder of childhood, but transforms it into religious awe and spiritual inspiration, instead of unbelief and cynicism.

As I contemplate the Buddha's face, the focus of spiritual power, which seems to dominate the chapel, I realise that he is truly special, different from the many Buddhas I have seen in other countries. He does not smile that often sad or compassionate smile in recognition of man's pain and suffering. Instead his features express a simple happiness, radiating an almost innocent joy, as though relishing the many pleasures that await him. It is the face of the Buddha before he had to bear the burden of enlightenment, before he put away childish things and came to know the grief inherent in human existence. I recede into a corner, captivated by his presence. It's almost as though he's alive, shining with new life, but also with an ancient life bestowed upon him by centuries of love.I gaze at him so intently, and for so long, that even when I close my eyes I see him etched golden before me.

After the Jowo the other chapels are hardly compelling: a collection of deities from Indian mythology, bodhisattvas on the way to becoming buddhas, lamas, guardian spirits, real kings, mythological kings, various aspects of Chenrezig, more images of King Songtsen Gampo and his two queens.

My interest is drawn to a small pillar against the wall with a hole in its top which Pascal told me to look out for. Pilgrims place an ear against the hole hoping to hear the Anga bird. The Jokhang is said to be built on the site of a lake where the Anga bird lives. If a pilgrim places his ear against the hole in the pillar, legend has it, he might hear the Anga bird beating its wings. I place my ear against the hole but hear only the shuffle of the pilgrims behind me, and wonder about my karmic hindrances.

One of the chapels contains a stone carving of the sacred goat, an important character in Tibetan mythology. It was this goat who filled the lake with earth, making it possible for the Jokhang to be built in its place. Just before leaving the hall I see a mural which depicts the legend involving the goat and shows how King Songtsen Gampo came to build the Jokhang. The king threw his ring into the air and said he would build the temple wherever it fell. The ring fell into the lake and a stupa miraculously rose from its depths. The sacred goat then filled the lake with earth, making the construction of the Jokhang possible. The lake is in the middle of the painting, the white stupa having risen in its centre. To the left of the lake, the Jowo is being carried from China to Tibet in a palanquin. Further to the left, the humble beginnings of the Potala can be seen, originally also built by Songtsen Gampo. It sits on the red hill waiting to become magnificent.

I leave the great hall as though emerging from some dim ancient wonderland with only partly revealed images, symbols, mythologies; stilled by the contact with a powerful spiritual presence, such as I have never before encountered. I feel lifted out of time, blessed by some essential mystery, deeply nourished. I emerge into the bright courtyard, dazzled by the light and energy, as though entering another time zone.

I look for Texas Dave, Tim and Doune, but they are nowhere to be seen. I've been so long with the Jowo they've probably gone upstairs without me. I enter a door leading into a passageway and find myself in a long alleyway with a thin path of sky covering its centre and prayer wheels lining its sides. A narrow roof supported by carved and painted pillars, similar to those inside the courtyard, extends over the prayer wheels. The holy walk winds around the Jokhang, entirely surrounding it. The prayer wheels, about three feet high, are made of brass, cut with intricate patterns and slippery with yak butter and grime from the continuous flow of supplicating hands. Ian said he counted more than three hundred wheels. Pilgrims move slowly along the passageway muttering mantras and turning the prayer wheels, the polished brass glinting as it rotates. The prayer wheels release the mantras within them as they spin, swirling an eddy of prayers, invocations, benedictions into the universe, committing them to the elements to be carried into the rivers by the rain, into the mountains by the sun, into the heavens by the wind, gaining merit for those who spin and blessing for the entire earth.

I turn the wheels as I pass until my hand is black and my arm sore but I can't find it in my heart to utter any prayers. I don't even know any. The Lord's Prayer is the only one I can think of and it seems woefully inappropriate. For a moment I consider chanting the mantra 'Om Mani Padme Hum', but don't feel I have that right. It's different saying it while meditating. 'Om' becomes an especially satisfying sound, a sound that has always lived within me, attuned to the rhythm of my breath, my heartbeat. The mantra helps me focus on my internal rhythms, eliminating the external world with its multiple confusions and putting me in an intuitively receptive frame of mind. It seems impregnated with psychic energy which in turn releases in me a pure clear vitality. But to utter the mantra as a prayer seems fraudulent, imitative. I'd rather be silent. Still I'm careful not to miss turning a single wheel.

The passageway leads back to the inner courtyard and I enter it, dizzy from the spinning. Suddenly Doune is beside me. 'Have you been upstairs?' She asks, her face glowing.

'No. What's it like?'

'Definitely worth a visit. Some of the chapels are closed, about ten are open. There's one shrine I thought especially interesting because it's the shrine of a female god. I met Texas Dave upstairs and he asked me if I'd been to the ladies. I couldn't make out what he was on about until I saw that shrine. The god, or rather goddess, is called Tara. She's very large and sits in the middle of the shrine and behind her are twenty one smaller Taras in glass cases. Tara is the female aspect of enlightenment the Great Goddess. (Trust Texas Dave to call her shrine " the ladies", he can't quite take anything seriously for too long.) But the best part is the roof. It's even more marvellous than it looks from below. All sorts of Buddhist symbols, dragonheads, small figures, the wheel of life and the two deer, and all that beaten gold. It's really lovely up there and there's a beautiful view of the Potala and of old Lhasa. You can see right into people's courtyards. Tim was photographing them. I must admit, so was I. Are you going up?'

'Not this time. I think I'll give it a miss for now. I tend to get overloaded, too much of a good thing.'

'I know what you mean,' Doune sympathises.

'I think I'll head back to the Banak Shol and have some tea,' I say.

'Sounds like a good idea. I never say no to tea.'

Late that afternoon I'm heading for my favourite place on the balcony when Pascal greets me, 'Ça va Niema?'

'Oui Pascal, ça va bien.'

'We go day after tomorrow to Nagarze. A jeep will come at eight o'clock in the morning to take us. You will tell Tim and Doune?'

'That's wonderful. They'll be so pleased.' He smiles. 'Where have you been Pascal? I missed you.' He hesitates.

'I was a little busy.' I don't press him.

'Where are you going?' He asks.

'You mean right now?'

'Yes, right now.'

'Nowhere, just sitting on the balcony.'

'Good. I will make some coffee and join you. Ça va?'

'Ça va indeed. Your coffee is ça va of the first order.'

'Ah, so that's what you missed, my coffee.'

'I must confess.'

Pascal goes to his room while I find a low stool to serve as a table and arrange a place to sit, leaning against the wall, facing the mountains. Pascal returns balancing a tray with his Arabic coffee pot and blue porcelain cups. We sit in the sun, the stool between us, the mountains sparkling. Pascal pours the coffee, hands me a cup and smiles, his eyes shining, showering me with affection, and at that moment everything is perfect, the sun warm on my face and arms, the snow, the mountains, the coffee, the blue porcelain cups, Pascal and me, we're all perfect. The coffee is delicious and as I sip it slowly, luxuriously, Pascal says, 'I saw Tashi today,' My breath catches. 'He told me that his plans have changed and he will not be leaving Tibet for several weeks more.'

The news does not surprise me. Somehow I expected it.

'If you agree, he would like to meet with you.'

This does not surprise me either. I accept it as part of some greater unfolding.

'He has something he wishes to give you.'

A surge of excitement causes me to lower my eyes. Pascal has not mentioned Tashi since our meeting with him in the tea house, leaving the choice to me.

He pauses, sipping his coffee, but when I remain silent, he continues, 'First he has some travelling he must do, some people he wishes to see, but when he returns to Lhasa perhaps you can meet with him?'

With eyes lowered into my cup, I ask, 'Will you be seeing him before he leaves?'

'Yes.'

'Tell him I'll be happy to see him and very much look forward to it.'

The thought of Tashi stirs some emotion within me to turbulence. I look up at Pascal, excitement escaping into my voice, 'Pascal you were right. Tashi is a very special person … very special to me.'

'I know, and for me as well … for me he is like a brother.'

'Thank you for bringing us together.'

He shrugs philosophically. 'Some things are meant to happen. I just arrange for the tea, or for the coffee, like now.'

'Where is he travelling to?' I ask, forcing my voice to sound casual, but eager to hear more.

'He didn't tell me and I didn't like to ask. You know he is very active in the affairs of Tibet, perhaps his travels are connected with that.'

'No, I didn't know. What affairs of Tibet? I thought he lived in India.'

'Well affairs concerning the Dalai Lama and his government in India.' Pascal registers my lack of comprehension and adds, 'In India he lives in Dharamsala where the Dalai Lama is the head of the Tibetan government in exile.'

'I didn't know the Tibetans actually had a government in exile.'

'Oh yes, for many years now. When the Dalai Lama escaped from Tibet to India in 1959, thousands of Tibetans also left Tibet. Now there are over 80,000 Tibetans in India. They have set up their own communities there so that they can keep alive their customs and religion, and their way of life, and the Dalai Lama has formed a Tibetan government in Dharamsala, their main centre … I was there before I came here.'

'Did you know about it before you went?'

'Yes. I knew about it in Switzerland. For a long time now there are many Tibetans living in Switzerland. You know my sister married a Tibetan man who came to Switzerland when he was a small boy. When I came back from travelling for the marriage, I met her husband and his father. I became very friendly with them, especially with the father. He knew Tashi's family, they were from the same place in Tibet, and when I told him I was going to India, he spent much time telling me about Dharamsala where he had been and about Tashi's family who are still there, and he asked me if I would visit them. I promised him that I would and so I did. That's how I came to meet Tashi. And that's the reason why I came to Tibet, I became very much interested in Tibet through Tashi, and also through the other people I met in Dharamsala.'

'Is that where you learned to speak Tibetan?'

'Exactly. Tashi taught me Tibetan and took me to meetings and translated for me. He also gave me a few books about Tibet which you are reading. He even took me to some of his classes in Tibetan medicine.'

'That's right, I remember you saying he was studying Tibetan medicine, and I meant to ask you if Tibet has a special kind of medicine of its own.'

'Oh yes, Tibet has its own medicine, a very old medical science for healing, developed for over 2,000 years. It goes back to the Buddha. The Buddha taught about medicine more than 2,500 years ago and he predicated modern diseases which would be brought about mainly by chemical pollution and wrong eating. The first Tibetan doctors studied with Indian and Chinese doctors, so it also uses the knowledge from Indian and Chinese medicine.' Pascal pauses, not sure if I want him to continue.

'Don't stop. I'm really interested. How is it different from Western medicine? What is it based on?' He needs little persuasion.

'It is based on the Buddha's teaching of harmony and balance in the body between the three main, what he calls, humours – wind, bile and phlegm – which are responsible for the body's condition. I learned about it from Tashi. When one of these humours goes out of balance, the person gets sick and has to receive special medicine made from herbs to bring back the balance. Tibetans are very advanced in their understanding of herbs and the special properties each one has for healing. In the West the doctors treat only what they can see, but a Tibetan doctor can also treat what is not seen. When a patient comes to a Tibetan doctor, he doesn't have to tell the doctor what is wrong with him. The doctor feels his pulse in a special way and perhaps presses on some points in his body, and then he tells the patient what he is suffering from. This takes many years of training. When the Tibetans got to Dharamsala, they built a medical centre as soon as they could so this special knowledge of medicine and herbs could not be lost. You know, Tibetan natural medicines are sent all over the world and Tibetan doctors also give lectures in Western

The magnificent Potala Palace taken from the gilded roof of the Jokhang Temple (Robin Bath)

Rock paintings and Prayer Flags fluttering prayers into the universe

Sera Monastery

The Sky Burial (Pascal)

Leaving Tibet

Huddled in the back of the truck with Tibetans.

Adorned yaks pulling a wooden plough. These animals are essential for Tibetan survival (Ian Crane)

Prostrating Tibetans in the Jokhang Temple

Milking sheep in the village of Nagarze (Tim Fowkes)

Tim outside the Banak Shol Guesthouse

Niema meeting the Dalai Lama in Toronto (Toronto Star)

countries. The West is slowly coming to realise the value of Tibetan medicine.

'Does the hospital here in Lhasa practise Tibetan medicine?' I ask.

'Yes it does. The Chinese have come to respect it, which they did not do at first, and all treatment is nearly free as it has always been in Tibet, only the medicine must be paid for. A Tibetan doctor practises medicine for reasons of compassion, not for money; it is part of his vows. You know, in Dharamsala I was told by many people that Tibetan doctors have been able to cure sicknesses Western doctors could not, like hepatitis, diabetes, and some cancers, even the common cold. There are Westerners who come there only for treatment. Also the Dalai Lama's personal doctor was put in prison for almost twenty years and would have died there like most of the other prisoners, but his knowledge of plants and flowers kept him from starving. Then the Chinese found out he could cure diseases that the Chinese doctors could not cure, so he was kept alive.' Pascal pours more coffee while I consider the questions I want to ask.

'Pascal, I must confess my terrible ignorance about Tibet. I knew absolutely nothing when I came and I'm just learning, very slowly, mainly thanks to you ... What you said before is confusing ... Didn't the Chinese invade Tibet in 1950? Why did the Dalai Lama leave only in 1959?'

Pascal, sensing he's in for some long explanations requiring the assistance of more than coffee, takes a cigarette from his pocket. 'Do you mind if I smoke? I think better.'

'Go ahead.' He lights the cigarette and inhales, half-closing his eyes to concentrate his thoughts. 'D'accord. Yes, you are right. The Chinese invaded Tibet in 1950 and the Dalai Lama gathered a small army to oppose them but they had very poor equipment and besides they were outnumbered ten to one. They had no chance against the

Chinese army with its modern weapons and they knew resistance would be just suicide. So then they tried to get help, but no country would help them, not America, not England, not India, not Nepal, not even the United Nations. They were all alone. I suppose no country wanted to get mixed up with China, and Tibet had been isolated for so long, nobody knew too much about it. So the Dalai Lama decided to negotiate with the Chinese, he had no other choice. Well it wasn't the Dalai Lama who decided – he was only fifteen or sixteen years old – but the people who acted for him. They were forced into an agreement with the Chinese, what they call the seventeen-point agreement.'

'What did they agree to? Surely not that the Chinese would run Tibet, like they do now?'

'No, no, not at all, just the opposite. They made the Chinese agree that Tibet would still have its own government with the Dalai Lama at the head, and they would be guaranteed religious freedom, something very important to Tibetans; also the full use of the Tibetan Language, and freedom for the Tibetan customs and culture. But they had to agree that the Chinese would take over everything that has to do with foreign affairs and defence. This meant there would be no more Tibetan army and that the Chinese would have the right to send their soldiers into Tibet. So, right away they sent 6,000 soldiers into Lhasa and a year later there were 20,000 soldiers, almost half the population. They brought nothing with them – the roads were too bad and they expected to get everything from the Tibetans, food, clothes, everything. You can imagine what terrible troubles this caused in Lhasa. For the first time that they could remember, the people knew there would be starvation. And of course the Chinese did not stick to their agreement, they probably never intended to. Even though they kept promising the Dalai Lama that they would make no big changes in Tibet for at least six years, and would not make them against the wishes of the people, they started to take away big pieces of land and join them to China, and they took away private land and land belonging to monasteries and turned it into collectives, like in China, and they forced the Tibetans – even the monks and nuns – to work on them, and they sent many of their own people into Tibet, not only soldiers and officials, but just ordinary Chinese settlers.'

'Tibet is so big and so uninhabited – someone told me it's the size of Western Europe – I guess the Chinese saw it as a good place to absorb their enormous population.'

'Yes. That's exactly right. And that's exactly what happened. Right now there are less than two million Tibetans living in Tibet, according to the Chinese, although the Dalai Lama says there are over six million, because he counts the Tibetans in the areas the Chinese took away from Tibet and made part of China – you know they took away about four-fifths of Tibet – and there are over one million Chinese not even counting half a million Chinese soldiers, and there are many more settlers coming. Even Mao admitted that he wanted to bring in four Chinese settlers for every one Tibetan. Here in Lhasa, before the Chinese came, almost all the people living here were Tibetans, but now there are more Chinese in Lhasa than Tibetans, three times as many. You can understand why the Tibetans felt they were being swallowed up by the Chinese and that they would lose their own way of living, so it is not a surprise that trouble started. It first started in Eastern Tibet in 1953, where there was fighting with the Chinese. Then the Chinese bombed some of the villages and shelled some monasteries and there was more fighting, especially with the Khampas.'

'The Khampas?'

'Those tall Tibetans with the high cheekbones and long hanging earrings you saw in the Barkor, the ones who sold Tim the necklace, they were Khampas. They come from the province of Kham in Eastern

Tibet. In Central Tibet the Chinese imposed their policies a little gently at first, but in Kham they used force almost from the beginning – they showed their true colours in Kham. They forced the policy of collectives with much violence. And they took Tibetan children by the thousands and made them children of the state and sent them to special Chinese schools. It was also in Kham that the Chinese settlers first arrived.'

'What did the Khampas do?' I ask, remembering how fierce they looked in the Barkor.

'The Khampas are famous for their bravery and their independence and they stood up to the Chinese. They fought guerrilla warfare against them. For this, many were killed and tortured and locked up in prisons or deported into China. The Chinese destroyed whole villages and held executions for the public, burning people alive and crucifying them. One man I met in Dharamsala told me that his father was given the chance to die standing up or lying down. He said standing up and so they dug a pit and put him inside it standing up. Then they filled the pit with mud and kept pressing the mud tighter and tighter and putting in more mud and pressing that until his father's eyes came out of his head. He saw the Chinese cut off his father's eyes. But his father was already dead. In all the history of Tibet there were never such terrible things.'

I can hardly hear what Pascal is saying, my identification with the man in the pit is so total. I press a pain in my stomach and Pascal's voice seems to emerge from it. 'But the situation only became worse and more serious, and from Kham it spread to the rest of Tibet. Refugees and guerrillas were coming into Lhasa telling such terrible stories about the torture and the rapes and the murders that the people became crazy with the wish to stop this.'

'And the Dalai Lama … What about the Dalai Lama?' I ask

with sudden intensity as though he was the man in the pit.

'He did everything he could to avoid the violence. In March 1959, the Tibetans were sure that the Chinese were planning to kidnap the Dalai Lama and this was one thing they could not suffer. They loved the Dalai Lama. He was the most holy, the most precious thing in their life, to kill him would be to kill Tibet. So they made a mass uprising and that is when the Dalai Lama escaped to India dressed up like a soldier. It's a good thing that he did this because two days later the Chinese shelled the Norbulingka, the summer palace where the Dalai Lama was living, and also the Sera monastery and Chakpori, the medical college; they even shelled the Potala. They also stormed the Jokhang where more than 10,000 people were hiding, and they put the red flag on its roof. The Chinese wiped out the Lhasa uprising very quickly and I must say, very viciously. It was a massacre. In three days they killed 10,000 Tibetans, most of them unarmed, and then they arrested all the men in Lhasa and there were mass executions. Even the Chinese admitted that 87,000 Tibetans were killed in the revolt. All over Tibet the Chinese took the valuables and the livestock for themselves and sent the precious treasures from the monasteries and from the Potala to China. Not many days after the Lhasa uprising was stamped out, the Chinese officially finished the self-government in Tibet and Tibet became a conquered land.'

As I listen to Pascal I become aware, from the intensity with which he speaks and from his familiarity with the facts and figures, that he has much more than a casual interest in the subject.

'Then, from 1959 onwards, Tibet's history became even more sad with terrible humiliations in the re-education and struggle sessions and with forced work gangs. And there was mass starvation. But as though all this was not bad enough, the ten years of the cultural revolution, between 1966 and 1976, were even worse. What the

Chinese did to themselves, they did even more in Tibet. The idea of the cultural revolution was to destroy the old – old ways of thinking, old ways of living, the old culture and customs – and to adopt new ways. Everything old was evil, reactionary.

'Of course in Tibet everything was old. Because of its isolation and the opposition to change by the monks and lamas, the old way of living, the old systems were hardly touched since the Middle Ages by anything new. So Tibet was considered especially reactionary and it needed big reforms. They said they wanted to "liberate the oppressed and exploited Tibetans" and to punish the nobles who oppressed them. And the Red Guards had a special mission in Tibet; they considered the Tibetans to be barbarians, superstitious, backward, uncultured, dirty, smelling from yak butter and they wanted to clean them up and clean up their "decadent" society.'

I am appalled and sickened by what Pascal has been saying, but suddenly I am angry as well. Only yesterday I was reading something by an Englishman, Hugh Richardson, one of only two Westerners who had lived in old Tibet for any length of time before the Chinese invasion, and had written about it. He found the Tibetans easygoing and cheerful and he specifically said they were not downtrodden or exploited, and that during thirteen centuries of their written history there was never any mention of mass discontent with their government. On the contrary, he said that their society was a highly developed one – not materially, but both spiritually and in terms of general intelligence – and that Tibetans led a contented, happy life. He certainly gave a different picture from the Chinese one and there is no doubt in my mind which version is true. If anyone exploited and oppressed the Tibetans, as far as I can see, it was the Chinese.

Pascal's voice interrupts my thoughts. 'The Red Guards had a real party in Tibet. There was a rally held to celebrate the beginning of the cultural revolution in the summer of 1966 and that started off what can only be called an orgy of destruction. Of course much of the violence was against Tibetan religion which the Red Guards considered a poison, the biggest obstacle in the way of advancement. Six thousand monasteries were destroyed, only thirteen escaped. Even the Muslim mosque was destroyed – it was rebuilt only very recently. Religious books were burned in bonfires or used for toilet paper, anything that was for religious worship was smashed and then the monasteries were blown up. Sometimes they forced the Tibetans to destroy their own monasteries and the young Tibetans were persuaded and bribed to be the leaders. The destruction took place to music and drums and to the waving of red flags, like a celebration. Monks were forced to give up their vows or to be executed. They were humiliated and spat on and were forced to make love with nuns, in public. Many of the great Tibetan spiritual leaders and teachers were killed, often the Chinese made their own disciples shoot them. And all the religious practices, even the private ones, were made illegal. It's all written down, documented. Oh Niema, the terrible stories I have heard.' Pascal stares into the mountains and is silent.

My mouth feels dry, gritty, and I take a large gulp of coffee. I don't know if it's because the coffee is cold or because I have come up against the dregs, but it tastes black and bitter. My impulse is to spit it out, but I swallow instead. The bitterness stains my tongue and the back of my throat. As we sit in silence, I recall the expressions of intense, joyous, almost mystical devotion on the faces of the Tibetans moving reverently in the Jokhang chapels earlier today, with their prayer beads, prayer wheels and offerings. It was apparent to me then that for Tibetans religion is not separated from living, something done on special days. For Tibetans religion is life, all of it. The Jokhang made it clear to me that spiritual dedication is a fundamental of their existence, a vital necessity like water and air, an element central to their well-being, nourishing, sustaining, life-giving, indispensable. To make their religion illegal seems inconceivable to me: it's like making breathing illegal.

'You mean Tibetans were not allowed to pray and to prostrate?' I ask in disbelief. 'What happened to the Jokhang?'

My agitation draws Pascal's eyes from the mountains and fixes them on his hands strangling the coffee cup. 'The Jokhang? To celebrate the cultural revolution the Red Guards raided the Jokhang. They destroyed and stole the holy treasures that had been there for centuries, since its beginning, treasures that can never be replaced. For days the two big courtyards were full of mobs burning scriptures and smashing images. It was wonderful for the Red Guards because the Jokhang was full of treasures brought from the other monasteries to keep them safe. Part of the Jokhang itself was also destroyed ... and afterwards the Jokhang was made into a headquarters for the Red Guards, and they used the outside areas for keeping pigs and for a slaughterhouse. That's how they treated Tibet's holiest place and one of the great spiritual civilisations on this planet. Nearly all the statues you saw today are new, they were made to replace the ones that they destroyed.'

I feel suddenly cold and notice that the sun has gone behind a cloud. The mountains, even the snow, look dark.

'You ask about prostrating ... Anyone prostrating anywhere could be shot. The Chinese wanted to kill religion completely, and it wasn't only religion they tried to finish, but the whole Tibetan way of living; the writing, the language, the medicine, everything. Tibetans were forbidden to follow their own customs, to have festivals, to sing their songs, to burn incense, even to wear their colourful clothes and jewellery, because everyone had to look the same so there would be no difference between ordinary people and nobles and monks. Even their long braids were cut off by gangs of Red Guards and they had to change their names to Chinese names. Besides the big terrors like the rapes, the public beatings and tortures and the thamzing (the re-education sessions where people were tortured and humiliated not only physically but mentally too), they had many small senseless punishments, like breaking to pieces the flowerpots in Lhasa, so Tibetans would have nothing colourful – you see how they love colour and flowers – and they were forbidden to whitewash or repair old Lhasa houses, and they killed their pet dogs, especially the Lhasa Apsos which they considered part of the decadent old way.

'But most important of all, the whole system of the economy was changed. Tibetans were not allowed to trade goods with each other. Even before the cultural revolution they were forced into communes, controlled by special party members, and which they considered like imprisonment. By 1975 there were almost 2,000 communes and all the Tibetans ever got from them was famine. They were forced to grow wheat, which the Chinese ate, instead of barley which the Tibetans have always grown and which is not only the main part of their diet, but for them is also a sacred grain, like corn is for the American Indians. The Chinese turned the whole agricultural system upside down. They didn't allow the land to rest, so it became barren, and that caused failures in the crops and then came great food shortages, so then they took food away from the Tibetans to feed their army and the settlers coming from China. They even sent food back to China because the Russians had stopped sending the Chinese wheat – there were some political problems.

'Then the food shortages turned into great famines. During the cultural revolution there was a famine for five years and tens of thousands of people died of starvation. Before the Chinese came, all

Tibetans, even the poorest ones, had food and clothing and a place to live, there was never any starvation. It was a bad time for Tibet. Many many Tibetans were tortured, many died in work camps (which were really death camps because there was no proper clothing and no food), and of course many died of starvation and sickness.' Pascal's voice and face are almost expressionless as he catalogues the disasters, as though the pain is too great to share, but now he sighs and his voice is filled with emotion as he says, 'There were close to a million Tibetans, one-sixth of the whole population, who died because of the Chinese invasion.'

Throughout the telling Pascal has maintained the attitude of an impersonal, almost objective narrator, his narration intense but the story a distant one, it's tone filtered through a sadness of long ago. But now the telling becomes immediate, impassioned, the grief evident, as though he is changing from narrator to participant. 'I tell you Niema, the Chinese have much to answer for,' he says with bitterness, the muscles of his face clenching, giving him a tough, almost vicious look, and I am aware that beneath his mild manner is a hardness, a stony commitment, a passionate single-mindedness.

'The Chinese killed most of Tashi's family. The town where they lived was bombed and their home blown to pieces. Tashi's family escaped; his father, his pregnant mother, his older sister, his baby brother and his father's younger brother with his new wife. They rode on horseback, trying to get to Lhasa. Many others were doing the same thing: refugees, groups of Khampa freedom fighters and nomads. Then on the flat plains the Chinese began to drop bombs on them and at the same time Chinese soldiers shot at them. It was chaos – horses and people falling, dying, screaming. Then a bomb dropped so close that Tashi, his mother and baby brother were thrown from their horse and the baby fell into a crater and was buried by the rubble. Little Tashi – he was only five then – tried to dig his brother out. That is Tashi's most terrible memory, trying to pull his brother out of the rubble and listening to the baby's cries grow weaker and then stop.'

I have a sudden vivid recollection of Tashi's face collapsing into pain when I related my nightmare about being buried alive.

'When his mother found them, the baby was dead. Then there was more shooting and bombing and Tashi lost his mother. In the confusion of bombs and gunfire, Tashi's sister and his aunt also got lost. His father was shot in the leg and Tashi saw him lying in the field bleeding, but he couldn't do anything; he was pulled onto a horse by his uncle, screaming for them not to leave his father. He didn't know if his parents were still alive until he got to Lhasa. But his mother managed to get the father on a horse and she carried the dead baby all the way to Lhasa, and on the way she lost the baby that was not yet born.

'By a miracle Tashi's father survived his wounds, but when they got to India starving and sick, after struggling for five weeks through the snow mountains, part of his leg had to be cut off. Then Tashi's mother got tuberculosis from the terrible conditions of the Indian camps and she could never have any more children and poor Tashi was so sick with cholera that he almost died. You know, Tibet is very high so there are few germs here, the Tibetans had no resistance to all the germs in India. Many quickly got sick and died.

'For over twenty years the family didn't know if their daughter was alive or dead or if the sister-in-law had survived, or about other members of their big family. They could receive no word from Tibet because the Chinese did not allow any correspondence with the rest of the world. The refugees who still came from Tibet could not help because they were stopped from moving around and did not know what was happening to people only a mile away. After twenty years they found out that both of them were dead. Many others of Tashi's family were killed or tortured or sent to China, some managed to stay alive. In the years of the cultural revolution his mother's older sister and her husband were made to watch their two sons, who fought in the resistance movement, being executed by the Red Guards and they were forced to clap. They both died of broken hearts. When Tashi's father told me what happened to their family, I was crying, it was so terrible to hear. But then I heard so many more stories, some of them much worse, that I had no more tears, only anger.'

Pascal stops and is silent, staring into the sky, his eyes bright and expressionless like a caged bird, and in the silence I feel helpless, unable to formulate the words to lessen his anguish. I feel compelled to touch him. Moving closer I put a hand on each shoulder. At first it's like touching a steel coil, but gradually I feel the knots loosen. He lowers his head. 'Pascal you don't have to tell me any more,' I offer.

'But I would like to tell you.' His voice is thin, pale. And before I have a chance to say anything, he continues as before, his features relaxed, his tone even, his voice soft, almost objective, as though determined not to indulge or even recognise his emotional lapse.

'Then in 1979, a few years after Mao's death and the end of the Gang of Four, Chinese policy began to change and to become more liberal. The Chinese government wanted to correct some of its terrible sins. Of course the Chinese had all the power even though Tibet was made into an autonomous region. But the communal settlements, which they saw to be a complete failure, were broken up and farmers were allowed to grow their barley or whatever they wished. Some monasteries were allowed to be restored and opened, and the Tibetan people were given more freedom to practise their religion. The Tibetan language was allowed to be used, but still not altogether. Tibetans were given permission to visit their relations who lived outside

Tibet and the refugees were allowed to come back home. The Chinese even asked the Dalai Lama to return to Tibet and promised him more money for schools, hospitals and other improvements. The Dalai Lama refused to return, for many reasons. I guess the main reason was that the Chinese wanted him to be in Beijing where they could watch him and have more control over him, instead of in Lhasa where the Dalai Lamas have always lived together with their people.

'The Dalai Lama doesn't trust the Chinese, they have broken too many of their promises, and even though he admits that they have made some changes for the better, he feels that basically the situation in Tibet has not changed, and in some ways is even worse, because in the last few years there has been a big increase in the number of Chinese coming into Tibet. He is afraid that the Chinese want to make Tibet into a colony – they already have many military airfields, and one of their biggest missile bases is in Tibet – and of course, there is Tibet's mineral richness and the forests they cut down without pity. He feels the Chinese want to turn Tibet into a Chinese territory with a small minority of Tibetans, and these will become one of China's "colourful minorities", an attraction for the tourists. The Chinese promised this would not happen and even promised to send back most of the Chinese population. They said that they are in Tibet only until they finish some projects, but then the government gives many incentives for Chinese people to come to Tibet, like more pay and higher pensions, because the Chinese consider Tibet to be like going to hell, and their official policy is to encourage settlers from China.'

'So the Dalai Lama remains in India?' I've become fascinated by the Dalai Lama, and am always eager to hear more about him.

'Yes, he remains in India, but he travels much in Western and also in Eastern countries and is very much respected in both. He talks not only about Tibet, but about world peace. He has become a leader for peace in the world. And he has offices in many countries which represent his government. There is an office in Switzerland and one in London as well. Through the offices he informs people about the real situation in Tibet. Most people don't know anything about Tibet, so he makes them aware of Tibetan culture and he also raises money to help the Tibetans in exile ... You know, in many ways I admire the Chinese and I admire many of the things they have done in their own country, their help and concern for the ordinary people, that is wonderful. But in the case of Tibet, what the Chinese have done is not forgivable.'

I am relieved that the emotional intensity has subsided, and wanting to sustain, to escape into, a conversational neutrality, an emotional quiescence, I say, 'Tim is somewhat of a socialist, and he says that in some ways the Chinese have had a positive influence on Tibet, they destroyed the old "feudal" system which was very repressive, and they built roads and communications. Do you think there is some truth in that?'

'Yes, it's true. Tim is right about that. For sure, there was no democracy in Tibet. Politics was only for the noblemen and the monks and lamas, the ordinary Tibetans never voted and had no say. Mostly a Tibetan was born either an ordinary person or a noble and unless he joined a monastery that is what he remained for the rest of his life. Only by marriage or through great sacrifice for his country or by becoming a monk, could the son of a poor peasant family have the chance to become a government official and get a high rank. But the monasteries were open to all Tibetans, rich or poor, it made no difference. And their leaders, who had great power to decide the issues of the country, were chosen because of their ability and not because of their birth. That's probably why so many Tibetans joined the monasteries, at least one male from every family. More than ten percent of the population were monks or nuns.

'The life of an ordinary person was a hard one. If he was not obedient to the nobles or monastery officials or if he committed some crimes, his punishment could be very cruel. The monks were hard judges. The Potala has underground chambers where people were punished in terrible ways; they could have their eyes taken out or their hands chopped off, even their tongues torn out. Although the Chinese like to exaggerate these punishments, some of it is true.

'The Chinese put an end to the old system, and it is to their credit that they did, today there is no "feudalism" as Tim says. But the Tibetans themselves were also making progress in these matters. The Thirteenth Dalai Lama, the one before this one, made many reforms, and he made the cruel punishments I told you about illegal. The present Dalai Lama, the Fourteenth, even when he was still young, knew that reforms were necessary for progress. He also knew that the policy of isolation was a mistake. Tibet was not even a member of the United Nations, and this made international involvement in its problems difficult. He understood that although Tibet was a spiritually advanced country, it was backward economically and socially and that there was much inequality, which was not according to the Buddha's teaching. He had already started to make reforms, like land reforms. Many noblemen also realised that Tibet needed changes. The difference was that they felt the changes must come from inside Tibet, not be forced on them from outside. It's like the Dalai Lama says. Tibetans are not against reform, or against communism, or even against the Chinese. They are only against having their country occupied by force by a foreign power. He says they have the right to govern themselves and to decide their own future.

'But getting back to the Chinese and their improvements. It's true they give large subsidies to Tibet and though most of it goes to support the Chinese in Tibet, it can't be denied that these subsidies help the Tibetans in some ways and improve their standard of living. From what I know, the life expectancy in Tibet has gone up from thirty years to forty years.'

'And in China? What is it in China?'

'In China it's sixty five years ... But about the roads Tim mentioned. Yes, the Chinese built roads but they were mostly for their own benefit – the roads take Tibetan trade away from India and give it to China, they make it possible for all those Chinese settlers to come to Tibet, and of course, the roads make it easy for the Chinese to bring in soldiers and weapons and to keep a big military force here. But the Chinese did not bring any democracy with their roads, they don't have it in their own country' ... He shrugs.

'But you know it's not really a question of comparing what existed before the Chinese invaded and what exists now. The fact is that the Chinese made an invasion, and they invaded one of the most peaceful nations in the world which for over 1,000 years had attacked no other country, and a nation which had only one desire, to continue its culture and its religion in peace. Tibetans are very proud and independent and do not want to live under Chinese rule and to be second-class citizens in their own country, even if it does give them some benefits.

'Just improving their living standards was never important for the Tibetans like it is for the Chinese communists. They feel that material gain cannot be a substitute for spiritual richness and for freedom. Tibetans are not free, they are crushed by the Chinese. And the simple truth is that in the past they were happy, now they are not. There is no longer an independent Tibet and that is the real problem. Even the International Commission of Jurists says that Tibet is an independent sovereign state in law and in fact. You know, the

Commission actually found China guilty of genocide for attempting to destroy Tibetans as a religious group. Tibetans want their independence back. It is for sure that an underground movement for independence exists here, especially with the young people, and is supported by the Tibetans in exile. Sooner or later they will make some kind of stand. It's only a matter of time. The Chinese are afraid of this, and the exiles who return to visit Tibet are closely watched by the authorities and some of them arrested.'

'Is that what Tashi is involved with?' I ask clumsily, immediately regretting the question.

'I don't know, and even if I did, I wouldn't like to say.'

'I'm sorry, it was stupid to ask,' I mutter, embarrassed.

'It is dangerous even to say the words "Tibetan independence". The Chinese are very strict about punishing anyone who speaks of independence, and for activities which they consider anti-Chinese, they execute Tibetans.'

Although we're sitting in a secluded part of the balcony, generally unfrequented, Texas Dave has spotted us and saunters over, arriving just in time to hear Pascal say 'execute Tibetans'.

'Hey,' he bursts in, 'this is no time to talk execution. It's the Buddha's birthday; a day of peace and celebration. I just passed the party room, it's all set to go and just crying out for the guests, that's us. We can't disappoint the Big J. So go grab your gear and round up the folks, it's party time!' He executes an impressive Spanish Heel-stamping routine, his inevitable cowboy hat tilting precariously, his sheepskin vest quivering. His instant sunshine manner burns through the dark clouds shrouding Pascal and me.

'Hey, that's terrific. Where did you learn to do that?' I say, clapping, genuinely impressed.

'I had private lessons from a Spanish signorita down Mexico

way. A great little teacher she was too,' he says smacking his lips. 'I'll tell you what. I have a tape of Spanish flamenco. I'll bring it along tonight. We'll dance some Spanish in honour of the Lady Margarita, the greatest little signorita who ever clicked a castanet.'

'Great. Don't forget, I love Spanish dancing.' Texas Dave moves off with more heel-stamping and finger-snapping. 'Olé, and on your bicycles,' he shouts and is gone, but his interruption makes it impossible to resume our conversation, and we're both relieved.

'Texas Dave is always ready for a party,' Pascal says with a narrow smile.

'He's a bit of a party himself,' I say, beginning to tidy up the coffee cups. 'I think I'll wash and change, it's getting late.' I get up to leave, momentarily infected by Texas Dave's party mood.

'I'll smoke another cigarette first,' Pascal says, needing more time to make the transition.

'OK. See you soon, and thanks for the lesson on Tibet, it's much appreciated and badly needed. I must get you to give me another one.'

'Any time. It's my favourite subject.' Pascal smiles and pensively lights a cigarette. I leave him gazing into the mountains.

The Party

When I return to my room the party mood vanishes. I can't keep the facts, questions, disturbing thoughts and images inspired by Pascal, from filling my head, and I sit on my bed trying to sort them out. I am especially perturbed by the question of religion. I've been reading a lot about Tibetan Buddhism in the past few days and I'm confused. I've always tended towards the marxist idea that 'religion is the opiate of the people'. But perhaps it's as Tim says and the Chinese have a point. Perhaps the old Tibet was a prime example of the common people living in poverty while their wealthy masters lived off their labour, able to maintain their status because of a religious belief that since everything is dependent upon actions in one's previous life, little can be changed in this one. The wealthier one is, the better one has behaved in previous lives, and the poorer one is, implies the reverse. So one had to accept one's lot and hope to do better in the next incarnation. A version of the 'pie-in-the-sky, but not on earth' idea many religions advocate, and seen by Marxists as a great con.

Organised religion had never endeared itself to me. It seemed a regressive force, not only by maintaining the status quo and thereby itself, but by inspiring killing on such a massive scale. History is full of religious wars with the condoning of violence, cruelty and torture, and it's still happening today in places like Northern Ireland, Iran, Iraq, Sudan, Afganistan, etc. I think of the vile crimes committed in the name of religion like torturing and killing those who have different beliefs, and the bigotry inherent in the idea of 'being saved'. I think of the arrogance of missionaries trying to impose their morality and religion on native peoples who have existed for centuries without the benefit of 'salvation'. I believed that throughout the ages, organised religion had been a compilation of terrible negatives – bigotry, prejudice, hatred, fanaticism, cruelty, violence - a repressive force catering to ignorance and greed. And, of course, the religion of politics was no better, based on many of these same negatives, expressing the same desire to force the individual into its thinking.

But I couldn't help feeling there was something different about Tibetan Buddhism. Pascal had told me that Tibetans don't attempt to convert anyone to their religion, least of all by force. He said that in Lhasa there were about 2,000 Muslims who originally came some 800 years ago with a Muslim delegation and there have been Muslims here ever since, recently joined by others coming from China. In the seventeenth century Muslims built their own mosque and have always been able to follow their faith in peace. They mainly married Tibetans who converted to Islam. There was never any objection to these conversions. Muslims did not have to convert to Buddhism – Tibetans respect all religions equally.

Not only were all religions equal in Tibet, but in the eyes of the Buddha all people were equal and therefore there was no caste system like in India. This tolerance seemed to me the great virtue of Buddhism. The Buddha's teaching was of peace and love, compassion towards all living beings, much like Christ's teaching, but Tibetans seem more convinced of these principles than Christians. The entire nation is devoted to them. Their daily lives bear witness to these spiritual values. Because they perceive that the natural world is sacred, they do not abuse it. They pray and make offerings, not only for world peace and the happiness of all living beings, but to make themselves better people, to eliminate hatred, greed and malice from within their own hearts. They have no confession to rid themselves of their sins, they alone are responsible for doing or avoiding evil, and must face the consequences of their actions. They believe that divinity is within. Every Tibetan carries an image of sainthood within himself and aspires toward it. Just by being amongst them, this becomes evident. They have a tranquil aura and their faces radiate a simple humanity. Their good humour and sense of fun seems even more incredible to me now, knowing the atrocities it has triumphed over.

I keep thinking about the Red Guards and wondering what could have been in their minds, in their hearts, as they smashed those irreplaceable treasures, and even destroyed beloved flowerpots to deprive Tibetans of anything beautiful and so break their spirit. In the name of what did they do this? For that matter, in the name of what did the Nazis do it? Red Guards, Revolutionary Guards, Hitler youth

– all those young men and women made even more vicious because they were motivated by a sense of mission rather than mere personal gain. Their desecration was inspired.

Yet the Tibetans survived this onslaught. The spiritual foundation on which their lives were built was indestructible. It had to be, for had it been destroyed, the very structure of their lives would have crumbled. Ironically, religion – the very thing the Red Guards wanted to destroy - gave the Tibetans the inexhaustible strength to preserve it, and to preserve themselves. As I sit on my bed mulling over the question of religion, I can't help feeling that in Tibet it is a positive force, exerting a beneficial influence over life. It's no coincidence that a people who have never seen foreigners should welcome them with tolerance, smiles, unguarded kindness and respect.

My reflections are interrupted by Doune wanting to borrow some thread. 'You don't look much in a party mood,' she observes, wrinkling her nose.

'I was thinking heavy thoughts.'

'Heavy thoughts? Not before a party.'

'You're right, later for the heavy thoughts. To quote Texas Dave, "It's party time at the Banak Shol," and I'm not about to let anything spoil that. It's a long time between parties.'

'Everyone seems to be going all out for this one. I just saw Gina in a skirt – she looks so different and Jaye and Ian are dressed for the prom. I wonder how everyone manages to produce all those smart clothes. I sent my skirt and dresses back with Graham … but I do have that new blouse I bought in Hong Kong. Remember?'

I nod, remembering well the mad consumer rush in Hong Kong.

'Trouble is, one of the seams is open and some of the buttons have come off. I hadn't even noticed … which leads me to the point of this visit, a needle and thread … What are you wearing?' She asks as I hand her my tiny sewing case.

'My purply dress. I save it for special occasions, and this one certainly qualifies.'

'I should hope so. I splashed out on my last drop of good shampoo. Will you be ready in half an hour?'

'I'll be ready whenever you are. I'm not going to eat, we had such a late lunch.'

'Me neither … Half an hour then. I'll collect you.'

Doune leaves and, making an effort to enter the party mood, I try to decide on what to wear. Laying my clothes out on the bed, I consider them carefully, enjoying their familiarity.

I travel with few clothes but these are painstakingly selected, not only for practical reasons, but because I like having things with me that are a source of pleasure. Whenever I buy something new, the main consideration is: can I take it travelling? This means it has to meet a stringent set of requirements. It must feel good, look good, be well-made, be affordable and be mainly purple. I become very attached to anything that qualifies and hate discarding it; it's like throwing away a friend.

My Indian shawl, unfolded, spreads over most of the bed. It's made of fine, almost silky black cotton, shot through with shiny threads of blue, lavender and silver, giving it a shimmering, iridescent quality. It's dominated by an enormous peacock, flamboyant in shades of purples and blues, its wings extended, poised for flight, against a surreal jungle of disembodied flowers and foliage. The old woman in the Barkor would have adored it.

My dress is sleeveless and long, the kind that ties up in a knot and shakes out into ripples. I wear it with a thin sash, woven in an Aztec design in lavender and gold, a gift from a dear friend. The dress is not only the mainstay of my travel wardrobe but a favourite treasure.

I harbour a sentimental attachment to it because of the remarkable, almost preordained way I acquired it.

I first beheld the dress about three years ago in a Chinese dumpling shop in Penang, on the back of a pretty blonde German girl, sitting on a low stool. She wore it tied at the waist with a satin ribbon, the blend of purples, pinks and lavenders flowing subtly in and out of each other, the skirt spreading around her like a purple rainbow. It was love at first sight. I followed the dress out of the shop to prolong the pleasure, and almost accosted the girl right on the street to find out where she got it, but couldn't quite make it.

Several weeks later, in a beach resort in Southern Thailand, as if by a miracle, the same girl appeared, wearing the same dress. Fate was giving me a second chance and I grabbed it. The girl's name was Goodie and she was pleased to hear how much I admired her dress. She told me she had bought it in the night market in Chiang Mai in Northern Thailand. The hand of providence now seemed undeniable. I was heading for Chiang Mai. The dress introduced us and Goodie and I became friends. Before parting we arranged to leave messages for each other in the Colombo post office in Sri Lanka, since we would be there at approximately the same time.

Obsessed with finding the dress of my dreams, I went to Chiang Mai earlier than planned. I located the right stall in the night market, and was within a whisper of fulfilment. The stall owner, noting the eager manner in which I inspected her stock, produced someone who spoke English, to finalise the all but certain sale. My description was so lovingly precise that the girl knew exactly what I wanted. But, alas, the dress was no more. There had only been one to begin with, and she remembered the girl who had bought it – German and blonde. In an instant a wide array of dresses were assembled before me, but I shook my head sadly and left the market with a heavy heart, not even examining the fascinating assortment of Thai crafts.

When I met Goodie a month later on a bench in Sri Lanka, I told her how fate had cheated me. She was genuinely disappointed. 'Never mind,' I said, 'it's only a dress.' Why should she feel bad? She wasn't to blame for my obsessions.

Goodie offered solace in the form of a beach café where we could have ice-cream with mangoes, papayas and fresh pineapple. There were many pleasures to override one small sorrow. Goodie left the beach resort before I did and I saw her bus off, waving a sad goodbye. I would miss her. When I returned to my room, there, rippling over the bed in purply splendour, was the dress. A note pinned to it read. 'A present from fate and Goodie. I am tired of this dress and want to buy a new one, now I have the chance.'

I look at the dress now with affection, thinking of Goodie, holding it against my cheek, anticipating the feel of the soft cotton brushing against my legs when I dance later tonight. I dress slowly and, being in a nostalgic, reflective frame of mind, recall the last time I wore it. It was only weeks ago in China, I ended up dancing then as well. It happened when we had been in China only a week. We were leaving Guangzhou, Canton, for Wuzhou by boat. It was an overnight trip and the boat had two tiers of bunks on either side of a long windowed room. We boarded the boat with the usual beginner's confusion, fumbling with a string of tickets and, with frequent recourse to our phrase book, looking for our bunks. We finally found them and were observing the other passengers from the advantage of an upper position when I suddenly did a double-take. Prancing towards us was a Chinese girl in a skin-tight red shirt, short shorts and spike-heeled shoes.

She had curled hair, heavily made-up eyes, moist scarlet lips and was covered in bangles. She would have been an eye-catcher any place, but on this boat, with its simply dressed, unadorned Chinese passengers, she was a phenomenon. I watched, fascinated, as she kicked off her pumps and climbed into the bunk next to mine. 'Hi, my name is Jean. Jean – that's my American name,' she greeted me brightly.

'Are you … are you … American?' I ask tentatively.

'I sure am,' she proudly retorted, chewing hard on a wad of gum to prove it. 'My father went to San Francisco when I was a small girl and I came to live with him five years ago. I go now for the first time back to China to see my mother and to visit my family. We live in Kunming, but first I visit my sister in Wuzhou.'

'We're going to Kunming too, in about a week.'

'Wonderful. You must come to visit us,' she smiled with enthusiasm. Most untypically Chinese, Jean sparkled with fun, sociability and warmth. She adopted us, and we gratefully submitted. She not only answered our numerous questions but made sure Tim got vegetarian food and that Doune and I did not eat dog, cat or worse. Before leaving us in Wuzhou she gave us her mother's address in Kunming and made us promise to visit.

We left the visit until the morning before our departure. Doune was at the hospital seeing to an ear that refused to unblock, so Tim and I went alone. I put on my purply Goodie dress for the occasion; after all it was the first time we had been invited to someone's home and I wanted to look my best. Jean's mother lived on a narrow shabby street where the houses looked like they were part of a neglected factory complex. Somehow we had expected something grander. Pushing open a weathered door we found ourselves in a yard surrounded by dingy rooms serving as workshops. We thought we had come to the wrong place. Nobody seemed to understand what we wanted. Finally someone led us around the back of the workshops, even shabbier than the front, and shouted up a rickety flight of stairs.

Jean herself appeared at the top of the staircase, looking like she was emerging from Vogue magazine, meticulously made up, hair piled in curls, nails polished red, dressed in tight shimmering trousers and matching blouse. 'Welcome. Come up. Come up,' she bubbled as she clattered down the steps and hugged Tim and I, beaming. 'I'm so glad you came. But where's Doune?'

'She couldn't make it,' I said.

'Oh, that's too bad ... But never mind. Come up. Come up.'

She took me by the arm, looking back to make sure Tim was following. At the top of the staircase we entered a chilly passageway which widened to form a kitchen with a wooden barrel for a sink. From the kitchen a door led through a bedroom to a sitting room. Here we were made welcome and given seats, while the others sat on a bed.

Although the house was extremely modest, it surprisingly contained a television set, a record player with large speakers and a tape deck. 'I send my family money from San Francisco,' Jean explained. 'My mother won't come to America, she loves China too much, so I send her money for some luxuries like we have in America.' Jean introduced her mother, a still very beautiful woman, with delicate features and a warm smile, and her two sisters and brother. Cigarettes were brought for Tim. Then tea was served, excellent jasmine tea, and steamed cakes. 'It's the first time we have Western guests in the house. My family is very happy,' Jean glowed. We all did a lot of smiling.

'Let's play some music.' Jean jumped up, putting a cassette in the tape deck. I was expecting Chinese music but, to my astonishment, out thundered loud, throbbing, all-consuming disco. I knew that disco music was taboo in China. In spite of the recent liberalisation it was still considered decadent. Jean registered my surprise, 'My family never heard disco music, so I brought some for them to hear. Maybe my mother will like it so much she'll come to America.' Then, impulsively, from nowhere, 'Niema and Tim, you dance for them.'

I smiled, sure she was joking. But she was entirely serious. 'They never saw disco dancing. They would be so happy to see it.'

'Jean, you dance for them,' I suggested.

'That's the problem. I don't know how. I never dance.'

'I never dance either,' Tim protested, with iron determination, as Jean tried to pull him to his feet.

Instinctively Jean knew Tim was a lost cause. I was her only hope.

'Niema you dance. Please do it for them. It is their only chance to see disco dancing,' she pleaded, desperately wanting to share her American life with her Chinese family.

More people had slipped into the room. They looked at me expectantly, hopefully. Here was their opportunity to glimpse the mysteries of the West. It rested in my hands. 'My mother begs you, specially for her, please dance.' The mother's eyes were imploring. How could I deny the plea of a mother? Jean knew I was weakening. Very unwillingly I allowed her to coax me to my feet, and at eleven o'clock in the morning, in the middle of China, in a cramped sitting-room, at the back of beyond, I began to dance, all alone. I knew it was a mistake as soon as I got to my feet. I felt ridiculous, jerking up and down like a yoyo in awkward spasmodic thrusts, my eyes glued to the floor, desperately self-conscious. Disco dancing at the best of times is no performing art, but right now it was downright pathetic. My body froze. It couldn't remember what to do next. I jiggled about foolishly, twitching repetitively, fists clenched, arms half-heartedly thrusting at some disinterested opponent, with the style of a lame grasshopper.

Serves me right. What the hell was I doing as a self-styled ambassador of disco culture anyway? The Chinese had survived remarkably well without disco, and would no doubt continue to survive, even thrive, without it. Why had I allowed Jean to convince me? It was acutely painful. When I finally dared look up I was confronted by more faces peering in at the windows and door. The room had become jammed. All the shop workers must have come up to witness the spectacle I was making of myself. Word travels quickly in China. There was even a policeman in the back row.

To my amazement, the faces reflected enjoyment rather than mockery or disgust. Miraculously they were loving it. Jean began to clap in rhythm and everyone joined her. Enthusiasm mounted. They clapped and swayed, shuffling and stomping with the beat. Somewhere in Kunming, during a morning tea break, the usually reticent, inscrutable Chinese, were alive and jumping. Infected by their enthusiasm, and drawing energy and excitement from it, I grew more involved in the dance. What the hell! Who knew me in Kunming? I began to let go – curving, twisting, twirling, gyrating, rocking and rolling, shimmying and shaking, my multi-purpled skirt swirling rainbows, brushing confidence against my legs. I became inspired. Magically my body revealed movements worthy of a Michael Jackson or Mick Jagger, emanating from some unconscious choreographic memory. In innovative abandonment I danced on and on, plugged into the electrical energy which charged the room. When finally it was over, I bowed, flushed with success. The applause was wild. I was an overnight sensation. 'Wonderful, wonderful, they think you dance wonderful,' Jean kept repeating. I felt like I had just danced the solo in the world premiere of *Swan Lake* and was being showered with bouquets of flowers. I was a star in China. Maybe Jean's mother would go to America after all.

I finish lacing my purple espadrilles just as Tim knocks on the door, interrupting further reveries. The sight of him begins the party. He is wearing the shirt he reserves for crossing borders, his good jeans, new Tibetan red and black leather boots and a colourful leather money belt he bought from the khampas, with pouches, studs and buckles. He looks quite handsome. I'd like to tell him but think it may embarrass him, so I say instead, 'I love your boots and belt, they're great.' Doune comes in wearing her best jeans and blouse and her newly acquired Tibetan jewellery. In a festive mood, dressed in our party best, we set off to celebrate the Buddha's birthday.

The manager greets us individually with smiles and a formal handshake. We're early. Few people have arrived, but predictably Texas Dave is already there and signals us to sit with him. He opens with, 'You're all spit and polish.'

'You look pretty grand yourself,' Doune retorts.

He does too. He's wearing a collarless gleaming white shirt, looking suspiciously ironed, with a pleated yoke and wide graceful sleeves, which gather at the wrist in a cuff. His sheepskin waistcoat has been replaced by a black velvet one with flashes of silver, and his leather belt by a colourful Tibetan sash. He is brushed and shiny with no trace of the cowboy. Even the hat has been removed and lies by his side, his hand resting on it, just in case. 'I'm all spruced up in honour of the Big J. He's one dude who deserves the best,' he says by way of explanation.

The room is large and decorated with Christmas lights, tinsel, streamers, posters and lined with mattresses covered with Tibetan materials and serving as seats. Each mattress has a little table placed before it, spread with a white cloth and set with saucers of boiled sweets, sunflower seeds and cigarettes. A giant ghetto blaster is at one end of the room with tapes borrowed from various Westerners.

The management has gone all out. The Banak Shol staff and their families are present, wearing their finest. They smile shyly, unsure of the protocol for a Western party. The children sit quietly instead of galloping about as they usually do.

More people arrive, among them Pascal, Jaye and Ian. They squeeze on to our mattress. Gradually the room fills. About twenty five Westerners sit on one side and the same number of Tibetans on the other. No one knows what to expect. We were told this was the first Western-style party at the Banak Shol, possibly the first in Lhasa, probably in all of Tibet. I would have preferred a Tibetan party. All of us would. But this party is the result of a genuine desire to please us and, touched by the gesture, we appreciate it as such.

The party begins officially with a speech by the manager, translated by Pascal. 'The management welcomes you and wishes to thank you for coming here tonight ... We would be happy to hear from you if you have any suggestions to improve the services given to guests, of if you have any complaints. The manager would like to remind you that you are not encouraged to bring your Chinese friends to the hotel ... he wishes you all a good and happy party.' We applaud formally and the manager smiles, pleased.

Immediately after the speech, Tibetan girls circulate with kettles of chang, the national drink of Tibet, a beer made from barley. So far I have managed to avoid chang – it's definitely an acquired taste – but now this becomes impossible. Dolma, the girl who sweeps our rooms, fills my mug and stands beside me, miming the act of drinking, discounting my resistance.

'Please, Pascal, tell her I don't want any,' I plead.

'No it is not possible,' Pascal shrugs. 'The guest cannot refuse the hospitality and the good wishes of the host. The host must stay with the guest until the chang is finished. They must share a toast together. That is the custom, it's for good luck.' He whispers something in Dolma's ear and she encourages me with cries of 'chairs', 'chairs'. Who am I to defy custom and meddle with fortune? I drink the chang, controlling my facial expressions, as the others clap and cheer me on.

Tibetan girls move among the guests filling one mug at a time and there is much cheering and clapping as each mug is emptied. The room becomes animated with shouts of 'skol', 'à votre santé', 'chin-chin', 'bottoms-up', 'salud', and 'L'chaim', as everyone embraces the custom. The manager toasts each of his guests personally, ensuring that every drop is drunk before proceeding to the next guest. It's a kind of enforced drinking session with the shouts and cheers growing in volume and enthusiasm with each passing kettle.

Several guests, notably Texas Dave and even Pascal and Ian, need little encouragement, downing the chang effortlessly, enthusiastically. 'Down in one. Mustn't keep the host waiting, he has many mugs to fill,' Texas Dave advises. In amongst the chang girls are sweets and cigarettes girls, pressing their wares on us although the saucers on the tables are still full. Doune and I attempt to hold out on the chang, but the best we can manage is missing several rounds. In fear of breaking with tradition and letting loose a deluge of bad luck, not only upon ourselves, but upon our host as well, we close our eyes, hold our breath and swallow.

From a low-key beginning, the party becomes decidedly raucous. Music is played – heavy metal, punk, rock, reggae, even the odd foxtrot. The room jumps to life. The Tibetans urge us to dance. Pascal, Doune and I are the first to comply. I feel giddy, reckless, spaced out on the chang and incongruity of the scene – a rock and roll party in a Tibetan retreat with the Tibetans providing what they imagine are Western essentials for a good time – booze, cigarettes and loud disco music.

More people dance and several Tibetan girls are dragged on to the floor, they in turn pull the manager to dance. Good-humouredly he obliges. Ian dances with two Tibetan girls, spinning them like colourful tops. Pascal dances with Dolma, who has offered to do his laundry – an offer which, he confesses, he accepted. Children are running about everywhere, encouraging people to drink, handing out sweets, climbing into laps, snaking between the dancers' legs, laughing and squealing when they are picked up and danced with. One has even wrestled Texas Dave's hat from his side and sprinted off wearing it, an action ordinarily strictly taboo. All shyness has vanished. It's quite unbelievable. If the Chinese had never seen Western disco, surely the inhabitants of this rooftop of the world have been spared its alien virtues. Yet here they are, not only accepting, but dancing, imitating what we are doing, laughing at their own and each other's efforts, playfully pulling everyone up to dance, some of the younger men and girls performing with such ease, it's as though they were born to it.

While the tape is being changed and I can hear myself think, I say to Pascal, 'The Tibetans are really getting into the party,' both of us leaning against Texas Dave, who is reclining on the mattress, chang'd out.

'Tibetans always like to have a good time. They believe that if they celebrate with a happy spirit and with much gaiety and fun, they will have good luck. So for them it's not only good but also lucky to celebrate,' Pascal says.

'I'll drink to those beliefs,' Texas Dave says, leaning on one elbow and lifting his mug.

'I'll second that,' I add, 'great way to be a believer, celebrating yourself into a better incarnation … look at that guy dancing with Gina, he must be a heavy believer … I'm sure the chang helps, he looks quite tipsy.'

'They don't mind if someone gets a little drunk, it adds to everyone's good time and makes the celebration better and luckier.'

'I'll certainly drink to that,' Texas Dave raises an enfeebled arm.

Watching the spirited dancing and recalling my success with the Chinese, I say, 'I'm convinced that every country should have an ambassador of dance, there's nothing like it for bringing the world together.'

'I'll drink to that too,' Pascal says.

'I already have,' Texas Dave mutters.

Suddenly flamenco guitar chords burst upon us with such dramatic intensity that Texas Dave recovers instantly with a stunning shout of 'Olé'. He rises from the mattress with such command, his posture so defined, that everyone stops dancing and retreats to make way for him. Clapping his hands above his head in flamenco rhythm, he moves sideways into the centre of the room with small staccato steps, his clicking heels punctuated by cries of 'olé'.

For a moment he stands motionless, his stance erect and proud, the matador about to strike. Then, with a toss of the head, he plunges into the dance, his heels beating a slow syncopated flamenco rhythm, while his arms held behind his back are released in opposing upward and downward thrusts, and his head moves sharply to one side, then the other. With sudden changes of direction he executes innovative rhythmic patterns, wrists flicking, heels stamping. The music grows faster and he moves in a small circle, striding, clicking, stamping, his body haughty, arrogant.

Without losing character he invites several ladies to dance, beginning with me. I move around him, my arms raised Spanish-style, my fingers snapping, my eyes fixed on him – a small signorita captivated by a *mucho grande hombre.* Gina, Doune and two American girls join us. A spontaneous choreography emerges: the five ladies dancing in turn towards and away from him, while he maintains a macho aloofness, mastering each lady in a few moments of dance, then stamping away in disdainful rejection. Texas Dave is superb, dancing a wonderful cross between Apache and flamenco, inspiring the ladies to compete for his favour in more and more wild and extravagant displays.

The music grows frenzied, guitar chords beat on each other, descending in a throbbing wild cascade, the ladies form a circle around Texas Dave pirouetting, clicking, snapping and shouting 'Olés', while everyone else claps encouragement. The rhythm changes, the music becomes slower with voices wailing over strumming guitars. Gina drops to the floor in relief. Ian seizes the opportunity of getting into the act and leaps toward her. Bowing low he offers his hand chivalrously, lifting Gina to her feet and executing his version of a gallant Spanish fandango in Highland fling style. He then vies with Texas Dave for the favour of the ladies in a unique version of tipsy highland fling coupled with debauched Russian cazatchka.

Now the tables are turned and the ladies do the rejecting. Three of us slip off-stage, but the two American girls remain. Texas Dave and Ian are hilarious, trying to outdo each other to impress the ladies. Texas Dave leaps high into the air, clicking his heels, and Ian performs athletic cartwheels and hand walks in comic disregard of all things flamenco. Everyone is laughing, but some Tibetans are laughing so hard, they're almost doubled over. Ian, unable to win over the American girls, dances them into the arms of Texas Dave, replacing them with his Tibetan ladies, one on each arm. Meanwhile Texas Dave crumples onto a mattress with his American prizes, Gina administering lifesaving measures to all three. The Western madness has not intimidated the Tibetan girls. On the contrary, they seem inspired by it, mimicking our Spanish stances and teasing attitudes with squeals of 'olé' and radiant smiles. The other Tibetans are splitting their sides.

All at once, the flamenco music whines to a halt and immediately a band strikes up, of all things, a rousing rendition of 'Roll Out the Barrel'. The Westerners are momentarily stunned by the incongruous transition but then see this as their cue to storm the dance floor, sweeping the Tibetans along with them. What began as dignified flamenco, deteriorates into a mongrel mixture of rock and roll, Irish jig, Virginia reel and German beer hall with a touch of everything else thrown in for good luck.

Pascal and I begin to dance a polka and find ourselves in a trio, then a foursome, then a conga line, swirled along by wave after wave of raucous party. It's an insane free-for-all, more than a little drunken and disorderly, with singing, dancing, children whirled by the arms, people hanging on to each other and falling to the floor as the altitude claims them. But it's Tibet and nobody minds. Everyone is having the time of their lives and luck is being churned out by the barrelful. The grand finale is an unruly rendition of 'Roll Out The Barrel', belted out by the English-speaking initiates, with the Tibetan and other novices shouting a chorus of 'olés' at the end of each line, Ian acting as inspired choirmaster. The song ends with gasping, panting, moaning, collapse and more chang.

Flushed and giddy, Pascal and I stumble to the balcony to recover. Alcohol usually dims things for me, diffuses them, but now my mind is surprisingly clear, sharp, the chang intensifying response, adding dimensions. It's midnight and a full moon. Leaning on the balcony waiting for the return of normal heartbeats, we watch as a cloud appears from under the mountains and the moon weaves through it creating magical patterns of silver, black and gold. I slip into a silver space, moving with the moon.

'Ça va Niema?' Pascal's voice is soft, etched with moonlight.

'Oui Pascal, ça va tres bien, vraiment formidable ... this is a beautiful time for me.'

'And for me,' he says, folding my hand into his.

We witness the moon sliding through the sky rippling the silver pathways, and listen to the music and laughter spreading over the balcony into the night.

'Thank you for everything Pascal,' I say, my voice hardly a whisper, fragile like a khata scarf floating over Pascal's shoulders.

'But for what do you thank me?' Pascal asks.

'Because you have brought Tibet close to me and me close to Tibet.'

He leans towards me and the moon hovering between us disappears. Slowly his fingertips draw my face closer to him, my head finding the curve between his neck and shoulder. For a moment we are still, held between the pulsating night and the magical sky. Then, almost imperceptibly, we begin to sway, our bodies a single incantation, moving to the rhythms swelling around us, rocking to the sound of throbbing drums ... or is it the throb of Pascal's heart ... or mine ... or the ritual drums beating in the Barkor ... or the pounding hooves of Khampa horses fleeing the Chinese.

Aware of another presence I lift my head to see Dolma beside us, smiling, a kettle of chang in one hand, two mugs in the other. As we continue swaying, she fills the mugs and hands one to each of us.

'To you Pascal.' I raise the mug, poised in the night.

'To you Niema.' Pascal downs his chang and refills the mug, handing it to Dolma. 'And to Dolma and Tibet,' he says, as she drinks.

'And to Dolma and Tibet,' I repeat, touching my mug to Dolma's and drinking my chang to the last drop.

Chapter Eleven

Inside the Potala

There is a slow start to the next day. Some people, including Tibetans, partied all night. I wasn't among them, but feel like I was. The balcony talk is exclusively about the party. Texas Dave is the man of the moment. When he finally makes an appearance and we enter the Banak Shol kitchen for late morning tea, he receives a hero's welcome. He is ringed by Tibetans shaking his hands, clapping him on the back and just gazing at him in silent acclaim. I'm sure if there was a palanquin big enough, they'd carry him through the streets of Lhasa. He responds with atypical low-key nods and a barely concealed desire to escape. We sit alone at a long table consuming cup after cup of tea, immersed in morose silence.

'Can I get you some aspirin or something?' I offer as much for my sake as his. His silence is making me nervous and I hate seeing him looking so miserable, it's like seeing a magician without his magic. He doesn't reply and I try a different approach. 'That was a very professional performance you gave last night.' I note a flicker of response and press my advantage. 'What are you, some kind of closet Flamenco Kid?'

Texas Dave surfaces, rubbing his temples, 'Something like that, I reckon.' Then, like a reluctant narrator obliged to relate a tale, he continues, 'When I lived in New Mexico I became a member of the Spanish Dance Club … I had to … I was in love with the teacher, the beautiful Margarita, and that's the only way I could get to her. I took so many damn classes, they made me president, and I ended up doing demonstrations with her. But that's all I ended up doing with her … Margarita had no use for Gringos, presidents or otherwise … Can't say as I blame her. Some fool Texan messed with her brother and to her I was just another no good Gringo.' He sighs, but the memory of Margarita has ignited a smouldering spark; he tilts his cowboy hat, winks and says, 'But I sure did learn to cut a mean Spanish rug.'

'You most certainly did.'

Ian wanders in looking uncharacteristically pale and depleted. Ian is the only Westerner I know who never suffered the effects of altitude, but at this moment he's suffering the effects of something. 'Someone spiked my chang,' he mutters between gulps of tea, his head heavy in his hands. 'It's that Chinese guy from the Number One, he did it in revenge for the Coco-Colas.'

'He wasn't there,' I am quick to point out.

'Doesn't matter. He did it anyway.' His voice is almost a monotone.

'How?'

'How did the Chinese take over Tibet? How is Lhasa on Beijing time? Don't ask me how the Chinese do anything. They just do it. "Vee haff vays und means of making you talk",' he says slowly in a thick German accent twanged with Australian. I desist from further comment.

One by one the others straggle in. Suffering celebration withdrawal, we drift into a party post-mortem, punctuated by moans in memory of last night's states of inebriation and this morning's worse sobriety.

'The main trouble with the party,' Ian complains, 'is that it's over.'

'The Tibetans have it sussed,' Doune muses, 'their celebrations go on for days.'

'These one-night stands just aren't good enough,' Ian agrees.

Ian and Doune have struck a responsive chord, an avalanche of agreement descends. We embark on one of those conversations where the total seems funnier than the sum of its parts, sparking each other with inane trivialities which somehow ignite into hilarity.

'Let's organise and form our own party,' Tim proclaims.

'Brilliant,' Doune agrees.

'We can call it "The Dance Party",' I suggest. The idea is embraced like the coming of the Messiah.

The enthusiasm is infectious. Texas Dave is unanimously elected Dance Ambassador to the World, and Doune his First and Foremost Secretary. Ian is elected Treasurer and immediately votes in a chang budget. I am not given a portfolio, but I'm granted the honorary title of Choreographer in or out of Residence in any Autonomous Region.

'Those who can't do things are best at talking about them,' Ian says, and votes in Tim as Minister of Dance Propaganda.

The American girls, whom Texas Dave has dubbed Cindy and Mindy for no apparent reason, are elected Awards of the Court, in absentia, as penalty for defecting to the Chinese guesthouse.

Pascal, also in absentia, is given the post of Foreign Minister. He's the only one among us whose mother tongue is not English, 'and that's foreign enough for me,' Texas Dave declares.

Jaye and Gina are elected the Chang Girls, with a sworn duty to replace the yin in gin with the yang in chang. Ian demonstrates the procedure with cheerleader movements, which the Chang Girls refuse to learn until fortified by the yang in chang.

'Roll out the Barrel' is voted the Party Colours.

Amid the enthusiasm and bursts of laughter, a Tibetan addresses

Texas Dave as 'Mr Olé'. The name is legally adopted. 'Hence-to-forth,' Ian announces, 'Texas Dave will be known as "Mr Olé", distinguished Ambassador of World Dance.' We all cheer.

There is so much merriment, I'm sure the Tibetans expect us to break into a chorus of 'Roll Out the Barrel' any moment. They are revelling in our carry-on, even though they have no idea what it's all about, but then again, neither do we. Finally the meeting is declared out of order, the participants congratulating each other on its success and on their much-improved spirit without recourse to spirits.

With great difficulty we tear ourselves away from the Banak Shol kitchen and each other. Energy renewed, we make plans for the rest of the day. Texas Dave wants to rent a yakhide boat for a trip down the Kyichu and Tim is to accompany him to the river to make arrangements. Doune and I decide to visit the Potala. Tim has already been there with Jaye and Ian, and we all plan a second visit after our trip to Nagarze. 'They keep opening and closing different rooms, so you have to go often if you want to keep up,' Texas Dave says, and then adds, 'and as members of the Dance Party, it is our solemn duty, not only to keep up, but to stay up.'

'Olé,' Ian seconds, and the meeting falls apart.

Doune and I return to our rooms for cameras and the torches necessary to negotiate the Potala's dark interior. With a sense of encountering a great unknown, we set off. From reading, postcard blurbs, photographs and discussions, I have managed to piece together some information about the Potala. The name originally comes from Sanskrit and means 'Buddha's Mountain'. When the mountain was dedicated to Chenrezig, Lord of Compassion, Protector of Tibet, the word 'Potala' came to mean the place where he lived, the abode of Chenrezig. It was only fitting that the Dalai Lamas, incarnations of Chenrezig, should eventually share his dwelling place, and it became the earthly abode of his incarnations.

The first person to build a palace on the sacred 'Red Hill' dominating Lhasa, was Songtsen Gampo, the same king who built the Jokhang. The mural in the Jokhang depicts this original palace, built in the first part of the seventh century. Apparently it was largely destroyed by fire in the ninth century. The Great Fifth Dalai Lama, credited with uniting Tibet as one nation and being its first modern ruler, is also credited with the construction of the Potala. By the middle of the seventeenth century he had completed the White Palace.

The building of the Red Palace is an intriguing story. The Dalai Lama died before it could be constructed. Knowing he was dying, and fearing the work would be stopped if his death were made public, he asked his Chief Adviser to keep his death secret. The Chief Adviser found a lama who resembled the Dalai Lama and produced him in extreme circumstances – from a distance. He pretended the Dalai Lama had withdrawn to retreat to meditate. It was a prolonged meditation. Twelve years later, the Red Palace was finally completed, and all that time the Chief Adviser managed to keep the Dalai Lama's secret.

The Potala was the home of the Dalai Lamas from the Fifth to the present one, and the Red Palace was where they lived and worked. It also contained the splendid chortens Tashi spoke of, where they were all buried, except for the Sixth Dalai Lama who died in mysterious circumstances. Tim estimated the tomb of the Fifth Dalai Lama alone, to be worth $4 billion, with its 3,700 kilos of gold, and gemstones the size of fists. The White Palace housed the Dalai Lamas' private monastery and its monks, the school for monk officials, as well as government offices and halls where the national Assembly met. Towards the end of the eighteenth century, the Potala became the winter palace and the Norbulingka, the summer palace.

The Potala remains the same as when it was first built, the fortress like Red Palace rising in the centre of the White Palace, which extends on either side. The only change is the addition of a chapel built to hold the chorten of the Thirteenth Dalai Lama. The Thirteenth Dalai Lama was deeply loved by his people because he did so much to improve conditions through his many reforms, and gave Tibet a long period of peace and prosperity. He was honoured with an especially grand tomb, two storeys high, and a special chapel to accommodate it. I was told that during the cultural revolution, the Potala was saved from destruction by the orders of Zhou En-Lai himself. Only the Chinese army could keep the zealous Red Guards out.

The Potala is one of the largest buildings on earth: over a quarter of a mile long, with thirteen storeys filled with over 1,000 chambers and halls containing 10,000 shrines, about 200,000 statues, all connected by a maze of passageways. It is said that even those who lived in it for years never knew all its secrets. It is built entirely of wood, earth and stone. Huge blocks of granite were carried up the hill on the backs of donkeys and men, and then shaped by skilled masons. The walls, up to nine feet thick and reinforced with molten copper, were built to resist earthquakes. No nails were used, and no technical devices. Only the efforts of 7,000 devoted workers who toiled day after day for almost fifty years. No wonder the building of the Potala is considered an architectural feat rivalling that of the Pyramids.

Doune and I have just begun the long hot walk to the Potala when the Banak Shol manager pulls up beside us in a miniature van, looking like he put it together himself with bits from a junk yard. He offers us a ride. Anxious to reserve our energy for the Potala itself, we accept gratefully. He drops us at the ramshackle houses clustered beneath the famous palace.

We climb the hill to the flights of wide zig-zagging stone steps, leading up the rocks to the Potala, designed with horses and palanquins in mind and ascend slowly, pausing often because of the heat and last night's exertions.

An old Tibetan woman, with grey hair, a brown wrinkled face and missing teeth, approaches us. From her bosom she takes a faded red candy in a chewed-up cellophane wrapper, and offers it with a small smile. Doune has a beaded Chinese change purse we were given as a souvenir on the Lhasa flight, and I have some respectable sweets from the same flight. We graciously pocket the old lady's candy and put our sweets into the purse, handing it to her. Her pleasure is touching. Her eyes sparkle and she grins widely but hesitates to accept the purse, unsure it's really meant for her, probably reviewing her recent offerings and prayers to determine which one could have merited such an inflated return. When we urge the purse upon her with reassuring nods and smiles, she tucks it into her bosom with unabashed delight. An experience in China has taught us always to carry some presentable treat with us.

One day Tim, Doune and I rented bicycles and cycled into the Chinese countryside. In amongst the hills we saw a cluster of dwellings and decided to explore. Down a dirt tack we came to an incredibly picturesque village, with white houses set against lone mountains twisted into enormous sculptures rising out of emerald green paddy fields. We parked our bicycles and wandered through the streets, intrigued by the setting and the beautifully crafted old wooden implements, buckets and ladles lying by the well, and wooden farming tools leaning against walls. As we passed a house right up against one of the strange projections with a dragon's head peak, a pleasant-looking woman, wearing the usual dark blue trousers and lighter-blue blouse, invited us in. We entered an almost bare room with a concrete floor, white walls, a table and several low stools. We were each given a stool to sit on and a bamboo fan to cool off with. Several children appeared and then two women and a man. We all sat in a circle, smiling, wondering how to make contact, the children staying close to the adults, unwilling to risk the strangers.

A primitive kitchen led off the central room and we could see a youngish woman washing her hair in a wooden tub. A hen and several chicks wandered in from the kitchen and were immediately shooed back in, one of the chicks waddling in from the street and cheeping to the kitchen. After a few minutes of awkward smiling, the girl washing her hair appeared with a wooden tray containing bowls filled with hot water. A bowl was handed first to the guests and then to the other adults. We smiled into the steam, wondering what we were supposed to do. Wash our hands? Our faces? To our amazement we saw the Chinese sipping the water. As I sipped mine, it dawned on me that these people were too poor to afford tea, and the hot water was the best they could offer their guests. I wished desperately I had something to offer in return, but I had nothing with me, neither did Doune.

We were feeling very annoyed with ourselves when Tim remembered he had a package of fancy Hong Kong biscuits at the bottom of his bag. They were in a box, prettily wrapped in blue and silver paper. Tim produced the box and, as if by magic, everything was transformed. The atmosphere became animated, the biscuits serving as catalyst, breaking the silence, plunging everyone into activity. The children left the security of laps and drew closer, the adults admired the packaging. A small boy was sent to fetch a grandmother to partake in the occasion. When Tim handed the box to the lady of the house, indicating it was to be opened, she ran for the scissors and cut the paper with such care, it might have contained the crown jewels. The thin layers of iced wafers were greeted with enthusiasm by adults and children alike, who crunched through the package with exclamations of pleasure and gestures of praises. The biscuits, and by association their deliverers, were an unmitigated success. When it was time to leave, everyone waved and posed for photos. Later when we passed the house on our way out of the village, we saw our empty box set on a shelf like a precious ornament, and the grandmother carefully smoothing the silver and blue wrapping paper, while several children watched, fascinated.

Now the old Tibetan lady adopts us and we climb the stairs together, an intimate trio, separate from the other Tibetans also visiting the Potala. At one point, the steps branch off, giving us a choice of staircases. Doune and I begin to climb the wrong one. Our lady sets us straight with a wagging finger, and takes each of us by the hand to prevent further mishap. At the top of one flight of stairs we come to a stone landing with an enclosure containing murals and an enormous carved brass prayer wheel over twenty feet high, encrusted with dirt from centuries of hands. Several Tibetan women unfasten the prayer wheel and whirl it. Doune and I whirl it as well, hesitantly at first, but then more boldly, as our lady, pleased with her devout charges, smiles encouragement. At this point we part company; she remains with the prayer wheel after indicating the path we are to follow. Her directions are invaluable as some staircases lead to dead ends and locked doors. There are no signs, nothing whatsoever to guide us. This is definitely the Potala before the advent of Pepsi Cola.

Fortunately there are few Tibetans visiting the Potala today. We were told that on some days visitors are buoyed along helplessly by the stream of pilgrims. As we pause to rest, sitting on the stairs, two young Tibetan men join us. They keep repeating a phrase. It sounds like 'pitcher Ali Baba'. Something to do with baseball? Arabian

Nights? That can't be it. Some kind of pouring pitcher, water, a drink? Finally we realise they are asking for a picture of the Dalai Lama, a much sought after treasure. They accept a CND badge instead.

As I sit looking up at the walls, rising sharp like a cliff, with nothing to cling to or clutch at, I remember hearing that monks used to throw themselves from the roof of the Potala, face first, sliding along a rope, in the annual feat of hanging the large Buddha tapestries from the outer walls.

At the top of another flight of stairs we come to a gate where we pay a nominal entrance fee. Inside the gate is a large terrace with a small kiosk selling postcards and reproductions of tangkas (religious cloth paintings) and murals. Doune and I each buy a set of seven prints and some postcards.

From this routine beginning we enter into what must be the ultimate magical mystery tour. The exterior of the Potala gives no indication of its sumptuous, diverse interior. It's fortress walls conceal a universe of dark musty passageways, steep staircases, chambers, halls, shrines, chapels, altars, sacred images, golden tombs, jewels, diamonds, pearls, frescoes, sculptures, paintings, brocades, silks; a labyrinth of cold dungeons, dim cave-like rooms lit only by butter lamps, pitch black corridors pierced by a torch beam; then sudden bursts of fierce colour leaping from walls, dazzling treasure, bright halls, sunshine, sky.

I move through the Potala as though I were moving through a dream potent with imagery and symbols too powerful to assimilate. Images collide. Impressions overlap, clash – demons, deities, swords, rosaries. A sudden flash of comprehension, then the mystery closes in again. A woman pilgrim weeps before the feet of a Buddha, her sobs tearing into the silence. I tremble. Overwhelmed, I creep silently along the walls, drifting among the gods, bodhisattvas, saints, robed in brocades and jewels, some huge, some minute, through balconies and courtyards covered with murals of a Byzantine complexity seething with events – the building of the Potala itself, history, mythology, legends, startling faces, good, evil, violently evil, human, super-human, non-human, worlds with all the realms of existence. Then replicas of bizarre places, one a large structure, the bottom strewn with hacked bodies, snakes, all manner of beaten and broken people, evil tidings, images of death minutely reproduced, and gradually the ascension to paradise perfection, ecstatic gods, benign animals and at last a blissful Buddha in lotus position at the apex, crowning another vision of the bliss of nirvana and the terrors of hell.

In the mysterious semi-darkness of one temple, many armed monsters embrace erotically through tongues of flame, while close by, saint-like figures rest serenely on lotus flowers, disciples at their feet. Goddesses with garlands of human heads dance wildly, ecstatically, while ascetics meditate beside them, blissfully oblivious. Suddenly the leers, the angelic smiles, the crazy grins, all the terror and beauty hidden in the deep blue spaces, seem to merge into a nightmare of cosmic opposition, pulling me apart. The impact is so intense that I can almost hear the screaming, the praying, the pleading, like voices of an undying past, as the images take on a life of their own, an almost supernatural reality, dancing around me fiercely, compassionately. I bolt from the temple hall, fire in my head.

Then I find myself inside the chambers of gods, bodhisattvas, kings, and I am suddenly calm. Some I have come to know. Tsongkhapa, the great reformer of Buddhism, founder of 'The Yellow Hats', the main sect of Tibetan Buddhism; the familiar King Songtsen Gampo and his two beautiful queens; Chenrezig, Buddha of Compassion. I find myself in rooms draped with brocades: brocaded ceilings, brocade covered pillars and walls, panels of brocades suspended like enormous lampshades; in assembly halls, grand, splendid, one with thirty pillars reaching to the roof, echoing with the steps of sacred dances, the ghosts of religious rituals, intricate ceremonies lavish with colour and music, joyful celebrations; in candlelit temples elaborately decorated with throned Buddhas, the great Buddha Shakyamuni, the eight medicine Buddhas, images of the revered Dalai Lamas.

I am startled by an enormous, ferocious figure guarding an entrance. Then the awesome chortens in which the Dalai Lamas are buried, shimmering gold in the light of butter lamps, their spires hidden in shadow, strewn with offerings; coins, white khata scarves, grain, jewellery, peacock feathers, coveted Dalai Lama photos. One stupa is solid silver studded with precious gems. Another, that of 'The Great Fifth', 'The Sole Ornament of the World', rises over sixty feet, three storeys, through to the roof of the Potala, covered in beaten gold, jewels, chunks of turquoise, coral, amber. Its curved base glows, lit by silver lamps, and ascends, slender, elegant, tapering into darkness. I pause – stunned by the power, the energy, the resounding echoes reverberating ancient greatness – and understand, even envy, the euphoria on the faces of pilgrims as they prostrate before the stupas.

As we follow the thin line of pilgrims muttering prayers, spooning melted butter into lamps, intent on perpetuating tradition and gaining merit, some who have travelled for years to make this pilgrimage without the reward of the Divine King at its end to bless them, our torch beam illuminates manuscripts filling entire rooms, ancient libraries of beautifully bound volumes; niches in walls with hundreds of miniature Buddhas gazing down on us; small images of lamas sitting row upon row along walls; detailed yak-butter carvings; and a sudden haunted or elated face – brief cameo images of a Buddha's universe. On one wall is an intricate painting of the wheel of life depicting the cycle of birth and death, the Lord of Death prophetically clutching the wheel in his mouth and claws, warning of the futility of attachment. On another wall is a portrayal of the 'stages on the path to enlightenment'.

Amid the gods and kings, sacred images and religious relics, hidden in musty corners illuminated by pale yak butter light, shabby saffron robed monks sit on mats, intoning from holy scriptures, meditating or sipping tea from thermos flasks. One monk raises his head briefly to ask for a Dalai Lama picture, and then lowers it in philosophical resignation. The smell of yak butter and incense permeates everything, and with each breath I am drawn deeper into a universe with an uncomprehended significance.

Suddenly we emerge into the sky on top of the Potala, the tombs of the Dalai Lamas bursting golden against a blue sky. The view is superb and the dazzle in my head gradually subsides, soothed by distance. Lhasa is cradled in green, held gently in a lush valley, the spires of the Jokhang reaching through leafy trees. The Kyichu river ('waters of pleasure') which runs the length of the valley flows through the heavy foliage, serene. The Sera Monastery climbs, white, red and gold, into the hills. Beyond is desert and beyond the desert the fierce embrace of blue-black mountains, 15,000 feet high.

I gaze at the panorama of mountain, desert and valley, and recall my entrance into Lhasa, the impact of that greenness after the dry stone mountains and parched sand, and my first mesmerising view of the Potala growing from those mountains. I knew then that the Potala was integral to the harsh landscape. But now, gazing at Lhasa from the Potala, after the many times I have gazed at the Potala from Lhasa, I understand something more of the forces which sustain the Potala, making it immutable, and something more of the forces which nourish the valley, making it green. The Potala has withstood the furies of man and nature, the ravages of centuries, acts of God (like earthquakes), even the wrath of the Red Guards. It has come to be indestructible, like the people who created it. And I wonder at the incomparable treasures hidden in a poor, remote, isolated corner of the earth.

The roof of the Potala leads to the private quarters of the Dalai Lama where he lived before fleeing to India. Usually it's visited early in the tour, but I have a strong urge to delay the visit until the end. We are able to manage this because the unusually thin trickle of visitors allows us to do some unorthodox backtracking. From the roof we enter the official reception hall, an opulent room hung with rich brocades and tapestries, its roof supported by twelve pillars in rows of threes. A skylight pours sunshine into the hall, mirrored in the smooth polished floor. A throne with a canopy of silks and satins and a portrait of the Thirteenth Dalai Lama on one side and the Fourteenth on the other, dominate the room.

We enter a small chamber behind the hall to reach the Dalai Lama's quarters. As soon as I cross the threshold I feel I've come to an oasis, an intimate moment in the grand scale of the Potala's magnificence. A boy grew to manhood in these rooms not so long ago. There is the sense of a living presence. The intermingling of that presence with its private griefs and triumphs and the surrounding antiquity with its deities and kings, give the rooms a human quality, a sense of life, a vitality, missing from the rest of the Potala.

The three rooms are like perfect gems hidden in a vast treasure chest, their ceilings and doorways carved in gold and red, their walls and altars adorned with silks, murals, frescoes and tangkas in brocaded frames, and their floors covered with bright Tibetan rugs – a microcosm of the Potala itself but with a particular energy, a quality of intimacy. First there is a sitting-room where the Dalai Lama received his guests, then a small altar room where he prayed and meditated, and a tiny ornate bedroom with a narrow yellow bed, where he slept and dreamed. They are exactly as he left them, as though holding their breath, poised for his return. There is a comfort about the Dalai Lama's private space. It is a refuge, a haven, and something makes me want to remain here.

Telling Doune I'll meet her outside, I enter into a strange communion with the rooms, part meditation, part contemplation, part imagination. But as I move from sitting-room to prayer room to bedroom, the sense of familiarity grows disturbing, fraught with apprehension. I struggle with a dim resonance haunting the edges of my mind. And both the diffuse dream-like sensation, and the vivid nightmare I experienced earlier in the Potala, when confounded by the profusion of images, colours, textures, jewels, gods and demons, concentrates into one overwhelming emotion – an acute sense of loss.

It is more than a sadness for the Potala mourning the absence of its exhalted divinity, its supreme love; more than the personal touches which make that absence so poignant, the intricate mural depicting the life of the Fifth Dalai Lama he loved to ponder, his books, clock, calendar, his beautiful jade teacup with the golden lid and an aura of eternity, now forlorn on its table. The sight of that teacup tears at my heart with the searing grief I felt when discovering my father's gold watch languishing in a drawer after his death. It is a personal loss, evoked by some mystifying familiarity. I feel abandoned, bereft, yearning for something … for someone…. And as I will myself to remember, struggling with an elusive significance, an almost visible spider thread I thrust at but am unable to locate, a vision of Tashi's anguished face flashes into my mind and then a tangle of wild images, frantic galloping, tumbling earth, plunging rocks, streaks of fire. The pictures racing in my head spin out of control. I twist my fists tight into my eye sockets to black them out.

Suddenly I am aware that Doune is beside me. Her presence reassures me, an anchor of comfort. 'Are you all right?' she asks, concerned.

'Yes ... No…'

She leads me out of the Dalai Lama's quarters and we rest against a pillar. 'What was that all about?' she asks sympathetically.

'I don't know. I guess I've been bombarded by too many stimuli … all those things Pascal told me … the terrible sadness of the Potala without its heart, its essence … maybe it has seen the last Dalai Lama … it's a tomb now, a wonderful tomb, but a tomb, empty, dead … it's that forsaken teacup with the golden lid … but it's something more … my father's watch … I don't know … I feel I've lived a lifetime today.' I battle to explain that which is inexplicable and know I'm failing miserably.

'Maybe it's a combination of climbing all those steps in the hot sun, too much chang last night and too much Potala today – we've been here over four hours,' Doune says, veering more comfortably toward the rational.

'I've been bombarded by an overdose of stimuli,' I repeat, returning my fists to my eyes, but more gently. 'I was beginning to hallucinate.'

'You can't see it all in one go, there's too much. We'll come back,' Doune says attempting to console me.

I nod, and Doune, shying away from things intangible, says, 'Well we can't complain about commercialism. There's nowhere here to get a drink of water, let alone a cup of tea … I'm gasping for a cup of chai … it won't last long though, the Chinese are too money-minded … Let's head back.'

As we walk, the sunshine gradually fades the sharp encounter.

By the time we reach Lhasa and enter the Tasty Restaurant, I'm feeling almost normal, having accepted the onrush of feelings I can't comprehend, and by the time I've finished my second cup of tea, my equilibrium is restored.

The Tasty Restaurant is close to the Banak Shol, but feeling fragile, we choose it to avoid a possible sequel to this morning's whimsy. The restaurant is half-empty. A few Tibetans are eating, the rest drinking tea poured by a lady circulating with a large kettle and plates of momos (Tibetan steamed dumplings). Needing the fortification and comfort of food, we decide on an early supper. The Tasty has the same set-up as the Banak Shol. In the kitchen we inspect the bowls filled with vegetables, peanuts, yak meat and eggs, and select the ingredients for a mushroom and scallion omelette, waiting until it's prepared. Returning to our seats, plates in hand, we find the restaurant has been livened up by a motley assortment of people and dogs. Several men, probably pilgrims run out of money and things to sell, scrape scraps from bowls, purposely left uncleared. Others linger against walls waiting for the diners to finish so they can have first chance at the leftovers or at empty beer bottles, returned for their deposit. Dogs sniff under tables. Immediately one selects me and hunches at my feet.

We have just begun eating when Lillian marches into the restaurant, chest out, head up, a stout captain with a determined manner. She brings a chair from another table, plonks it down and sits with us. Lillian is another American phenomenon, an older New York lady in her mid-sixties, with straight grey hair chopped below the ears, a body like her walking boots, short and sturdy, and a heavy Brooklyn accent. She's a grandmother, a healer, a part-time mystic and a full-time traveller. She is travelling alone, and has more energy and stamina than Tim, Doune and me put together. People tend to be put off by her at first, finding her somewhat overbearing and bossy, but when you grow accustomed to her brashness, she's quite likeable, full of travel titbits, good advice and esoteric information willingly shared, gleaned from many solitary years on the road.

We first met Lillian in China on a bus going from Kunming to the Stone Forest. That is, we heard her on the bus – her loud Brooklyn accent causing Tim and Doune to wince visibly – and hoped we'd be spared meeting her. No such luck. That evening, eating in the hotel restaurant outside the Stone Forest, Lillian appeared with a young blonde girl in tow, who we presumed was her daughter.

'My name's Lillian,' she informed us. 'If you don't mind my asking, I'd like to look at your menu, I want to see the prices.'

Tim handed her the menu. The meals were set and more expensive than the usual à la carte dishes.

'They're robbing you blind,' she said, slapping the menu on the table. 'I won't pay these kind of prices.'

'It's a full meal,' I explained, feeling obliged to defend the restaurant's superior effort, 'lots of courses and plenty of good tasty food.'

'It's good value,' Doune agreed, 'and they're obliging people, they prepared a special vegetarian meal for Tim.' I think Doune was feeling sorry for the blonde girl who looked like she was about to expire.

'I don't care how obliging they are, I don't pay for obliging and we don't need a full meal.'

'Why don't you order one meal between the two of you? I'm sure they won't mind,' I suggested.

The blonde girl, who turned out to be Danish and temporarily sharing Lillian's room in Kunming, looked relieved by this compromise.

'I would like to do that, we can share a meal,' she said timidly, hopefully.

'No.' Lillian was firm. 'We can't afford it.'

'There are no other restaurants, and the food stalls are closed,' Doune volunteered.

'So that's it. They have a monopoly. It's a mafia. No wonder they have the nerve to charge these prices.'

'Look, I can't finish all this food. You're very welcome to it, if you don't mind leftovers. There's lots of rice and sauces,' I said, intrigued by Lillian's style. 'We don't mind.' She was seated before I could complete the invitation.

The Danish girl hesitated, but gratefully followed suit. 'Thank you very much, it's very kind of you,' she said.

Doune and I handed them the plates we had finished with, some half-full. Lillian cleaned plate after plate, tucking in with gusto. Then, oblivious of all else, she began tucking into plates we hadn't finished, had hardly begun, even appropriating Tim's hard-to-come-by vegetarian dishes and the special bits Doune and I were saving for last, while we looked on in polite disbelief.

After that we didn't see Lillian until we arrived in Lhasa. Once again her voice preceded her. 'Give me a break,' Tim groaned, 'there goes our dinner.' She was staying at the Banak Shol and embraced us like long-lost buddies, an embrace not entirely reciprocated. Actually I grew quite fond of Lillian, and so did Tim and Doune. She'd come into my room with a bunch of radishes and a tin of fruit, we'd whip up a snack, make tea, and I'd listen fascinated, to the story of her life: how, at the age of sixty, she abandoned her middle-class existence, complete with country cottage, lawyer husband, two model children and three grandchildren, to 'discover who she really was', and had been travelling throughout the world ever since, with very little money, often sleeping on beaches or on floors and living with the locals whenever she could. You had to admire the woman. She certainly had gumption and she was always up to something interesting, like convincing a young Tibetan to take her to his university classes, or crashing a buffet dinner given by the Chinese authorities for wealthy American tourists. Nothing stopped her. She walked and hitch-hiked to places she was warned not to attempt, and besides detailing her extraordinary adventures, she could always be relied upon to report all the news and gossip.

Now, in the Tasty Restaurant, she relates her latest adventure. This morning she was up at dawn and climbed the hills behind the Sera Monastery to caves inhabited by Tibetans, a difficult and dangerous climb. It's a wonder I didn't break my neck, those rocks are a lot steeper than they look. I had to pull myself up by my nails inch by inch, I kid you not. Look, my hands are raw, the skin is all scraped off.' She regards her hands dispassionately, then holds them up for our inspection. They are torn and bleeding, some nails broken.

When we express concern, she says, 'It's nothing. I have a first aid kit in my room … I had to jump over spaces between the rocks with big drops underneath. Thank god for my shoes, they're the kind that don't slip – expensive, but worth every cent – they saved my life. But I'll tell you something … I was scared … I didn't think I was going to make it, and Lillian the dumb-bell, didn't take her hat.' She slaps her forehead in rebuke. 'I though I'd get there before the sun got hot. Schmuckelainy. There wasn't a drop of shade. My head was like a fire. When I got to the caves I was so knocked out and so thirsty, I could hardly talk, and for me that's something.

'A kind lady gave me a jug of water and let me sleep in her cave on a blanket. Bless her. I slept for hours. When I got up she gave me some bread and cheese and showed me their temple. Can you believe it, they have a temple way up in those caves, with prayer wheels and

Buddhas, and paintings on the rocks. It's really remarkable. Leave it to them. When it comes to religion nobody can beat the Tibetans, nothing is too much trouble or too much expense. They are such good people, so kind. One of the men helped me climb all the way down, so I wouldn't get hurt. I just got back. I'm lucky I'm living,' she says flippantly. 'And I'm starved.'

True to form, she fills a momo with some of my omelette and munches away happily. She fills another and then another. 'Where were you gals today?' She asks, wiping her mouth on the back of a bruised hand.

'We went to the Potala,' I answer.

'The Potala … oh yeah … that's a magical place … very powerful. I had some very high mystical experiences in the Potala … Get that damn dog away from my feet. He's biting my shoes.' She lashes out at the dog who skulks to my chair. 'Lets get out of this place. I hate those dogs,' she says, the magic of the Potala forgotten. As though sensing our imminent departure, the beggars close in on us, intent on salvaging the scraps. But Lillian has left nothing to salvage.

Chapter Twelve

Trip to Nagarze

Next morning, despite apprehensions, our jeep arrives at eight-thirty sharp to take us to Nagarze, driven by a young smiling Tibetan called Norbu. We are only planning a two-day stay so we take very little. Nagarze is a small town on the Tibetan-Nepalese road, about a four-hour drive south west of Lhasa. It sits on a thirty mile long lake, reached through a high mountain pass. The jeep is ancient and rattles along, clattering like a sack of old bones, the windows don't open, the doors won't shut, it's held together by prayers and offerings, but for two days, thanks to Pascal, it's ours, and we rejoice in the luxury of our own transport. I sit in front with Norbu. Tim, Doune and Pascal squeeze into the back, as a penance for smoking.

Once out of Lhasa, a rural peace descends. We pass settlements enclosed by walls, with red brick and mud houses, vivid prayer flags tied to branches, fluttering from their roofs. The setting is idyllic: green pastures carpeted with wild flowers, grazing goats and sheep, sapphire skies, golden sunshine, even a meandering river. But an upward glance shatters the pastoral illusion, revealing the stark mountains in stern command, a harsh reminder that this is Tibet. We drive along the Lhasa river, passing small shrines and rocks painted with Buddhas and Gods and carved with script, again a reminder, now spiritual, that this indeed is Tibet. Norbu tells Pascal that when he was a small boy these same rocks were covered with Chinese Mao slogans. We shout with excitement and wave frantically when Tim spots Texas Dave doing his yak-skin boat trip along the river, but he's too involved with manoeuvring the boat to notice us.

We stop for petrol and wait our turn in a long queue. Petrol is rationed, but somehow our driver produces legal coupons for our illicit journey – we have no permit for Nagarze – and we are on our way again. Alongside the river, about twelve miles from Lhasa, we pass a large rock sculpture. A Buddha sits in the lotus position, cradled by stone cliffs, his image held unbroken by the flat timeless water. Norbu obligingly stops for photos.

Suddenly we lurch to a stop. Breakdown. About two dozen Tibetan men and women working on the road hacking rocks and heaving buckets of earth, gather round, welcoming the intrusion. Norbu lifts the hood and a plaintive 'Ay-yah', the Tibetan-Chinese expression of woe, cousin to the Jewish 'Oy Vay', wails to the heavens, echoed by Pascal. He then crawls under the jeep, his tinkering punctuated by muffled sighs and increasingly plaintive 'Ay-yahs'. Pascal is dispatched to the river and returns carrying a large can, slopping water over himself, smiling sheepishly as Doune and Tim surprise him with cameras. Nothing helps. The engine refuses to start.

A mini van taking a group of Westerners to Nepal, among them Banak Shol residents, breaks down at the exact same spot, a veritable bonanza for the Tibetans. Norbu joins the mini van driver under his hood and a duet of 'Ay-yahs' emerges, Pascal intermittently counter-pointing a trio. This is their second attempt to reach Nepal. They broke down yesterday as well and had to return to Lhasa for repairs. Meanwhile we indulge in a third farewell scene, examining their last-minute purchases which the Tibetans help to assess with nods and thumbs-up signs. Eventually with the advice of potential mechanics and much engine cranking, our jeep starts up. We leave the mini van behind and drive off sputtering and wheezing.

Soon after the breakdown we begin the long climb to the Khamba La mountain pass, almost 16,000 feet high, 4,000 feet above Lhasa. We all refrain from asking the nagging question, 'Will the jeep make it?' The smooth surface quickly changes to rough, but the green fields, trees and clusters of white-washed houses endure. Before we get into serious climbing, Norbu stops at a house selling tea. Immediately the jeep is surrounded by a group of curious dirty-faced children, who look on half-bewildered, half-smiling, as Tim photographs them. Inside a room with a dirt floor and a long wooden table, sweet milky Tibetan tea is served. We are joined by the husband and wife who live in the house and who point out which of the children are theirs and then add two more, a baby and a toddler, making a total of six.

Unlike the Chinese, who are allowed only one child, Tibetans can have as many as they like, and unlike the Chinese, girl babies are as welcome as boys. When I first heard of the official policy limiting child-bearing to one child per married couple, by means of persuasion, incentive and penalties, I was shocked. My Western sensibility was appalled by this authoritarian incursion into individual freedom. Not having brothers, sisters, uncles and aunts was inconceivable to me. 'Only one child allowed to be born,' a Chinese teacher told me in Guangzhou (Canton), 'the others not allowed. This is most sad, but for now it must be so.' Brainwashing I thought, the man has been brainwashed into accepting an unforgivable government invasion into the ultimate privacy of its citizens.

But later when I saw Chinese children (surrounded by affection, cherished) and compared them with children in India (maimed, diseased, dying on pavements), and when I walked, crushed shoulder to shoulder, on Chinese streets, I had to concede that the severest measures were necessary to curtail a population which was already barely able to support itself. Eighty-five per cent of Chinese land is unusable and the remaining fifteen per cent has to feed a quarter of the world's population – relentless statistics. I had seen no begging in China, no starvation; everyone looked neatly dressed, healthy, with a sense of dignity. There were no crippled people with parts of their bodies rotting or falling off (some purposely maimed as children to increase their begging potential), as in other parts of Asia where population control was either unknown or ineffective. Surely this was a vindication of government policy. The Chinese simply could not afford the luxury of population explosion, and, to their credit, took effective steps to avert the horrendous suffering it caused elsewhere in the world. Although the one child per family policy was enforced in cities where the problem was at its worst, it was loosely adhered to in the country where it was less acute. In Tibet it was ignored entirely.

After a vigorous engine-cranking session, performed before an audience of delighted children, the jeep coughs to a start. Leaving all traces of valley behind, we begin a slow struggle up steep mountain faces, into a bleak landscape. The ride is terrifying. The narrow dirt road winds through mountains, climbing curves, zig-zagging around hairpin bends suspended on the edge of slopes with sheer drops of hundreds, then thousands of feet. It's dizzying to look down. The houses become white flecks on a slim strip of green carpet, and still we climb.

We can see the Himalayas covered in snow, their frozen peaks almost within reach, and still we climb. In the sky above us truck engines trail smoke, straining up mountains, their wheels churning dust and stones in an effort to grip the loose gravel. The front seat changes from blessing to curse. I am on the cliff side. When a truck approaches and we pull over to let it pass, my fingers grip the seat and

I feel grey with terror, shuddering with the engine on the edge of a looming void, waiting to suck us into eternity. No road is visible under the wheels. Our tiny jeep clings to a slanted ledge of gravel, hanging in space.

'He's a good driver,' Pascal reassures me.

'But the road has no shoulder. It can crumble away. We can slip on the stones. Please tell him not to go so near the edge,' I plead for our lives.

'But he can't help it.'

'Let the truck pull over more.'

'Where? Into the mountain?' I realise my position is illogical. But better illogical than dead.

'I hope we have Michelin tyres,' Doune comments wryly, looking only straight ahead. Tim, although he sits on the wall side of the mountain and sees road not void, has his eyes shut tight.

'Don't look over the side,' Pascal advises.

'I have to. I can't help it.'

That exchange leaves me grim and silent, leaning my weight into the road, pulling the jeep away from the edge, as though the sheer concentration of my effort will keep us from plunging into the cosmos. It works. We reach the summit of the pass shaken, but intact. Norbu rests the over-worked engine and we leave the jeep shivering, our hearts pounding in the cold wafer-thin air. The temperature had fallen considerably, but we were too scared to notice.

Now the view greeting us is so spectacular, that we forget the temperature. Bare mountains, crumpled into rough pleats of sun and shadow, with colours ranging from sharp white to blue-black, surround us. Far below, the exquisitely still lake Yamdrok bathes the land in azure, above it snow mountains float into the sky. I love seeing snow mountains. There is something about the way they suggest infinite reach that frees my spirit. Through Tim's zoom lens I witness a white bird dive towards the lake, ski on its blue surface and sail over the black carpet of yaks clustered at its tapered end.

The summit of the pass is a small stony field crowned by an improvised stupa – a round structure of layered stones from which tall branches jut haphazardly, bowed by a heavy tangle of coloured prayer flags set solidly in the stones, but extending into the spaces of eternity. In an oven-type opening, several truck drivers are burning juniper branches and incense and tying yet more prayer flags to the overloaded branches, in the ritual thanksgiving for safe passage. Norbu makes a slender base of four stones topped by a large flat one, his toadstool offering to the deities protecting our journey. I notice many such offerings in the field. Tim discovers his own thanksgiving, a bright pink flower with a golden heart, spreading delicate petals into the broken stones. He takes a photo.

The descent into Nagarze is faster and feels safer. We're on the wall side of the mountains and it's now the turn of oncoming vehicles to hug the void. The peaks and lake are magnificent, and Pascal says more dramatic than the Alps. Green gradually makes a tentative appearance and then grows more confident. Further into the valley we pass lone farmers working small patches of land with yaks and wooden ploughs. By the lake, herds of sheep are grazing, dotted with the occasional shepherd on horseback. About two pm we arrive in Nagarze. Norbu pulls up by a truck stop, the only place offering accommodation. The large sooty kitchen has a pot boiling on the stove waiting for the few travellers who stop. We have a quick lunch of tired noodles and exhausted vegetables, redeemed by good tea. Doune wants to stand by the lake and Pascal goes with her. Tim and I head into Nagarze.

It's exciting to be inside a Tibetan village, our first. Few

Westerners come here. The Tibetans interrupt their work to greet us, smiling from windows and doorways, tongues sticking out in the traditional sign of greeting. Snotty-nosed children gather in knots to giggle and shout 'Bye-bye'. Women, with heavy loads on their backs, pause to nod. Nagarze makes Lhasa look like Beverly Hills. It's a small village climbing a hillside which leans into barren mountains with snow peaks reaching stark white above the faded buffs and browns. A walled fortress rings the hilltop, its rear side crumbling down the slope, returning to the earth. Narrow dirt paths twist through the village, edged by stone fences and whitewashed houses in need of repair, their traditional flat roofs stuck with branches laced with prayer flags, like festive TV aerials. Dogs sun themselves on roofs, wagging their tails, stretching lazily as we pass. It's a treat to see dogs. Tibetans are probably the only Asians who show them affection. Whereas they avoid killing animals, the Chinese eat every animal they can, and dog meat is a delicacy.

Several children induce us to follow them. Like pied pipers in reverse, they lead us through the streets, hopping and skipping, shouting encouragement each time we falter. They bring us to the courtyard of a house which we enter through a thick wooden door, shut firmly behind us. The courtyard has a stone floor and high stone walls. A herd of sheep are milling about and two women in bright Tibetan aprons and boots, their hair tied with woollen scarves, are separating out the rams. We sit on the steps in front of the house and watch. Through some ancient choreography of women and sheep, the great tangle shuffling and twisting, pressing into corners and against walls, magically transforms into four straight rows facing each other, like the pattern of a square dance. The women move through the rows, their red and green kerchiefs bobbing up and down as they tie the sheep together by the legs. Then, beginning one at each end, they weave among the sheep, leaning over them, their rounded backs repeating the curve of hunched sheep. Milk jets against their tin pails, beating a rhythmic accompaniment, counterpointing the staccato milking movements.

We sit with a young mother who displays the baby she is nursing with a beautiful smile, and of course, a clump of cheeky, dirty kids. Tim produces a bag of sunflower seeds which he shares. The finest sweetmeats couldn't evoke a more enthusiastic response. He then takes the last cigarette from his red pack of Marlboros and begins to crumple the box. The mother eyes the empty packet so lovingly that he offers it to her. Delighted, she accepts, and puts several pebbles into the cigarette box. Shaking it like a rattle, she gives it to the baby. The baby is even more delighted. He plays with it, laughing and kicking with excitement, unwilling to relinquish it to anyone. Tim further increases his popularity by allowing the children to look through his zoom lens. They pass the camera carefully from one to the other, holding it like a magic chalice, spellbound.

By the time we leave the milking session and make our way to the fortress the sun is beginning to set. We watch it slowly disappear over the village, floating above the electric blue lake, into the mountains. Then, without warning, gusts of wind race up the hillside, whirling dust, causing my eyes and ears to sting with cold and dirt. In a moment black clouds fill the sky. We hurry through the village shivering and vulnerable, while the Tibetans continue their business unperturbed. Pascal and Doune are back from the lake with stories of shy earless rabbits sitting on hind legs, and exotic birds bathing in the clear unpolluted water.

Again the Tibetan family are in the kitchen. I admire two toddlers, intrigued by their nappy arrangements, or rather lack of them. In Tibet, as in China, small children wear no nappies. They wear trousers, slit front and back, with nothing underneath. Small bums and genitals dangle precariously. When I first became aware of this dangerous custom, I was understandably nervous in the presence of small children, especially those sharing my train compartment or sitting beside me on buses, expecting disaster to engulf me momentarily. None ever did. Chinese and Tibetan parents seem to have a sixth sense when it comes to their offspring's toilet needs. I never saw a wet lap, an out-of-place puddle, or worse. Now, in the cold bare eating room, the toddlers are wearing the customary slitted trousers. The slit, however, is covered front and back by a small fur apron tied from the waist. This ingenious arrangement does not interfere with elimination, but keeps the exposed bits warm and cosy.

The same pot is on the stove, bubbling with the same indefinable ingredients. We give it a miss and settle for our instant Chinese noodles, biscuits and tea. Clutching thermos bottles filled with hot water, we dash from the kitchen to a low building with dormitory-like rooms where we are to sleep. Outside it's black and freezing cold, the sudden icy wind a reminder of the snow mountains hovering above us. Lowering our heads against the searing wind and shielding our ears from the biting cold, we follow Pascal blindly. If this is the middle of summer, I dread to think what the winter must be like. Once again I am filled with admiration for that inner resolve, that harmony with earth and spirit which allows the Tibetans not only to make a home of this bitter land, with its continuously aggressive elements, but to embrace it with laughter and love.

Our room is basic: a table, an enamel washbasin, a bare light bulb, and six narrow beds, heaped with pillows and thick quilts. It's almost as cold inside as out and my hot water bottle is a comforting thought. I never travel without it, but Lhasa was so hot I was tempted to leave it behind. Luckily I didn't. Norbu and a friend are already in the room, apparently sharing it with us. Two of their female acquaintances join us as well, pretty Tibetan girls, smiling and giggling. When I pose for a photo sitting on Norbu's lap, they shriek with delight.

Our bedtime rituals are observed with the fascination usually reserved for rare theatrical events. They can hardly believe the enigmatic activities we indulge in, like creaming our faces, washing, and brushing our teeth. Even our props intrigue them: a strange assortment of bottles, jars, tubes and brushes, mysteriously appearing from zipped pouches within zipped pouches – a travelling magic show. I delight them further by dabbing perfume on wrists and ears. But the highlight of the show is the hot water bottle act. My bottle has a furry coat, like a cuddly animal, with a fat body and small head. The four Tibetans watch in amazement as I pour hot water into the animal, its belly swelling as it drinks. Then, in a flash of comprehension, Norbu jumps up, rummages in his bag and produces a packet of tea.

'He says you must put tea in the water, otherwise it has no taste,' Pascal translates.

Now it's our turn to laugh. They look on in utter disbelief as I place the swollen bottle in my bed and cover it with a blanket. I am putting this half-animal, half-teapot to bed. It is going to sleep with me, water and all.

When Pascal explains the purpose of the bottle they break up with laughter. 'I told them it keeps your feet warm, like a husband.'

The hot water bottle routine is hard to follow, but we do our best. Our acts of undressing are almost as entertaining, certainly more comic, and even less comprehensible. Desperate to get into bed, and not having a clue when the girls are leaving, or indeed if they are leaving, I choose a discreet moment when the others are occupied with Tim's *Furry Freaks* comic book and begin by kicking off my shoes. Hopping on the cold floor, I slide my trousers down, while modestly pulling hard on my undershirt, attempting to cover bare thighs. Glancing up, I am greeted by expressions of such shock and bewilderment that for a moment I am struck by stage fright, forgetting my next move. I stand in knee socks and a T-shirt dangling misshapen from under my blouse, intent upon stretching the shirt to its limit to hide my nakedness.

'They think you are crazy taking off your clothes, you should be putting them on,' Pascal explains.

Crazy is better than obscene. Regaining my composure, I whip off my blouse and leap into the pre-warmed bed, in one fell mysterious swoop. All eyes turn to Doune who performs with tactful refinement, in a calm unfrenzied manner, revealing less flesh than I had, but confusing the Tibetans even more by removing, God forbid, her socks. Tim and Pascal do a joint performance, their hairy legs a source of great merriment. Norbu and his friend put on an extra sweater and slip into bed fully clothed. The show is over. The girls depart, well pleased with the evening's entertainment. I pull the quilt over my head, gratefully cuddling my hot water bottle husband.

Early next morning I awake to a winter wonderland and remember that we are over 14,000 feet high. It has snowed during the night and everything is covered in powdery white. Looking out of the window above my bed, I see a group of Tibetans – men, women and children – sleeping on the ground against the wall of the building, huddled in blankets, their hair white with snow. I recall hearing voices during the night and being too tired to investigate. They must have arrived very late. Having to pee, I dress quickly and once dressed decide to walk through the village before the others are up. Wrapping myself in a blanket, I head into winter.

It's early morning in a Tibetan village, blanketed by snow.

Everything is still, the air crisp and clear. An old lady carrying a basket moves through an alleyway in unhurried silence. A lamb bleats, a rooster crows, a dog barks, the sounds rising into the new morning like the first sounds on earth. The village awakes. Through an open doorway I see into a courtyard which contains the family altar, a small igloo-shaped structure with an opening in the centre and a hole on top. A teenage boy is preparing offerings, placing incense in the opening, then lighting it. The escaping smoke wafts towards me. I inhale deeply, the smell exquisite in the clean air, evoking a thousand sacred mysteries. A young girl sweeps the courtyard with a hand-made broom. Her mother prostrates before the altar. Her father offers fresh incense. The scene has the ritual dignity of a medieval miracle play, the tranquillity compounded by the soft hush of snow and the ancient stillness of the mountains. I walk through the village smiling like a Tibetan, feeling a superb peace, a buoyant hopefulness, like the first day of a new life which is yet eternal.

Chapter Thirteen

Pema

By the time I return to our room, the camping Tibetans are gone. The others are up, dressed and surprised by the snow. On the way to the dining-room Pascal and Tim engage in a snowball fight, pelting Norbu with fluffy snowballs which burst into powdery showers, lacking moisture to bind them. Doune and I join in. It's Westerners against Tibetan. Unfair odds. I switch to the Tibetan side.

After tea, we wander into the Chinese part of the village – a wide concrete street with blank uniform buildings and a few shops selling the usual boiled sweets, tins of fruit, pots and pans, jackets and caps. Tibetan women are bent over, sweeping snow from the streets. They smile. Children pass on their way to school bundled in Tibetan odds and ends, striped aprons, sashes, bits of colourful embroidery. They wave. All else is white and grey, cold, grim. Norbu is worried about road conditions over the pass and would like to leave early. Doune waxes lyrical about the home comforts of the Banak Shol. We agree on an early start.

The road is icy and gutted with snow. We creep through the white mountains, our jeep struggling with the unexpected winter. But we're on the mountain side and compared to yesterday's death ride I feel as safe as a baby tucked in a pram. At the top of the pass Norbu stops for a quick offering. The stupa is transformed into an igloo, its branches fingers of snow dangling ghostly tatters, the prayers frozen in the grey sky, over a lake shrouded in clouds. It's hard to believe this is the same place we stopped at only yesterday. But as we descend into the valley, everything changes. The sun is shining, the air is warm, the grass green, flowers, trees, blue sky. In just minutes the bleakness of the Chinese street in Nagarze is hard to recall. I make a point of remembering.

Because it's earlier than expected, Norbu suggests we visit his relatives who live on a farm close to Lhasa. We're happy to accept. The house is entered through the back yard. Outside the door is a neat patch of potato plants – nothing to write home about until Tim points out that they're entwined with marijuana plants. Tim always notices these things. We refrain from comment. Although we're not expected, the family welcomes us as though they've been waiting weeks, even months for our arrival, honoured to be receiving guests. At the sight of us there is an explosion of joy – shouts, smiles, handclasps, embraces. The whole family is there to greet us: grandfather, grandmother, mother, father, big children, small children, even several chickens and a dog. We're ushered into the main room and given the best seats, a bench covered with blankets set before a table. The others sit on wooden chairs or on floor mats, the younger children held in the laps of the older ones. A baby lying snugly in a basket outside the door is brought in to join us. Almost before we're seated, the woman of the house begins to churn yak butter tea in a corner of the room, using a wooden vat like a tall old-fashioned butter churn.

The room is dark, with only the open door and a hole in the roof for light. Posters of guru-like figures seated in the lotus position meditating in fields and on mountaintops, decorate the walls, as well as bright posters advertising relevant Chinese products, like loo paper, presumably hung for colour as it's unavailable in Tibet. Within minutes hot tea is served. Freshly made yak butter tea has become almost palatable, although the salty taste is still surprising and the drinking requires special adjustments. I have to ignore the greasy patches of floating butter and swirl the first few mouthfuls, while trying to think of the tea as something other than tea – soup perhaps. This particular tea is actually good and the family respond to our praise by pouring cup after cup. Refusing is out of the question, especially when accepting gives so much pleasure. But after the third cup, when I see the kettle approaching. I know I must make a stand. My distended belly can't tolerate another mouthful and my back teeth are floating. Besides the tea is good, but not that good, and I'm feeling slightly nauseous.

I look to Pascal for help, for a graceful way out. Mistake. 'It's a question of spacing,' he tells me, 'you drink too fast. You must learn better spacing.'

I've been accused of bad timing, but never of bad spacing. With a philosophical smile I allow my fourth cup to be poured. Learning good spacing doesn't come easy. But finally a point is reached in the tea-drinking ritual when refusal is permissible. This, however, brings no relief to our overworked kidneys. Refusing tea is the signal for the chang to be broken out. This task falls to the grandfather. He disappears for a while and returns with several milky looking bottles. Our cups are changed and he pours out the chang amid laughing and talking, waiting for each of us to drink, encouraging us to do so. My spacing is still less than perfect. I sip slowly, and depict a busting belly with such descriptive gestures, that I'm a great disappointment to my hosts. Pascal, on the other hand, is not. He redeems us; even Tim and Doune help restore the faith. And in the fullness of time I manage two cupfuls of chang, much to the delight of all present, especially Pema, the young daughter of the house, a girl of about Eleven. Pema seems to have developed a special affection for me. She removes the delicately chiselled silver and turquoise pendant from around her neck and places it around mine, and then repeats her name over and over until I say it correctly. She says mine, 'Niema', with a quality like music.

Pema is exceedingly beautiful, with black hair spreading like a shawl and a delicate way of moving, each gesture sustained and held, as though she were moving through a painting, framing each moment. Her eyes are remarkable, soft like a doe's in repose, then leaping with intelligence and humour as she perceives something. I am fascinated by Pema as soon as I see her. If someone were to tell me she was the incarnation of some great spirit, I would know it was true. Every time I catch her eye we both burst out laughing as though we share a secret.

Actually we're all smiling and laughing, feeling comfortable and relaxed, enjoying ourselves with the kids and adults alike. It's the kind of comfort that in the West is normally achieved only with close friends, certainly not with strangers. There is a total generosity here not only with things, but with spirit. There is no weighing or measuring. No points to score. Nothing needs to be done. Nothing needs to be said. The acceptance is unconditional. Their joy in the process of living spills over on to us. I have the sense that, unlike our Western families there is no banging of heads against walls with frustration or anger, no raging at the environment, trying to tear from it that which it can't give, or raging at oneself or each other for similar reasons. There is instead an attunement with the rhythms of being, a grace towards each other which embraces everyone else. And in this sparsely furnished room, with no windows and a bare earth floor, living may not be easy, but life is good. The children play with each other or with us, the adults chat and laugh, glad to be drinking tea with guests, glad to be here, now.

Once again I realise that happiness does not lie in the possession of material wealth. Whereas we admire the person who achieves worldly success, who pushes his way to the top, Tibetans admire the person who renounces worldly success, but who achieves spiritual wealth. And as I watch the grandfather, delighted by my acceptance of more chang, and the grandmother, happy as though she was attending some great festivity, and Pema, smiling at me as she touches the velvet ribbon tying back my hair, I experience a surge of love, a desire to embrace. I smile and drink a silent toast.

While Tim and Doune are outside the house amusing the children and themselves, and Pascal and Norbu are talking to the adults inside, Pema takes my hand. 'Niema … Niema…' She repeats softly, in that musical way, and smiling a secret smile, leads me through a door off the main room. I find myself in the altar room, a prayer space found in every Tibetan home, even in the poorest yak-hair tents of nomads. I have never been in a prayer room before and understand that this is a gift from Pema. As soon as I enter the room I know it is her special place. I sense a change in her breathing, in the way she holds my hand, even in her appearance.

The room is glittering with light from butter lamps arranged in rows on a low bench before a shrine. The lamp light illuminates the Buddha seated in the centre of the shrine, his imperceptible smile smiling through the centuries. He is surrounded by holy objects, sacred books wrapped in cloth, silver offering bowls, a framed picture of the Dalai Lama, lamps burning incense. The wall behind him is covered by a tangka. I recognise Chenrezig, the protector of Tibet, his eleven heads and a thousand arms, issuing forth boundless compassion. Incense smoke curls around him. The other walls are covered with paintings of deities, some of which are familiar.

As I move around the room examining the paintings, I realise

Pema is no longer beside me. I find her in a corner, on her knees, facing the Buddha. Her expression has assumed an intensity, a purity, removed from present consciousness. Her face is magic. In the light of the butter lamps it glows with a serene beauty, lit from within. The beads of her rosary move through her fingers, catching the light, as slowly, over and over again, she chants 'Om Mani Padme Hum'. The prayer moves not only her lips but her entire being so that her body seems to rise up and up, her neck becoming longer, her eyes opening wider and wider, as though she were growing, coming alive before the Buddha. Her intimate connection with the powerful prayer, the powerful deity, makes her shine like a new star.

When it is time to go, I leave the house with Pema's mantra humming within me and her face suspended before me, like a beacon.

Chapter Fourteen

Sera Monastery

Several days after our return from Nagarze, Pascal tells us that Tashi has arranged for Tim, Doune and me to visit Sera Monastery. There is a special celebration the following afternoon for the monks living there, and Tashi's relative, the high lama who speaks English, will be at Sera and is expecting us. Tashi can't come, Pascal wants to go climbing first and will meet us there later. We decide to get an early start so we can see the monastery before meeting the lama and Pascal.

Although I have been reading a great deal about Tibet – Pascal keeps me supplied with mysteriously acquired books – I haven't found out much about Sera itself. I do know it was built below the tiny hermitage where Tsongkhapa, the great Buddhist teacher and reformer, born in 1352, retreated for several years to meditate and write about the Buddhist scriptures. He believed that Buddhist principles were being abused by the monasteries, and spent his life making monastic reforms. These reforms led to his founding of the Gelukpa sect ('the path of perfect virtue'), known as 'The Yellow Hats', which remains the dominant school of Tibetan Buddhism. Sera Monastery was founded by Tsongkhapa's leading disciple in 1419, the year of his teacher's death.

Sera is one of the three pillars of Tibetan Buddhism. The other two are Drepung and Ganden, all close to Lhasa. Until the Chinese invaded Tibet, they were the great centres of learning, monastic universities, really monastery towns. All three served as academic centres where Tibetans came from every part of the country to receive long years of monastic training (becoming a monk was considered the highest form of service to the community). It was in these ecclesiastic universities that Tibetan culture flourished. The higher studies of literature, medicine, arts, architecture – the entire body of knowledge derived from Buddhist teachings – were taught in these academies. They were the world's largest monasteries, with Drepung housing about 7,000 monks and Sera 4,000. (Sera now has fewer than three hundred monks.) Like the other two monasteries, Sera consisted of various colleges where the different subjects were taught, each with its own assembly hall and chapels; a main assembly hall where the monks from different colleges came together on special occasions; four main temples; as well as numerous houses where the students lived. I'm not sure exactly what remains of Sera. I know that Ganden was destroyed during the cultural revolution, but I understand that Sera's main buildings are pretty much intact, although many of its residential buildings were razed, and that it is once again operating as a monastery school.

Sera is about two and a half miles from Lhasa. It lies at the foot of mountains on the edge of the Lhasa Valley. We decide to cycle there, and set off early next morning, me riding on the back of Tim's bicycle. The road is good and the bicycles have to be pushed on only two occasions. We pass small groups of Tibetans also making their way to Sera, who stop to smile and wave. Most are dressed in the traditional manner, the women wearing bright aprons over long black skirts with colourful sashes and dark jackets. Some have babies tied to their backs. The men wear blankets tied with sashes, long chubas with wide sleeves, or trousers and jackets, and the usual wide variety of hats. A group of women pass in entirely different dress. They wear rigid black pillbox hats, embroidered in gold, and black tunics with embroidered triangular designs, about hip-level. They look very elegant and I wonder what part of Tibet they are from.

In less than an hour we're at Sera. We tie our bicycles to trees and proceed on foot. Sera has the feel of a medieval village with winding cobbled streets and white stone houses rising in rows against mountain cliffs. Stone steps lead to buildings with wooden balconies and carved painted doorways and eves. The occasional donkey walks by, a load tied to its back. A number of pilgrims climb the streets with us, carefully balancing jars and small brass bowls filled with melted yak butter, come to worship and make offerings. As we twist around corners, through archways, along alleyways, we pass temples with golden spires spun on their roofs and blue and white canopies hanging over their entrances. Before visiting the temples, we decide to climb the mountains above the monastery to see the rock paintings and carvings while it is still cool.

Lungs rasping for oxygen, we climb high into the steep cliffs, the monastery receding beneath us like a white nest. A sharp glinting light coming from a golden emblem on a temple roof – two deer on either side of the Dharma wheel – follows us as we climb. This image, seen in many places, symbolises the teaching of the Buddha and commemorates his first sermon, given at Deer Park, Benares, in India. Spokes of light radiate from points in the wheel and as we sit down and stand up the Dharma Wheel seems to turn, like the name of the sermon itself, 'Turning the Wheel of Dharma.'

Suddenly we arrive. Soaring out of the rocks are fierce demons painted in bright primary colours, alongside blissful Buddhas and other deities. It's a wild mountain temple splashed with brilliant decoration – demons, deities, holy script – rising and falling into the sky. In a crevice below us a Buddha is carved into a giant rounded boulder, his eyes gazing from deep within the rock, his head adorned with an elaborate headdress. The boulder is crowned with heaps of stones stuck with burning juniper branches and incense. A halo of smoke floats over the Buddha's head, ascending like a soft veil to enfold the deities and demons above.

Between the rocks, lines of bright prayer flags hang, creating an aura of festivity. Tibetans climb among the sacred boulders (touching them with their hands, their foreheads, their backs), burning incense, saying prayers, sitting among the Buddhas whirling prayer wheels, meditating, or simply eating and talking. In these desolate mountains, the barren rocks have suddenly sprung to life, blossoming with colourful deities who enshrine them and with people come to pay them homage.

As I sit on a rock enjoying the scene, I am aware that it is not a strange or unusual one, but integral to life in Tibet – ancient monuments, open, unguarded, alive. And I marvel that these remarkable paintings, these religious relics, these ancient carvings, are not fenced in, but freely available to everyone. Tibetans don't come to look. They come to feel, to participate, to express the religious beliefs which make life meaningful for them, which give them continuity with the past, hope for the future. They come to pay their respect to their deities and to the mountains which shelter them.

The climb down is difficult, the rocks loose, the ground steep. Doune nearly comes to grief slipping on a stone. She becomes dizzy and breathless. We pause to calm trembling legs, ease pounding hearts, and to gaze at the spectacular view across the valley and the mountains beyond. Finally we are down.

After a rest, and some tea, bread and jam, which we brought with us, we are ready to explore the temples. We enter a temple hall filled with brocaded pillars, murals, tangkas and carvings. Huge lantern-shaped fixtures hang from the ceiling, made from strips of brocade shaped like men's ties sewn together. Padded benches line one wall. Huge old tangkas faded and dusty with age, cover the others. Off the hall are chapels where offerings are made. Buddhas sit serenely, hands stuffed with money. Yak butter lamps burn, filled by passing pilgrims. The smell of yak butter permeates the chapels, the cool darkness penetrated by candles burning in front of giant Buddhas, powerful, yet peaceful.

One chapel is shared by Shakyamuni, the Buddha of the present; Maitreya, the Buddha of the future; and Dipamkara, the Buddha of the past. A monk sits cross-legged, saying his prayers contentedly in the presence of three great Buddhas. Another chapel, dark and mysterious, is like a chamber of horrors. Evil-looking black figures with bared fangs and long fingernails, loom like demons of death. In the centre of this chamber is a dark curtained box which the Tibetans stick their heads into as they file by. I put mine in gingerly. Something wet, perhaps a cloth, touches my forehead and I withdraw, flinching as though something has passed over my grave. Doune sticks her head in a little way and pulls back quickly. Tim waits outside.

Too early to meet Pascal, we wander through temples, halls and chapels. All are of a similar style, some more lavish than others. Tsongkhapa seems to be the outstanding figure of the monastery, always wearing monk's robes and a yellow hat. Many chapels are devoted to him and he appears in statues, on tangkas, in murals. The popular Fifth Dalai Lama, responsible for building the Potala, is also well represented, as of course, is the Buddha Shakyamuni. In one main hall he is the central figure, a beautifully made Shakyamuni, with a fine sensitive face and delicate features. In another place I find an image of him with a small figure of Milarepa, the poet-saint, sitting by his side. Tara, the female Buddha, mother of compassion, symbol of unlimited fertility, born from a tear of compassion dropping from Chenrezig's eye, is also prominent. There is a stone figure of her, as well as several large images and hundreds of small ones. In the main hall of one temple is a statue of the beloved Thirteenth Dalai Lama. On one side of him is an empty seat reserved for his successor, the present, Fourteenth Dalai Lama, when he one day visits Sera.

Each temple has two storeys. The upper storey of one has a balcony-passageway, painted with murals, and chambers leading off it. Some chambers are filled with old manuscripts and scriptures, some with shelves of small figures and religious articles. In one room monks are busily engaged in cutting thin strips of ancient script from larger sheets, then rolling the strips into tiny scrolls, prayers for the inside of prayer wheels. In another room, several monks sit around thick wooden tables carving printing blocks, their chisels moving swiftly and accurately. Throughout the monastery monks are working at various tasks, some repairing the monastery itself, others cleaning it. Unlike the Potala, there is a sense of life in Sera; even the halls have a more lived-in look, the atmosphere is lively and cheerful.

As we approach the main assembly hall, the largest building in Sera, a droning singsong sound drifts towards us. Inside the hall about a hundred monks of all ages, including a sprinkling of boys, are seated cross-legged on flat cushions, in rows forming a semi-circle, swaying rhythmically. Their faces rise out of dark orange robes and veils of incense, lit by hundreds of yak butter candles burning before them on a low altar. We stand at the entrance to the hall, entranced, but reluctant to enter, not wishing to disturb the proceedings. A young monk passing by urges us in and signals us to sit, bringing pillows from stacks of cushions and neatly folded robes, piled on long benches. The chanting continues uninterrupted, the monks oblivious to our intrusion. I listen, fascinated, never having heard such chanting before.

It is a strange sound, part music, part speech, with a rhythm that keeps repeating, swelling, and receding in waves, lifting and falling, echoing with a powerful resonance. I become engulfed by the deep vibrations which seem to emanate from the womb of the earth. I am surrounded by them, held by them. Litanies are intoned three notes at once (a uniquely Tibetan sound) by a chorus of deep mellow voices, further enriched by an undertow of muffled drumming and the clash of tiny cymbals. It is like a river of sound flooding the hall, then flowing onwards, twisting, meandering, rumbling, rushing into the next flood.

I am absorbed into the waves, the cadences, floating, drifting, when suddenly the chanting stops. Silence. The air is hung with stillness. The monks sit motionless, eyes unblinking, as though fixing an inner image, a perception, a sound. Suddenly the leader snaps his fingers and the silence is engulfed by liquid sound. Further snaps penetrate the chanting, punctuating the plaintive ebb and flow. Fluid hand and finger movements blend into the sound, drawing it onwards, upwards, inwards. Palms are pressed together, moving in unison from heart to forehead, then held above the head, arms framing meditative faces in a triangle of devotion.

The rhythm of the chanting swells and wanes, over and over, hypnotically, filling my head with the sound of invisible forces summoned from the earth, the sea, the sky, carrying me along the crests of sound, lowering me into curves and dips, until the strangeness becomes part of my heartbeat. I ride the swells, lifted higher and higher, transported to a point where I am about to know something, break some barrier. But abruptly the chanting ceases. The monks rise from the cushions, adjusting their robes, returning effortlessly to this place, this time. Acknowledging our presence with grins and nods, they file out of the hall, the smooth stone whispering against their bare feet. I remain immobile on my pillow, listening. The chant lingers but reveals nothing.Tim tells me it's time to meet Pascal. We are to meet outside the temple. Doune and I sit on the steps to wait. As Tim walks over to join us, he slips on the floor, polished by centuries of yak butter drippings, and slides down the stairs, crashing into a group of Chinese soldiers, knocking two of them over and scattering their rifles. Several passing Tibetans break into fits of laughter. The soldiers are not amused. Neither is Tim. They spring to attention, brushing off their weapons and themselves and march off briskly, determined to preserve a semblance of dignity.

The shock of this misadventure is compounded by the impact of Pascal's arrival. He looks as if he's seen a ghost and collapses beside me, mopping a dripping brow.

'Are you all right?' Doune asks. 'You look very strange.'

'I feel very strange,' he answers weakly. 'I have just had the most strange experience of my life … You know I went climbing up there.' He waves his arm in a broad gesture, encompassing the mountains above Sera. 'I was very high up, sitting by myself, very peaceful, looking at the wonderful view of Lhasa and the mountains, when quite far away, in the rocks, I thought I could see dogs attacking some person. I knew they could be wild, so I picked up stones and a stick and, very carefully, I went to have a look. I got close up to them without them seeing me and then I began throwing stones to frighten them. I hit some of them and they ran away. Then I climbed up to where they were.

'A girl was lying on a rock, on her back, dead. She was very beautiful with smooth skin like the colour of coffee. Her arms and her breasts were naked and her hair, very black, was spreading over the rock, shining … But there was only one half of her, the top half, perfect, not touched … the dogs had eaten the other half, everything

… I stood there like a stupid man. I thought I should do something, but what was there to do? I didn't even know what I should feel.

'Then I remembered … Tibetans who can't afford the sky burial (you know it is very expensive for them, one quarter of what they earn in one year), well if they can't afford it they put their dead on high rocks for the birds and dogs to eat. But that was just a fact I heard about. I didn't expect to see anything like that … It wasn't like the sky burial. In the sky burial there was some … ritual … some ceremony. This was so raw … I don't know … I stood staring at the girl for a long time. Finally I left her and came down. When I turned to look I could see that the dogs had come back and were eating her again.'

'How awful for you Pascal,' I say, taking his hand and pressing it with my anxieties. For a moment he considers, then says, 'yes, it was awful, but you know, it was not so awful. The girl's eyes were open and very calm. She looked beautiful, very peaceful, I would say even happy.'

Pascal's story is interrupted by the lama who has come upon us unnoticed, so absorbed were we. Pascal jumps up. It's all I can do to focus on the introductions and make myself smile, my head is so full of that half-eaten girl lying on the rock. I do manage to see that the lama is tall with a kind face and twinkling merry eyes, and that Pascal has produced a khata scarf from somewhere and placed it around the lama's neck in greeting.

We follow him back into the hall and he leads us to an alcove strewn with pillows and lit by yak butter lamps. It's good to get out of the hot sun. I appreciate the cool and quiet, and the incense smells like flowers. Yak butter tea is brought and served by two young monks with shaved heads and orange robes. While we sip the tea a discussion begins, everyone has questions for the lama. Doune asks about Sera, about its history and its present situation. Although I'm interested in the answers, I can't seem to listen, the image of the beautiful girl being eaten by dogs at this very moment, sits heavy, like a lump in my throat I can't get rid of. I ask nothing. I can hardly swallow my tea, let alone talk.

Then I hear the lama say something about the disappearance and death of many monks, and I burst out with, 'Pascal saw a dead girl in the mountains just before. The dogs were eating her. She was already half eaten, only the top part of her was left.' I fall silent, feeling like a child spilling over an anguish to a revered adult, who, by some miraculous accumulation of experience and wisdom, can make it all better. I look hopefully at the lama. He sips his yak butter tea meditatively and says nothing. I feel foolish, exposed, as though I were in the midst of some religious procession in my underwear.

Slowly the lama looks up from his tea. 'I am happy for Pascal. It is good for him to see this girl.' His voice is full of robust energy. We are all taken aback.

He continues calmly, carefully, but with that same undertow of energy. 'It is necessary to become familiar with death, to see it, to contemplate it, because that which is familiar to us is no longer fearsome. As Buddhists we believe that we must meet all the death demons, picture them in our minds, become accustomed to them, so that death can hold no terror for us. That is why our tangkas and our paintings show us these demons. We send novice monks to caves to meditate with the remains of the dead, so that they can face their fears of death and so overcome those fears. For it is only by facing death that we can understand life. And so like that.' He pauses for a moment. No one moves.

'You too must contemplate your own death, meditate upon it, learn to understand and accept it. For only when you understand that life and death are not two opposites but only different sides of one reality, will you have no fear of death. For life is a candle which burns in the wind, its light can be gone in a moment. Death comes to all that lives. We must therefore never forget how precious this human life is, with its wonderful possibility of wisdom, which we should take advantage of before our death.'

As the lama speaks, I am struck by how different our Western approach to death is. We are terrified by death, yet obsessed with it. Our television and newspapers are filled with death but we spend our lives avoiding the idea of our own mortality, refusing to confront death, deal with it, accept it.

The lama looks into each of our faces and suddenly breaks into laughter. 'You all look so worried. You must not take me so seriously.' He smiles and the sun bursts into the room.

But in the glow of burning incense, the image of the girl returns, rekindled by memories of the sky burial. 'Lama, to see dogs eating a girl's body …' I stop, unable to finish my sentence.

The lama spares me its completion. 'We Tibetans regard the body as a precious gift, but once that body has no more life, it no longer has any purpose and it is right and kind to give it to some living being as a last gift. Is this not so?' he asks gently.

No one answers.

'We must all know that there is nothing which is permanent. If we cling to anything, even to life, we can only cause ourselves great suffering, and it is the aim of Buddhism to release mankind from suffering. The Buddha teaches that suffering comes from desire. Desire has no end, for no matter how many desires we are able to fulfil, there are still more that we cannot fulfil. To be released from suffering we must first be released from desire.'

'How can we be released from desire?' Doune asks.

'For a beginning we can meditate upon impermanence, upon death. As we become truly aware that death is inevitable, for it exists within us as soon as we are born, we also become aware that living from one desire to the next has not made us happy. It has not given us peaceful minds. The present does not fulfil us. We remain striving for something in the future. We have only to think of all the people we know who have lived their lives striving to fulfil desires, only to die unfulfilled, in disappointment. A peaceful mind will not fall out of the sky, we must create it, and to create it we must eliminate desire. And so like that.'

There is a long silence as we consider the lama's words. Then Tim says, 'Can I ask you about reincarnation?' The lama nods, focusing on Tim, giving him his entire attention. 'If Buddhists believe that man is reincarnated into another life when he dies and therefore this life is only a preparation, doesn't that make it easier to accept this life however bad it is, and not try to change or improve it, for only the next life is of real concern? Doesn't that make it possible for people with power to take advantage and increase their power?'

'A Buddhist does not concentrate on his past lives or on his future ones. These lives are either over or will begin in the future. Knowing this is sufficient. What is most important is this present life. Buddhism teaches that each person is responsible for his own deeds in this life, both good and bad, and as human beings we have the will to choose which they shall be. This life must be lived well. The Buddha's teachings all have this as their aim.'

'What would you say is a life lived well?' Tim asks.

'A life lived with kindness and compassion for all living beings, a life which does not abuse the gifts of heaven. Even as monks we can do all the correct things, not eat meat, be celibate, meditate in our cells, worship in the temples, but if in our hearts we feel no true compassion for every creature that lives, and do not devote ourselves to helping them, our lives shall be barren. We must wish to achieve enlightenment not only for our own happiness, but to be a greater betterment to the world and to all that lives in it. Respect for life, compassion and love are the main principles of our Buddhism, and compassion is the most important one. And so like that.'

I know that Tim has been wanting to ask his big question and now sees his chance. 'Speaking about compassion, there is something which has been troubling me ... If you believe that compassion to all living beings is so important, how do you justify eating meat? Animals are being slaughtered right in the middle of Lhasa, the Barkor is full of dead animals.'

'Yes,' the lama says, his voice saddened, 'that is truly a troubling question. I wish I could answer it well. But I cannot. I can only say that we know the lives of animals are being taken daily and we wish it was not so. Yet very often a man must eat meat or he would die. Our climate is a hard one and we do not have many different foods, often meat is all we can get. Drokpas, nomads, for example, must eat meat to live. Yet they are very religious people and do not believe in taking life. Because they must do so to stay alive, they become even more devoted in their efforts to relieve the suffering they see about them. In this way they make an attempt to atone for the sin of taking life. They also pray for a rebirth in which taking life is not a necessity. I know that this reasoning can be used by some as an excuse for eating meat and I can only feel sorry for those who are not sincere in their thinking, and also sorry for those who kill animals. Tibetans believe it is sinful to kill an animal for any reason but we allow Muslim butchers to do our killing for us, so that we ourselves do not kill but only buy the meat of animals already dead. But I believe that those who take pleasure in the eating of animals are also gratified by the taking of life.

I consider this to be bad, but there are those who must eat meat to live. This I cannot consider to be bad, but neither can I consider it to be good. When people eat meat they must always eat it thinking with compassion of the animal who gave its life for them and try to make the life of other animals easier and better. They must vow to try even harder to bring comfort to all living beings. They must use their eating of meat as something from which they can learn, as we must learn from all things in life. For life itself is our greatest teacher. And so like that.'

The lama speaks with such compassion, such humanity, such simplicity, that everything he says is touched by a gentle peace. Somewhere among his words, his smiles, his humour, the way his robes distend like wings when he lifts his arm, my agitation has left me. My disquiet has somehow been absorbed by his inner peace and I can hear his words with renewed calm. I feel in the presence of a great wisdom, a great beauty, a rainbow light of tranquillity. For the first time I understand the impulse which causes people to seek out a guru. I would like to remain soaking up the lama's ambience, his embrace. But I see Pascal looking at his watch, aware that we must not take too much of the lama's time and energy. 'We must go now,' he says. 'We are grateful for being with you. You have been very generous with us.'

The lama's eyes twinkle and he smiles that sunshine smile. 'If you find not much use in what I have said, you must forget it. My brain is finished with all this unaccustomed talking, so I will now stop. But before we part I would like you to hear some lines of poetry written by Tsongkhapa, one of our great Buddhist teachers who spent many years meditating above this monastery.'

He pauses for a moment, his eyes sparkling with candlelight, then in a rich mellow voice says:

'The human body, at peace with itself,
Is more precious than the rarest gem
All worldly things are brief, like lightning in the sky
This life you must know as the tiny splash of a raindrop
A thing of beauty that disappears even as it comes into being'

When at last I look up, the lama is gone. We remain still, meditating as he had wished, each on our own discoveries. Most of all I am aware of 'the human body at peace with itself'. I feel as though something has changed within me. It is not so much the words of the lama, but something more powerful. I remember reading somewhere that 'a single man striving to achieve perfection, radiates perfection', I have just met such a man.

On the way back from Sera, Pascal takes me on his bicycle. I hold his waist, remembering the way I clung to him on the ride back from the sky burial. That seems a long time ago. As we ride I watch the wispy clouds moving high overhead, like white birds in flight, and it occurs to me that the Tibetans know how to live, precisely because they are so in tune with death. I hold Pascal gently now, with serenity.

Chapter Fifteen

Reincarnation and the Dalai Lama

I have never thought much about reincarnation, at least not seriously. But in Tibet I can't avoid it. The concept is so prevalent, accepted with such unqualified assurance by people I respect deeply, like the lama of Sera and Tashi, that some of the certainty filters into my consciousness and I am continuously wondering, troubled and intrigued. It wouldn't be exaggerating to say that the subject of death and rebirth has become something of an obsession, a haunt which leaves me hovering over shadowy landscapes. Since the visit to Sera the preoccupation has grown even stronger.

The supreme reincarnation is the Dalai Lama. Although the Dalai Lama is the undisputed ruler of Tibet, the temporal and spiritual head of the country, he is not elected, he does not inherit the position, he doesn't compete for the title – he is reincarnated. He is the incarnation of the preceding Dalai Lama who was the incarnation of the one before him, going back to the first Dalai Lama and then through a line of saints, yogis, philosophers and kings, to the time of Buddha. All were in turn reincarnations of Chenrezig sent by the Buddhas to protect Tibet, a sacred duty inherited by each successive incarnation. When a Dalai Lama dies, his incarnation could be anyone, appear anywhere. The search for him is a spiritual endeavour, a holy mission of profound significance, for upon its success rests the well-being of all Tibetans.

Tenzin Gyatso, 14th Dalai Lama

The search for and discovery of the present Dalai Lama, the Fourteenth, is a modern tale of ancient magic and miracle. When Thupten Gyatso ('Gyatso' means 'Ocean of Wisdom', the name given to all Dalai Lamas), the Thirteenth Dalai Lama died in 1933, Tibet was plunged into terrible sorrow. Not only was the grief personal, for every Tibetan loved him dearly, but the loss was a great national one. The divine ruler was dead. The heart of Tibet had ceased to beat. Nothing could be more vital to the life of the nation than to find Thupten Gyatso's reincarnation. A search was begun immediately. This was a mystical task, the complexities of which were governed by ancient traditions. Since Tibet is a vast country, the direction of the quest had to be determined. It was believed that portents and signs would be given, but these would need to be recognised and interpreted. The State Oracles and the most learned lamas, were consulted for this hallowed purpose. Employing methods centuries old, they sought divine guidance, then prayed and meditated, watched and waited. All Tibet prayed with them.

Signs appeared. Strange cloud formations were seen in the north-east of Lhasa. Although the Dalai Lama's body had been placed on a throne facing south, his face gradually turned east. This was considered especially significant. (Often the previous Dalai Lama will give some indication as to where his reincarnation will be found, or in which place he wishes to be reborn.) Near the Dalai Lama's body, on a pillar in the north-eastern part of the shrine, a star-shaped fungus appeared. It soon became apparent that the direction to look was north-east.

Then, in 1935, Tibet's most sacred lake, Lhamoi Lhatso, about ninety miles from Lhasa, famous for the visions seen in its waters, was consulted. The Regent, himself a high incarnation surpassed only by the Dalai Lama, and a man of exceptional ability, who had been appointed to rule Tibet until the new Dalai Lama was discovered and of age to rule, visited the lake personally. After days of prayers and meditation, the vision appeared. Three letters from the Tibetan alphabet, 'Ah', 'Ka', and 'Ma', followed by a monastery with gold and green rooftops and a house with turquoise tiles. This vision was held in strict secrecy.

The following year, high lamas and special dignitaries, entrusted with the secret of the vision, were dispatched not only to the north-east, but throughout Tibet, to find the places revealed by the sacred lake. However, in accordance with the portents, those sent to the north-east succeeded. They discovered the monastery of Kumbum with its green and golden roofs, near the village of Taktser, in the province of Amdo, a province governed by the Chinese. In the village itself, they found a turquoise tiled house, which precisely matched the house in the Regent's vision, down to the mottled brown and white dog. The peasant family who lived in the house had a boy almost two years old. The miracle was unfolding. Excited by their findings, they were most eager to see the boy.

In order to allay suspicion, the Abbot of Sera Monastery, who headed the mission, was disguised as a servant and the visit made to resemble an ordinary one of passing travellers seeking lodging. Since there were no hotels or restaurants in Tibet at the time, not even in Lhasa, it was customary to extend hospitality to all travellers. The guests were made welcome. Then a remarkable thing happened. When the little boy saw the disguised servant, he was immediately drawn to him. He rushed over and insisted upon climbing on to his lap. Then he took hold of the rosary he was wearing and asked if he could have it. It was the rosary belonging to the Thirteenth Dalai Lama. When asked who the man with the rosary was, little Lhamo Dhondup replied without hesitation. 'A lama from Sera'. The disguise had not deceived him. His spiritual powers were so impressive that it seemed he must be the incarnation they were seeking.

However, further tests were needed to be certain. One of the tests given to children suspected of being reincarnations, is to see if they can recognise articles belonging to the deceased, for they are known to have memories of their earlier lives. Two identical rosaries were shown to the little boy and he unerringly chose the one belonging to the Thirteenth Dalai Lama. Next he was shown two drums, a small unadorned one belonging to the Dalai Lama, and a large ornate one. Again he chose correctly. Lastly he was presented with two walking sticks. He took the wrong one, hesitated, then changed it for the right one. It was subsequently discovered that the first stick had at one time been used by the Dalai Lama, hence his confusion. He had passed the tests.

The visions of the three letters were interpreted as, 'Ah', for Amdo, the district where Lhamo Dhondup was born; 'Ka' for the nearby monastery of Kumbum, or 'Ka' and 'Ma' together for the monastery above the village, Karma Rolpa Dorje, where the Thirteenth Dalai Lama himself had once stayed and where he had left a pair of his boots. The search party needed no further confirmation. The Fourteenth Dalai Lama had been found.

A telegram was sent in code from China via India to Lhasa, the only telegraph route, with a report. The answer came: 'Bring the boy immediately to Lhasa.' Permission, however, first had to be granted by the Chinese governor. His help was requested to take possible candidates for the Dalai Lama to Lhasa. The fact that the final choice had already been made, was not revealed to him for fear he would create problems. The fear proved justified. The Governor would not release the boy. After inspecting the group of likely candidates, he suspected that Lhamo Dhondup was the one chosen, and ordered that he be held in Kumbum monastery. He then demanded a huge ransom. The ransom was paid.

Realising he was on to a good thing, he demanded an even larger ransom, so enormous that the treasury of Lhasa did not have the means to pay it. Negotiations to raise the money were begun. They lasted almost two years. During this period the strictest secrecy was observed. It was never admitted to the Chinese Governor, the Tibetan government, not even to his parents, that the Dalai Lama had been found. Meanwhile little Lhamo Dhondup was held in the monastery where he was lonely and unhappy, separated from the warmth of his family.

Finally the money was raised. The Governor was paid and the boy was freed. A week after his fourth birthday the momentous journey began. A large caravan consisting of Lhamo Dhondup, his parents and about fifty others, set off for Lhasa. The journey lasted over three months. Until the 1970's the routes to Lhasa, even from India or Nepal, took at least two months to negotiate and were blocked for a good part of the year where they crossed high mountain passes. At the time of this journey there were no wheeled vehicles in Tibet, and therefore no roads to accommodate them. The little Dalai Lama rode in a carriage supported by two mules, and when the route became too difficult, he was carried.

As soon as the caravan was safely in Tibetan-controlled territory, the National Assembly was given a full report, detailing how the Dalai Lama had been found. It was emphasised that the search had been conducted in strict accordance with the advice given by the leading oracles and lamas of Tibet. The National Assembly issued an official proclamation declaring the discovery of the Fourteenth Dalai Lama. Senior officials were dispatched to welcome the Dalai Lama en route to Lhasa. It was only when these government officials met the caravan and offered symbols of reverence and homage, that his parents knew their son was the Fourteenth Dalai Lama. They had suspected nothing so momentous before this. Their eldest son had been recognised as the reincarnation of a high lama, and they supposed their trip to Lhasa was to determine if this son could be a similar incarnation. Lhamo Dhondup's peasant clothes were taken from him and replaced by monastic robes and from them on he was carried in a golden palanquin. A little boy plucked from his peasant heritage, rode into Lhasa hailed as a divinity on earth.

By now the people of Tibet had been informed that the Dalai Lama had been found and there was great rejoicing. Along the remainder of the way they welcomed him with festive processions, with the music of horns, flutes, drums and cymbals, with clouds of incense and with dancing. The Prime Minister, members of the cabinet and leading abbots of the three main monasteries, Drepung, Sera and Ganden, came personally to welcome him. Not far from the holy city of Lhasa the procession was greeted by thousands of monks lining the route with brightly coloured banners, groups of people singing and playing instruments and soldiers of all the regiments in the Tibetan army presenting arms. The entire Lhasa population came out in force, dressed in their best clothes, to welcome the new Dalai Lama, shouting 'A happy sun now shines in Tibet,' and 'The day of our happiness has come.'

Soon after his arrival in Lhasa, in 1940, the Dalai Lama, now four and a half years old, was enthroned on the Lion Throne in an elaborate official ceremony held in the Potala Palace, with chanting, prayers, mime, dance and intricate rituals. Little Lhamo Dhondup handled the occasion with impressive poise. When called upon to bestow his blessing upon the distinguished guests, he did so with a seriousness, self-possession and dignity, which foreshadowed his remarkable ability to handle difficult situations with calm and composure. Through this ceremony the Dalai Lama was proclaimed by the government and people as the spiritual and temporal ruler. Tibet was jubilant.

My thoughts about the Dalai Lama and reincarnation are interrupted by the appearance of Lillian bearing a bunch of radishes. 'Come with me to the truck stop,' she says, chewing a radish, 'I want to check out the chances of getting out of here by truck via Golmud,' I am taken aback. The days have been peeling from the month, slowly almost imperceptibly, beautifully, like veils in a dance, unfolding, revealing, creating new shapes. It comes as a shock that Lillian is considering departure. Our group here is so satisfying I resist any threat of dismantling it, but Lillian forestalls my protests. 'Hold your horses, I'm not going anywhere, I'm just doing the preliminary research. In my position you gotta be two jumps ahead.'

The truck stop we are to check out is in the Muslim quarter, behind the mosque. The dirt alleyways here are even narrower than those around the Barkor. Stone walls make the houses invisible. Set into the walls are wooden doors, several ajar. We can see into courtyards, some quite pretty, with wells, outdoor ovens, birds and flowers. Goats and donkeys stand idly on the narrow streets, motionless against the walls. As we squeeze past them they observe us with mournful patience, but don't give an inch.

The truck stop is a large dirt patch where beat-up Chinese trucks, and some surprisingly luxurious Japanese ones, are parked. Several Tibetan men are milling around the yard, working on the trucks. Lillian quickly establishes which ones drive the Japanese vehicles and makes a beeline for them. The drivers are surprised to see two females in the yard, brazenly inspecting their vehicles, but are friendly and smiling. Lillian marches over to a man cleaning a Japanese truck. I hang back. Without preliminaries she repeats the word 'Golmud' with a no-nonsense firmness, points to the man, herself, and then to the inside of the cab. Her manner is businesslike, efficient. The driver looks bewildered. Then, thinking he understands the strange charade, he bursts out laughing and shares the joke with his friends.

The laughter is good-humoured, without malice or derision. But Lillian is not amused. She shouts over to me, 'Wait till he's seen the colour of my money, he'll be laughing on the other side of his face.' Briskly withdrawing her wallet, she pulls it apart and flashes several bills. Still smiling, the man, displaying indifference to the money, reaches instead for the wallet. Thinking she's initiated some type of bargaining, she hands it to him. But he's simply interested in the velcro fastener, tearing the wallet open and pressing it shut with scientific curiosity and nods of appreciation. She grabs the wallet from his hand.

Lillian goes from one driver to another, lowering her standards, settling for battered Chinese vehicles which look like they couldn't make it to the Banak Shol, let alone to Golmud. But all she gets is more of the same, amused disinterest in her insistence on a ride and fascination with her wallet. The drivers refuse to treat her request with the seriousness she expects. They are accustomed to large rugged male travellers making arrangements for rides to Golmud. This little irate grandmother with man's boots, big bosoms, and a tricky wallet, confuses them. What can she want with them? Surely she wouldn't be attempting the long hazardous truck journey to China, a small elderly lady, all alone.

I have a sneaking suspicion they want no part of her, despite the intriguing wallet, and are relieved, when completely frustrated, she throws up her arms. 'You're all a bunch of macho male chauvinists,' she shouts and stomps out of the yard, me trailing behind. The drivers smile and return to their trucks. Foreigners are a strange lot.

As compensation I suggest we go to a Muslim dumpling shop near the mosque and offer to treat Lillian to momos and Muslim tea. Food always pacifies Lillian. Actually she needs no pacifying. The encounter hasn't fazed her. 'Now you know why I have to do preliminary research,' she says. 'But don't worry. I don't take no for an answer, and there's no way I'm going to waste my good money on a plane ticket. Tomorrow I'll get Texas Dave to handle things for me. They can't refuse him anything. I'll be sitting pretty in the cab of one of those Japanese trucks, trust me.' I trust her implicitly.

When we return from the trucking expedition, I find an envelope from Pascal. It contains some Tibetan poetry he had promised me at Sera. The poems are copied in a beautiful script, not Pascal's handwriting. Most of the poems are composed by Milarepa and by the Sixth Dalai Lama, two of my favourite Tibetans. I'm very pleased.

Tsangyang Gyatso, 6th Dalai Lama

The Sixth Dalai Lama, popularly known as Tsangyang Gyatso ('Ocean of Melody'), is for me a very touching figure. Because the death of the Fifth Dalai Lama in 1682 was kept secret to ensure that the Potala would be completed, the search for his successor was not begun until twelve years after he died. Unlike the other incarnations, discovered as small children, by the time Tsangyang Gyatso was declared a reincarnation, he was a young lad accustomed to a life of liberty and the adventure of growing into manhood. He knew the pleasures the world offered. But the abrupt confinement to a monastic life meant they were no longer his. Aware of the enormous responsibilities which had suddenly fallen upon him, he tried to concentrate on his religious training. However, he never adapted to the seclusion and discipline of the monastery. Unable to reconcile the spiritual aspects he aspired to, with the earthly ones he yearned for, he lived his life in an uneasy limbo between heaven and earth, desiring both. A dualistic lifestyle resulted. During the day he devoted himself to religious studies and spiritual practices, and lived in a manner so simple and so austere, that he chose to do without servants. Although never fully ordained, he lived like a monk. But at night his ascetic life was abandoned. Slipping out of the Potala to the tiny hamlet beneath it, he would visit the houses of love, drink chang and enjoy his lovers, a practice which not only did not endear him to the other lamas (all celibate), but was a source of deep conflict within himself:

In my Palace, the place of Heaven on Earth
They call me Rigdzen Tsangyang Gyatso,
Chenrezig Reincarnate
But below my Palace
In the little town of Sho
They call me Chebo Tangsan Wongbo
The profligate
For my loves are many.

The conflict tormenting his soul found expression in his poetry, the struggle between Tsangyang Gyatso – the Dalai Lama, the reincarnation of Chenrezig, divine ruler of Tibet – and Tsangyang Gyatso, the sensual youth, who loved the pleasures of women and love-making, and who unsuccessfully attempted to subdue them by monastic rigour, 'the man of many loves':

I came before my accomplished guru
To receive a mystical communion
But my mind could not be contained

And slipped away to thoughts of love.

His religious teaching, however, affected him deeply, informing both his love-making and his poetry; his embraces were interwoven with a poignant spirituality. And it is this combination of spirituality and sensuality which gives his poetry such haunting beauty:

Although I try to meditate upon
The countenance of my sublime guru,
His face will not stay in my mind;
Yet without effort the face of my love
Appears again and again.

He died in strange circumstances which have never been revealed. He was not quite twenty-five. Despite stories and rumours circulated about him, the Tibetans have always loved and revered him. His chorten, however, is absent from the Potala, the only Dalai Lama not to be buried there since its construction.

In the short walk of this life
We have had our shares of joy
Let us hope to meet again
In the youth of the next.

Milarepa

My first encounter with Milarepa was extraordinary, like a moment of reprieve in an anguished nightmare. It was as though I had been drowning in a black sea and he appeared to save me. That day I visited the Potala and became enmeshed in the terrible array of monsters, demons and gods, dragged into a surreal world, so agonised, so afflicted, so grotesque, that the circuits of my brain exploded, there was one consoling figure I returned to again and again. He sat in the lotus position, one hand raised to his ear, listening; the other cradling a bowl. Through the chaos of screaming colours – of death visions entwined with images of sublimity, tender angels superimposed on madness, torment and agony – he remained tranquil, dignified, attentive, his features delicate, his complexion pale, surrounded by an almost visible aura of gentle compassion, gentle love.

Later I discovered that he was Milarepa, Tibet's beloved poet-saint. Perhaps because he composed poetry and songs, perhaps because Pascal told me he was a sinner who became a saint, no doubt because of our significant encounter, he captured my imagination. Finding out about him was not difficult. Almost every book I consulted contained some reference to Milarepa, and the story I eventually pieced together was not only fascinating but very moving.

He was born in the eleventh century near the Tibetan-Nepalese border and given the name 'Thopa Ga' ('Joy to Hear'). The name proved prophetic for he grew up with the gift of music and poetry. When Milarepa was very young, his father died. But before dying he entrusted his wealth to his brother, who promised to care for the boy and his mother until Milarepa came of age. The uncle, however, was one of those cruel, greedy men, and as soon as his brother was dead, he plundered the inheritance, robbed Milarepa and his mother of all their possessions and treated them with cold-hearted ruthlessness. It is not hard to understand why Milarepa's mother craved revenge. Out of deep love for her and deep resentment against his uncle, Milarepa, spurred on by his mother, vowed to destroy him. He devoted himself to learning the black magic of destruction and used it with devastating effect. During a wedding celebration given by his uncle, Milarepa caused his uncle's house to collapse, killing all the guests. He then caused a fierce hailstorm which ravaged his crops. The uncle was ruined and Milarepa and his mother were avenged. But revenge brought him no joy; instead it filled him with remorse. He realised that his desire for vengeance had resulted in the accumulation of black deeds.

With terrible agony he became aware of the karmic consequence of those deeds and was consumed with regret.

Wishing desperately to atone for his sins, he was advised to seek out Marpa, the renowned Buddhist teacher, to ask for guidance and instruction. He remained with Marpa for several years, attempting to undo his great karmic obstruction by meditating, by patiently carrying out the brutally difficult tasks Marpa set him, by studying Buddhism and by seeking self-purification and spiritual enlightenment.

Then, in the solitude of the Himalayas, he continued his Buddhist practices. He wandered alone in remote areas hoping to find the path to liberation in a life of asceticism. The mountains became his monastery. He lived in caves clinging to slopes, with no possessions except for a cotton robe, a wooden bowl, a cup made from a human skull (to remind him of the impermanence of life), and only nettles to eat. In both summer and winter he wore a light cotton robe, and became known as 'Milarepa', ('Mila', his family name, 'repa', 'clad in cotton'). He grew to love the wild country and the animals, birds and plants he shared it with. Here, in its inaccessible reaches, he composed his mountain poetry, singing his Buddhist perceptions, encapsulating their truths and releasing them in music and poetry. Despite his isolation people came to know and to love him. He attracted many disciples who listened to his spiritual teachings and he became one of Tibet's most revered mystics, a Buddhist bard, spreading his wisdom through poetry and song. It is said that when he died, the heavens wept blossom tears.

Milarepa's story has an unusual power and fills me with admiration. He personified those Buddhist principles the lama in Sera was talking about. Milarepa had truly liberated himself from a conditioned existence, which fuels in us the all-consuming desire to acquire the perishable things of the world. He had developed a way of living free from desire, free from attachment to things that pass away. All those things we accumulate, living in a technological society, considered unquestionably necessary, and for which we are willing to trade most of our time and energy, even our health, he would consider 'impediments to right living'. He believed that they impede the discovery and expression of the beauty inherent in each of us, and the beauty inherent in life itself. Although Milarepa had none of these things, or precisely because he had none of them, he was free to perceive that beauty, to celebrate it in song, to bring it to others. And because he had created a mind at peace, a mind in harmony with his surroundings, which he loved, he was able to share that peace with others, just as he had shared it with me in the Potala.

Since that day, I have located many paintings, tangkas and figures of Milarepa. He is always portrayed as I first saw him, his right hand against his ear, as though listening to the poetry and music within himself, or perhaps within the rocks, sky and streams; his left hand balancing his bowl of nettles. Locating his poems, however, has been an entirely different matter. I could find very few and those only increased my desire to find more. Finally I allocated the task to the resourceful Pascal.

Now, reading his poetry, I understand why he is so well-loved. Milarepa, in renouncing his ordinary life for a life of solitary wandering in the mountains, without ambitions, without desires, without needs, became part of those mountains. He sang from within them, his songs the essence of the Tibetan spirit, the singing of Tibet itself:

Hermitage admidst the solitude of mountains,
place where the marvellous jina receive their bhodi,
region where holy men are residing,
spot where now I am the only human!
Red-rocked chonglung, eagle's nest,

clouds from the south are piling above you,
far below swift-running streams are snaking,
high in the air the vulture is circling;
every kind of forest tree whispers,
splendid trees sway like lissom dancers;
bees are humming their song khorroro,
flowers exude the secret of chillili;
birds are melodiously chirping kyurruru
up on red-rocked chonglung
birds big and small are practising their wing-beats,
monkeys big and small are practising their leaps,
stags and does are practising their running.
I, Milarepa, am practising spiritual powers,
spiritual powers and inner holiness I practise;
with the local deity of the hermitage
I am in peaceful harmony.
Spectres of evil who are assembled here
imbibe the juice of love and of mercy
and depart from hence, each to his place!

As I am returning the poems to the envelope, suffused with the poetry of Tibet, a piece of paper flutters to the floor. I pick it up and read: 'My friend Pascal. It is soon time for me to go so I have copied out some of the poems you asked me for. Kindly give them to our dear friend with my good wishes and thoughts.' Signed 'Tashi'.

Chapter Sixteen

The Mani Stone

I have been patient about seeing Tashi, enjoying the certainty of the coming pleasure. I know I will see him, know it will be good and postponing the pleasure is itself pleasurable, heightened by the assurance of still greater pleasure. It's like anticipating a journey. I long for it to happen but never want to rush the moment. The waiting has its own delights, an excitement, a quickening heartbeat entwined in the calm of certitude. Seeing Tashi is yet to come. I enjoy living with the promise, holding it in my mind. The waiting brings him closer.

Late one afternoon, several days after receiving the poetry, Pascal startles me. 'I have arranged a meeting with Tashi at the tea house. Are you free to come?'

I am flustered, unprepared. 'Tashi? When?'

'Now?'

'Now? Right now?'

'Yes. He is there already. I was just with him.'

My tongue tangles, but my head manages to signal yes. I rush into my room, can't focus on what to do, and rush out again.

We ride on Pascal's bicycle. By the tea house he leaves me, saying he has things to do. I am abandoned, fragile, my heart trembling. I enter alone. The tea house is empty. But Tashi is there. He is more beautiful than I remember, his ear pierced with turquoise, his body lean, wild, his smile magic. Seeing him I want nothing else. Some troubled yearning I hardly know exists is quietened, yet I am wonderfully excited. His glance draws me like gravity.

Am I laughing? Crying? Did I speak? He rises to embrace me. My blood is singing. I hold him with such intensity that to separate from him would tear my flesh. It is not the wild elation of the first five minutes of being in love. It is the sustained power of a profound love eternally there, eternally here, begun at this moment. As I recognise it, believe it, I hear other voices. His embrace quietens me. Gently we draw apart. Two men are drinking tea.

As if it were prearranged, Tashi and I follow the road to the Potala. His serenity flows through me. I am stilled, wanting only to walk with Tashi, just like this, on and on, yet wanting to postpone the next step indefinitely. All the questions I wanted to ask, all the things I wanted to know, do not exist. I have no questions, no answers. The menagerie of desires is satisfied. By the Potala we find a rock. It seems curiously familiar. Had Doune and I sat here? Had I come this way before? I think I hear Tashi speak, but know he is silent. As I sit contented, I am compelled by Tashi, by the Potala, by Tibet, to some realm where we exist together. United.

Tashi reaches into his pocket, withdraws his hand and slowly opens it. In the centre of his palm is a stone the size of a pressed rose. Its remarkable icy blue colour catches the sun as he hands it to me. As soon as I take it in my hand I know it is no ordinary stone. Tashi watches with that total serenity that makes no demands but only enhances experience, as my fingers move over its worn surface. At first it feels cool, removed, like silk, but as I hold it, folding my fingers and palms over it, it's as though my hands are drawn into it and filled with energy. It is warm, significant. I seem to know it. Perhaps it recalls the stone the masseur used in the Chinese tea house, stroking my forehead, temples, cheekbones, suffusing me with calm energy. I finger the ridges, deliberate like script.

At last I say, 'Is this Tibetan writing?'

Tashi nods.

'What does it mean?'

'This is a mani stone,' he says, 'a very special stone that has the characters of a prayer carved into it. This stone contains the prayer to Chenrezig, the Bodhisattva who looks with compassion in a thousand directions, his compassionate spirit reborn into each Dalai Lama. The prayer to Chenrezig is "Om Mani Padme Hum", the six holy sounds, and the characters of Mani are carved into the stone.

'It's beautiful,' I say, realising this is the mantra I have been chanting in my impromptu mediations, but was unable to say in the Jokhang. 'I love holding it. It feels like it has an energy, a power of its own.'

'Yes. It does. It was given to me by a very great lama and contains his love and his blessing. Because of that I wish to give it to you. It is my gift to you.'

'But it was given to you,' I protest.

'And to you,' he adds simply. 'It will remind you of Tibet and of Tashi.'

As though I could ever forget.

'And it has special healing powers, it will heal your fear of being buried while you are still alive.'

His voice is quiet with caring and I recall once again how his face darkened with pain at the telling of my nightmare. He wants to shield me, protect me from my fear.

I am deeply moved, deeply grateful. 'Thank you Tashi. I am so over-whelmed. What can I say?'

'You must say nothing. There is no need.'

He's right, there is no need. He understands more about me

than I understand about myself. I sense that he possesses an attunement with the profound rhythms that shape and connect events. I hold the stone in both hands, like a prayer, and lower my head to it. Tashi reaches out, his fingers spreading through my hair, his fingertips coming to rest in the hollow of my neck. I hold them like a nest cradling new birds. The exquisite surprise, the exquisite familiarity, stirs something within me to ecstasy. It is an ecstasy I could never imagine. The sensation is so vivid that when Tashi withdraws his hand, it remains. My head stays bowed, unwilling to disturb it. We sit for a long while under a still heaven. It is perfect being here, not talking, not touching, a deep bond between us, a recognition of the unlimited alternatives for love and affection that exist in life, and the even more profound bond that makes of this moment a lifetime.

'There is a story I would like you to know, an old Tibetan tale.' Tashi says, 'but sadly I do not have it with me here in Lhasa.'

'Tell it to me then.' All at once I have an urgent desire to hear it.

'I do not wish to spoil it. But when I return to Dharamsala I will send it to you. We will make arrangements.'

'Please … Promise you will send it, that you won't forget.' My urgency surprises me.

'I cannot forget.'

We walk back under the silence of the sky, my mind spreading slowly, like the moon on the sea, quietly embracing Tashi and Tibet. When we reach the Banak Shol we turn to each other. I am supremely happy. 'Go with love.' Tashi's voice is absorbed by the mountains, the rivers, the skies. Did he say that now, yesterday, many years ago? I enter the Banak Shol, holding the mani stone and trying to remember.

Chapter Seventeen

Leaving Lhasa

About a week later, sitting comfortably with our tea and bread, Texas Dave makes a surprise announcement. 'Folks, I'm leaving for Golmud in two days.' When he made arrangements for Lillian's ride, negotiations which took several days, he also arranged for the driver to take him along on his next journey to China. He's just had word that the driver is leaving the day after tomorrow. A mini scene erupts between Texas Dave and Gina. 'You don't care about us splitting up,' she accuses, 'you've got another lady …. Other ladies. You're going to Golmud with that Cindy and Mindy.' She darts him looks charged more with pathos than anger. We all know the Americans girls are flying back to Chengdu. Gina knows as well, but her distress at separation from Texas Dave must take some direction.

She is going to Nepal, he to China. She knew their being together was temporary, but this knowledge doesn't help now. She's grown attached to him, wants to be with him, and the inevitability of the separation – travellers whose roads no longer merge – gnaws a hole in her gut. His announcement, made so casually, so finally, panics her. 'You don't give a damn … you didn't even tell me,' she blurts out and bolts from the kitchen in tears. Texas Dave attempts no defence. There is none. As in an American Square Dance, partners are always changing, groups whirl together and then split apart, forming new patterns, new sets.

'I've also made my plans to leave,' Pascal says quietly. 'I will take the plane to Chengdu, Guangzhou, then to Hong Kong and then back to Switzerland. I'll remain there for a while.' Tashi too has left. Pascal gave him the address of a well-known hotel in Xian where he can write to me. We'll be in Xian for sure, and even if we don't stay at the Remin Daxia Hotel, I'll check there for mail. Ian and Jaye ask Texas Dave for particulars about his Golmud ride.

Tim, Doune and I look at each other with that uncomfortable winding down look. Departure is contagious, like a song everyone is suddenly humming. Like dominoes, one goes down and an invisible momentum is set up, affecting the others seemingly standing tall. I'm not sure what calls but we know it's time to go. Things happen quickly after that. We decide to leave with Ian and Jaye the day after Texas Dave, the day before Pascal. If we can manage a lift on the same day, we can all meet in Golmud. Texas Dave will wait. The thought is pleasing and makes separation less difficult.

Tim, Doune and I have a problem. Truck drivers take one person in the cab, two at most, if there's no second driver. We are three. It's decided that Doune and I will go in one truck, Tim in another. Sometimes trucks travel in convoys. Perhaps we'll be lucky. Discussing the technicalities of departure makes me anxious, uneasy. I don't want to pursue them any further and return to my room. In times of emotional fragility I have developed a technique for putting everything away from me except that which needs to be done immediately. Alone in my room I call upon that technique to help me with leaving Tibet, and concentrate on revising a list of things that need doing.

Next morning we meet to check out two truck stops near each other – 'preliminary research'. We have excellent front men. Ian has everything worked out. He's learned the necessary words both in Tibetan and Chinese, and Tim keeps the phrase book ready. Both truck stops, however, are empty of activity; no drivers, few trucks. We've obviously come at the wrong time. Ian approaches a Chinese lady sitting on a chair by the entrance, sewing. She tells him to come back at three o'clock when the drivers will be there and she'll arrange rides for us. Encouraged, we go our separate way, planning to be back by three pm.

Doune and I wander in the Barkor, trying to drink it to the dregs. We're invited into a small temple on a narrow dirt street and observe people restoring it, making the image of a deity, shaping the body, painting the face; colouring yak butter for butter sculptures. We're offered tsampa, then yak butter tea. In the Jokhang there's a special ceremony to celebrate the unveiling of a Buddha. Horns are wailing; special robes and hats. We watch, but are restless, wanting yet more. Coming out of the Jokhang, we trip over construction work. The Chinese are building a square with shops and boutiques, part of their tourist plan for Lhasa. I'm glad I won't be here to see it and think how lucky we are to be in Tibet now, before the Chinese desecration. We manage a hurried look at the Potala and a stroll in the park around the Norbulingka, but soon it's time for the truck stop. We're all there on time except for the Chinese lady. We wait – three-thirty, four, four-thirty. No drivers, no lady, nothing at all. At five o'clock we decide to try again tomorrow.

That night Gina gives Doune a pair of padded down trousers. 'I hear it's a cold ride,' she says, her eyes filling with tears. Texas Dave is taking that same ride. He's given me an improvised sleeveless sheepskin poncho. The skins, left over from his jacket are sewn together, leaving a hole for my head. It reaches my waist but doesn't quite come together at the sides.

Pascal insists that I take his sweater. 'I won't need it any more,' he says.

I resist, allergic to wool.

'You won't be allergic to anything when you start freezing in the mountains.'

I remember Nagarze and accept. I bought Tibetan boots but have no other warm clothing, nothing with sleeves except one cotton blouse. Travelling in Asia I expected to be too hot, not too cold. I was flying from London to Bangkok where the temperature in February was in the high nineties. I took only the lightest clothes. Hating to be lumbered with anything extra, I even sent my jacket back with Ronit when she drove me to Heathrow. I lived to regret this.

I was flying with Tarom Rumania, the cheapest airline to Thailand. The flight originated in Brussels, stopped in London and went on to Bucharest where we were to change planes for Bangkok. Brussels was immersed in fog and the plane couldn't take off. We spent the first night in a Piccadily Circus hotel. Next morning was still foggy and all Tarom passengers to Thailand were advised to make other arrangements. Most did. I didn't. I wasn't pressed for time; nobody was meeting me in Bangkok; and I didn't want to spend extra money on a ticket; besides I sensed adventure. When we finally got to Bucharest that night, we discovered the connecting flight had departed without us. The next flight to Bangkok was in one week. There were thirteen of us in this predicament.

The Bucharest airport was modern, swanky and freezing cold. I remembered the beach towel in my bag, a going-away present. I intended using it on the Thai beaches and then trading it. It was too large to carry – deliciously large I discovered as I wrapped myself in it and waited in the visa queue, watching my breath. 'Freak! Freak!' one of the guards exclaimed when he saw me. I wasn't surprised. I certainly looked like a weirdo, arriving in the north pole at night in sandals and a beach towel. Still I cast him a cold, disdainful look;

though not too hostile, he was carrying a rifle. It turned out he was saying ‘frig’ (‘cold’) sympathising with my condition, but I didn’t discover this until the next day when everyone else was saying it – too late for apologies. Chris, a six-foot-four Swede, was standing in the queue behind me. When he learned I had nothing warmer to wear he took off his Scandinavian sweater and insisted I have it. He said he was used to the cold, even liked it. I didn’t dare reveal I was from Canada. Actually I hated the cold. In London central heating was my big fantasy. Now I really looked like a freak, smothered in an enormous sweater encased by a jaunty beach towel.

Visas arranged, we were taken by bus to a hotel. It was twenty degrees below zero. Everything was covered in snow, the streets cold and dark, exceptionally dark. It occurred to me that when we were landing Bucharest seemed to be lit by candles. It probably was. We found out later that because the Rumanians had participated in the Los Angeles Olympics, the Russians punished them by charging hard currency for oil. As a result there was no heat, no light, no petrol.

The hotel was surprisingly grand. I shared a room with Ruth, an English girl going to Bali to shop for her boutique in Cornwall. The room was spacious with two double beds and a large bathroom, featuring a bidet. There was only one problem – no heat. The wall thermometer read twelve degrees below zero. The radiators were like undulating blocks of ice, and the water so cold it was painful to turn on the tap. We wrapped ourselves in blankets and in a mood of quiet despair joined the others for dinner. The dining-room was splendid but even colder than the bedroom. Dimly lit chandeliers, tall candles, white linen tablecloths and napkins, crystal wine glasses, real silverware, fresh flowers - a veritable ice palace.

Our Tarom group was seated at the long beautifully laid table, each of us covered in layers of snowy white blankets ripped of the beds, some reaching over the head and fastened at the neck like hoods. This was an elegant dinner party transported to the Arctic Circle with a guest list of polar bears and Ku Klux Klan. Surreal. Waiters appeared, bearing large platters of food, towels draped over their arms, their immaculate uniforms supplemented by fur hats and fur-lined gloves. Our waiter served French-style. When the meat hit my plate it congealed instantly, a ring of fat surrounding each bite-sized morsel. The gravy stood stark still in shock, and the piles of vegetables huddled together for warmth. The cutlery was so cold my fingers stuck to it. I ate with sweater sleeves covering my hands.

The staff and the other guests acted like it was business as usual. The waiter poured wine, aloof and dextrous, despite the gloves. A trio of musicians played for our dining delight. They wore jackets, fur hats and gloves with cut-out fingers. After dinner a chanteuse took the floor, blowing kisses. She wore a full-length fur coat which she flashed open at intervals to reveal her low-cut gown and glittering jewellery. She sang, 'I just called to say I luff you', in a heavy Rumanian accent, while we froze. But we listened to the bitter end. It was either the Snow Queen in the ice palace or stiff bedsheets.

In the morning a committee was dispatched to the Tarom office to inform them officially that we were going to die of pneumonia. They moved us to the Bucharesti, the best hotel in Rumania, one of the two with heat. We thawed in our individual suites with hot showers, closed-circuit TV, room service and excellent food and wine – guests of Tarom Rumania. Back at Heathrow two British girls working in the Bucharest Embassy had advised us to bring cartons of Kent cigarettes. (Only Kent would do.) We sold these for so much money that we were unable to spend it. Shops had little for sale. Most things were rationed. The one item easily available was Russian vodka. We became very popular with the staff, very unpopular with the management.

I enjoyed Bucharest. The wide boulevards and squares were empty of traffic. Everywhere cars were hunched like sheep stranded in deep snow, waiting out the winter. All private vehicles were banned, only taxis and public transport were permitted. The city had a special quiet grandeur. Thanks to Chris, I was able to explore it fully. He was married to a Thai girl called Nit, and was bringing back clothes she had left in Sweden. Blessed be Nit, her Adidas sneakers were a perfect fit. Some Somalian students donated a bundle of clothes to our cause. The Rumanians were well-dressed in fur coats and hats and fashionable leather boots. We appeared among them draped in blankets, in clothes that didn't fit, with protruding pyjamas, and no boots or hats. Someone asked us if we were a pop group. Our week in Bucharest was luxurious, walking until our feet got cold, then driving around in taxis, partying every night. But I couldn't help feeling sorry for Tarom Rumania who had to foot the bill. The country seemed so poor.

With the Bucharest freeze in mind, first thing next morning, I go to the Barkor and buy long Chinese underwear – red. We get an early start at the truck stop but to no avail. The trucks left for Golmud at six thirty am, one containing Texas Dave. There is no further movement. After a day of hanging around and futile attempts at negotiations, Tim and Doune are somewhat discouraged and begin to think about the plane to Chengdu. Even Ian is considering it, but Jaye and I remain determined. We're going to Golmud, no matter what. In the end we decide to show up at the truck stop next morning at six am, with our belongings, and take our chances.

The following day has a bleak beginning. We get up at five am and are at the truck stop by six. Pascal comes to say goodbye, riding his bicycle together with me and my bag. At the first stop there is a depressing lack of activity. The gate is locked. We trudge to the second stop. No trace of life. We hang about, a morose knot of six.

After a long hour, Tim says, 'Let's fly.' Pascal is quietly subversive, secretly voting for Chengdu. Doune too is convinced we won't get out and discusses going to the CAAC office with Tim and Pascal. Ian checks the plane schedule to Chengdu and the train schedule from Golmud to Xining. Jaye and I try to inject hope. It's hard. Gloom too is contagious. Someone locks the truck stop gate and we retreat to the first one. It's chilly. We sit on the cold pavement gazing despondently at a pack of dogs playing.

About seven-thirty our luck changes dramatically. A man appears wearing a corduroy jacket with a pen clipped to one pocket and a notebook protruding from the other, signs of authority. He asks where we're going. 'Golmud,' I answer brightly, sensing that this man wields power. I'm right. He's our man. There's a truck leaving for Xining at eight o'clock. Xining is even better than Golmud; about five hundred miles further along our route into China, a total distance of approximately 1,250 miles from Lhasa. We would have had to take a train to Xining from Golmud. The price is so low we forego bargaining. He opens the gate and shows us the truck. Not quite what we hoped for. It's plain Chinese rather than fancy Japanese, and covered by a suspicious tarpaulin, but as Ian says to Tim who makes a cursory inspection, 'Don't look a gift truck in the tarpaulin'. There will be fifteen or us. No matter. We climb aboard and set out our bags, staking our claim, before our man can change his mind.

All through the excitement of seeing our ride materialise, I carry the pain of parting from Pascal like a letter I'm loath to open. I climb from the truck now, unable to delay any longer, the driver signalling he is ready to leave. In a corner of the yard, by the shelter of a truck, I take his hand. Two seasoned travellers accustomed to goodbyes, adieus, farewells, but for this one I am unprepared.

'Ça va pas Pascal?' I say, pushing back the pain.

'Oh, oui Niema, ça va bien.'

He is more accomplished. We embrace. I feel him close and once again listen to his heart.

'Pascal, I know you will stay in my life.'

'Many people pass, but a few stay. I will stay.' He presses me closer, sealing his promise.

The driver honks the horn.

As we draw apart, Pascal gives me a small package. 'Open it somewhere when you are on the road.'

I shove the package into my pocket, beside the mani stone, my fingers clinging to both as we run back to the truck. A minute later it pulls away, me waving an emotional goodbye, Pascal promising to write, me shouting thank yous.

It's eight o'clock, exactly on time. It seems too good to be true. It is. Instead of leaving Lhasa we begin an extensive tour of it, driving from one part to another with long waits in between, loading people, bags, bundles, sacks, three drums of petrol. With each stop our space diminishes, our stake shrivels. One wait is so long that Doune and I go off for breakfast. All we can find is a grubby restaurant. Doune orders an omelette, I settle for a boiled egg. The omelette arrives swimming in grease. Hungry, Doune eats it anyway. By the time we get back to the truck, she's violently ill and throws up in front of the Tibetans, acutely embarrassed. But they express no disgust, only sympathy, and help her back on the truck, squeezing together to give her more room. One man produces tea from a thermos.

The corduroy-jacketed driver disappears. He's replaced by two others, an older Muslim in his sixties, with a hooked nose and a great smile, and a young Tibetan, who we discover is an apprentice, learning to drive. Despite the heat, both wear caps and heavy sheepskin coats. Eventually there are fifteen of us packed into the back of the truck: ten Tibetans, including a woman and a child under two; and five of us. By the time all the goods are loaded we've been compressed into a small area, unable to stretch out. The drivers make repeated reference to our scanty clothing, their faces expressing concern, their heads shaking in disbelief, their shoulders finally shrugging, resigned to our folly. We don't understand. Jaye and Ian are well-prepared with storm jackets, hoods, sleeping bags and inflatable mats. Doune has Gina's down trousers plus a sleeping bag. Tim has a windproof jacket and hood. I have Pascal's sweater and Texas Dave's poncho. True, the Tibetans have rolls of bedding and long sheepskin coats. But how bad can it be? It doesn't take too long to find out.

At two o'clock we finally leave Lhasa buried in a cocoon of bundles, sacks, bedrolls and each other. As soon as I'm certain we are leaving, I extricate myself to stand in the opening of the truck, waiting for the Potala. More than anything else I will miss the Potala and the many ways I have come to know it. It has become more than the picture I saw before coming to Lhasa, an image embodying my fascination with Tibet; more than the powerful first sight, when it welcomed me like an epiphany rising out of the dry hills; more than the symbol of Tibet, a place of great power, a people of great strength. In some inexplicable way the Potala has become fused with my being and I know I will always be drawn back to it. Slowly it appears. Although I have been wanting this moment, I find myself fearing it. Some moments release a lifetime. My fingers reach for the mani stone filled with blessing, the blessing of Tibet, Tashi's gift to me. And as I see the Potala for the last time, my eyes fill with tears as they did the first time. But between those tears and these exists the journey into Tibet. I have touched Tibet; Tibet has touched me. I hold the vision carefully, closing my eyes to better preserve it, as the truck moves out of the forbidden city.

Chapter Eighteen

Leaving Tibet

Not far out of Lhasa we join the Qinghai-Tibet highway, the highest road in the world. We're heading north-east through Tibet into China, the same direction the wise lamas and state oracles took to search for the Dalai Lama fifty years ago. For the first hour the road is good if bumpy. At one point it winds through a gorge with fairytale walls of pink-striped stone and purple rock. Shortly after that we begin to climb: high mountains, villages in hills. Our engine struggles as the road grows worse and we tilt from side to side. It begins to get cold.

During a pee stop I put my second pair of trousers on top of the first, my long underwear underneath both. Jaye lends me a windbreaker. Tim, Doune and I huddle under Doune's sleeping bag. I'm pressed into the woman and baby, grateful for the warmth, but unsure about the baby, my legs slotted into someone else's. Last night Ian, who is big on maps, told me that Qinghai province alone, which we will probably reach tomorrow, has three mountain ranges running east to west, with high plains in between, so I know these mountains are only a beginning.

Road works begin. All vehicles are forced off the road, driving in wet grooves, jolting over stones and sliding through mud, crossing streams, climbing rocky inclines, each driver improvising his own detour. We are bumped to death. The Tibetans are quiet, patient, accepting. Not a peep from the baby. We are noisier, fidgety, chewing on biscuits, groaning over bumps. Ian sits with the drivers. He's their obvious favourite. Later he changes with Doune. He's too uncomfortable squeezed between the two men, sitting in the crack dividing the seats, his legs perched high on a tool box, his knees pressed into his chest. About five hours out of Lhasa we pass two pilgrims prostrating toward the holy city. They barely raise their eyes, so engrossed are they in the great pilgrimage to reach 'the Place of the Gods', and fulfil every Tibetan's dream – to see Lhasa before he dies.

At midnight we stop high in the mountains at a truck stop. We pile out eagerly, cold and stiff, thankful for the stretch. The Tibetans, except for the drivers, stay in the truck to sleep. It's cheaper. We wait while the drivers wake the man in charge. Without complaint he leads us to his cell-like office and makes arrangements for our rooms by candlelight. There is no electricity. The five of us are given one room and charged four RMB each (about sixty cents). It's basic, but clean: narrow beds with heavy quilts, a table, candle stumps. It's colder inside than out. We eat some soggy noodles and biscuits and fall into our beds fully clothed, Tibetan-style.

Next morning, we leave at seven am. Suddenly we're in the depths of an arctic winter. I have to keep reminding myself that this is high summer. The drivers were right, we're dismally unprepared for the weather, even Jaye and Ian. Nobody wants to sit in the cab; although warmer, it's acutely uncomfortable. I'm smallest so I volunteer; besides I'm so cold that heat at any expense seems a blessing, and the back of the truck isn't exactly the Ritz. Reluctantly I return Jaye's jacket and relinquish Pascal's sweater to Tim. The cab is certainly warmer, pressed between two sheepskin coats, but there's no space for my blood to circulate. Soon I find myself contending with pins and needles and wishing I'd paid more attention to an aerobic exercise book I saw at the Banak Shol.

The cab is crammed with tools, boxes, bags, rags, food, cigarettes, even a broom and shovel. The seat, with a space and a gear stick separating the driver's section, is covered by a rancid sheepskin. Whenever the driver changes gears I'm prodded by his elbow or the gear lever itself. But the drivers are cheerful and friendly, especially the older one who does most of the driving. The younger one is a little shy. They have only one major flaw – they insist on force-feeding me.

First they present a brown and yellowish delicacy, some kind of biscuit I assume, hopefully part chocolate. It turns out to be a lump of yak meat, and when I unsuspectingly bite into it, the yellow, pure fat, congeals on the roof of my mouth. The brown, far from being chocolate, is tough, sinewy, unchewable. It's like eating leather laced with lard. Once in my mouth, however, I have no choice except to swallow. Later the driver sniffs that particular lot of meat, wrinkles his nose in disgust and flings it out the window. It's gone off. I feel instantly poisoned. Next I'm offered a stale bun from an uncovered cardboard box, which has collected a layer of dust and grime. The driver blows at the dust and wipes the bun against an even grimier coat. I break off a very small piece. Next jagged pieces of what look like crystalline stones are pressed on me. I lick at one with a suspicious tongue. It turns out to be rock sugar, an amplified version of the kind used in Muslim tea. Thank goodness. Now I can be gracious by accepting something.

During the eating bouts we keep pressing forward. We're in mountains patchy with ice and snow, twisting through barren passes, swept by freezing winds, a bleak ravaged landscape, the dark side of the moon. Boulders cling precariously to mountain slopes, crashed to rubble below. There is no humanity here. Isolated army camps are the only signs of life. Miserable soldiers working on the road. A thin convoy of army trucks, like a row of straggling ants, strains toward the camps, overloaded.

Again and again we are forced off the disintegrating road into rutted mud, swerving between rocks and ditches, charging at streams, bumping so violently my eyes are knocked against my skull, each driver striking out on his own, churning up tracks, carving out an individual route to Golmud. The Chinese are investing millions to widen and asphalt the road – it is one of the few arteries into China – and after eleven years of work, it's still considered the worst ride on earth. Periodically the engine gives up. The driver is our salvation. He knows exactly what to do and eventually we lurch forward. I find it incredible that the trucks move at all. Some don't. They sit abandoned, sunk in a sea of freezing mud. At one point we pass though a herd of yak, grazing invisible grass. They don't move as we approach, but as the horn is sounded, look up with panicked eyes, and slowly disperse. Later we see drokpa tents made from yak-skins. A cold draught coming from the floor, makes me shiver. I remember someone telling me that during the summer months all drokpas sleep outdoors in yak-hair blankets, and that children up to the age of five go naked. I can't decide if this thought makes me warmer or colder.

Sometimes we find ourselves on paved road. It's like driving on satin. My internal organs reorganise, grunting their way back into place – until the next onslaught. Mohammed, the older, more experienced driver, navigates the treacherous parts. Jigme mainly helps, cranking the engine when we get stuck and passing tools, like an intern assisting at an operation. Although they are not related, Mohammed treats Jigme with the affection of a father, and Jigme is gentle with respect. Despite the strain of keeping the engine going and the truck moving, despite the agony of making repairs with numbed hands, they never become bad-tempered, are never sharp with each other, never lose their humorous view of things. Inside the cab a routine develops. Each time Mohammed spots a particularly wretched patch of road, he sighs a deep 'Ah-yah' like a vast lament and I sigh a wailing 'Ah-yah' in sympathetic response, followed closely by a bleating 'Ah-yah' from Jigme. We have occasion to sigh many 'Ah-yahs' together.

Eventually we climb through the mountains on to a high windy plateau, intensely cold, with fields of stone and rubble on either side of us, slashed like wounds. The mountains have receded to distant white peaks. Wild, empty, desolate. It begins to snow. The snow becomes a blizzard. Almost no visibility. Snow hurtling against the windscreen. In the back of the truck blasts of wind hurl snow through gaps in the badly fitting tarpaulin. Tim and Doune occupy a corner with holes in the tarp acting like funnels, blowing snow over them. They wear dust masks to protect their faces and stoically shelter their cameras. It becomes impossible to continue. At six o'clock we mercifully pull up at a truck stop, clouds of snow making it barely visible. Again the Tibetans remain in the truck, drinking thermos tea, chewing on yak meat, dried cheese and flat hard bread, uncomplaining. At least our departure gives them more room. Blinded by snow whipping into our faces, we run for cover, our clothing white.

We enter a sort of eating place, with wet floors and dirty tables. There's no food available except stale, slimy buns and tea, but at least it's warmer. We prepare our own food – more instant noodles. Ian fills his large thermos with hot water. Even in these nowhere places, there's always hot water. We limp-up the noodles, throw in a few damp onions and cold tomato sauce, and sing praises to our biscuits and hot life-saving tea. I try to write in my journal but soon give up. It's too dark, my hands are too cold, Doune's sleeping bag keeps slipping off my shoulders, and besides I'm too exhausted to write.

The amount of energy expended eating soggy noodles has done me in. It's not surprising. The altitude here is about 15,000 feet. The route from Lhasa to Xining encompasses altitudes up to 18,000 feet, and we've been riding high since leaving Lhasa. Tibet is the highest country in the world, and it feels it. Doune has been complaining of chest pains. I've been all right but thankful for not having to undertake anything more strenuous than breathing. Even that is exhausting. I remember someone saying, 'In Tibet everything is difficult, even breathing.' I close my journal. Tim says riding in the back of the truck is surreal. Everything is covered in snow. The Tibetans are bundled in yak-hair blankets, their eyes peering from sheepskins. The Westerners are huddled in high-tech fabrics, under new-age sleeping bags, their eyes peering from surgical masks. Twilight silhouettes, alien shapes, silent and still.

We have to be up at three am to leave at four am, so shortly after we've eaten, Ian announces bedtime. Our room has an earth floor and damp walls streaked with dirt. It smells of mould and is bitterly cold with wind blowing in from a broken window pane. There is no form of lighting. The five beds are crowded next to each other with no space to move. But we each have two quilts and the thought of being able to stretch our stiff, aching limbs is paradise.

Paradise, however, eludes me. I have to go to the loo. The others have returned to the truck for our bags – we weren't sure when we stopped if we were staying the night. I sit miserably on my cot, colder than I can ever remember, hating the prospect of finding the loo. The cold is like chill fingers, creeping relentlessly, reaching precisely into unreachable places, running up the nape of my neck, along the path to my armpit, the space under my knee, the inner seam between my thigh and torso. Nowhere is inviolate. But nature gives no reprieve.

Alone I head into the night. It has stopped snowing. The sky is clear. The moon lies against the snow in an immense silence. In the vastness of this wild open space I experience a superb sense of freedom, a sense of release from the confines of 'civilised' existence. It occurs to me how circumscribed, how insular that existence is and how high a price we pay for its coddled security. In the absolute coldness of pale moonlight the land has a formidable power. I understand why the world has left it alone for so long. To cross continents, to sail oceans, to climb earth's highest mountains only to find a vast silence of frozen peaks seemed an ordeal without reward. The land itself protected its people who alone loved its wild heights, its silences, who populated it with heavenly spirits, yogis, gods, filled it with miracle. And now somehow I am here, allowed to partake in that miracle. I pause for a moment in the snow and cold to give thanks.

At three am Ian's alarm shatters my brain and I drag myself from under warm covers into cold darkness. I'm wearing almost all the clothing I have: two T-shirts, long underwear, two pairs of trousers, three pairs of socks, a glittery Indian blouse, a long-sleeved tie-dye shirt, a sarong, a towel, my sheepskin poncho, a kerchief, my peacock shawl, and of course my Tibetan boots, but I'm so cold it's as though I'm naked.

After tea from the thermos and damp chilly biscuits, we head for the truck to take up our positions, me in the cab, the others climbing over Tibetans to find their slots. But alas, the truck won't start. It's too cold. Mohammed and Jigme crank the engine in turn, again and again and again, but it refuses to catch. I'm banished from the cab. The seat has to be removed to get at the tools. I jump up and down to keep warm but my fingers and toes soon become numb. A dismal dawn chisels through the night and in the grey light I feel even colder.

To keep from freezing to death, I walk through the yard where the trucks are parked, to the gate, and look down the road, beating my arms like a broken bird. It's so empty, so forbidding, that I run back to the truck, relieved to see that Mohammed and Jigme are still alive. More drivers appear. Frozen shadows cranking frozen engines. I watch Mohammed and Jigme cranking until they're exhausted and finally give up. There is nothing I can do except freeze. Mohammed returns to the truck and looks for something under the seat. It's a blow torch, the kind that works under pressure and gives off a hissing light. He gets it lit, I think to warm their hands. To my horror he places it under the hood, next to the engine, to heat it. I panic. I'm convinced we're going to explode, blow up in flames. In the first flush of panic I run away from the truck, then in a moment of guilt, rush back. I must tell the others. They're probably asleep. Should I wake them? By the time I decide to save their lives, the blow torch has disappeared. Other arrangements are under way. A truck comes to pull us. I'm invited back into the cab, wondering if burning to death is better than freezing. At least it's warmer. The engine starts. It's seven-thirty am, cloudy and very cold. A raven flies by, black against the snow. A new day on the road begins.

After two hours of driving we enter a small town with a bridge, its only distinctive feature. For us, having been deprived of human activity for so long, it seems like a hub, bustling with action. People move about with purpose, trucks honk their horns, men roll empty barrels into a yard stacked with full ones, yaks stream down the street, children, dressed in layers of rags, smile and wave. Best of all, Mohammed stops at a tea shop for a quick cup of tea and a chat with buddies. The shop serves yak butter tea, preferred by older Tibetans, and also sweet milky tea, which the younger ones like as well. We drink what is probably our last cup of Tibetan tea, hot and sweet and delicious.

As we drive along, the temperature becomes warmer. The sun slowly burns through the clouds and when we stop to adjust some flaw in the engine, the weather is almost pleasant. While Mohammed and Jigme tinker with the motor, we leap from the truck, unzipping jackets, pulling off hoods, removing masks, and treat ourselves to a leisurely photo session. We photograph the Tibetans smiling as they emerge from their huddle, and we photograph each other balancing on the edge of the truck. So far we've managed only a few brief photo sessions, wedged into pee stops.

Once, as I sat squatting in a field of rubble sprung with tufts of grass and stunted shrubs, a strange vision appeared over the horizon. Two powerful yaks slowly materialised, yoked together, their enormous curved horns meeting between them. They looked like twin Cinderellas dressed for the ball. Their shaggy matted heads were festooned with large red tassels and smaller black and white ones, their black long-haired backs adorned with red and white woollen squares. On their foreheads were red circles with raised white and black centres, like decorative third eyes. Even the thick ties which bound them together were festive, woven with intricate designs. The herdsman following behind wore a matching woolly red head band and a broad red sash. Quickly I pulled up my trousers and took a photo, as they plodded by me, huge and solemn, oblivious of their finery. Tibetans are dependent on yaks, 'the ships of the plateau', for all the essentials of life. They provide food, shelter, clothing and transportation; their dung is burned as fuel, even the ashes are used, spread on yak-hair buntings to keep babies dry. As such they are highly valued, respected, well-treated. I've seen many yaks rewarded with a tassel or pom-pom, which danced jauntily as they worked the fields. But I couldn't help thinking that these two yaks must have performed some wondrous deed to merit such splendid attire, or perhaps, as the lama in Sera explained, they were being recompensed for their fellows' slaughter.

After leaving the town, the countryside is pleasant, filled with grazing yaks and sheep. We pass a river. Then more detours. Stones, ditches, puddles of water, patches of ice, trucks limping and heaving, somehow making it back to the road. The last vertebra of my spine feels like it's been whittled away and I'm sitting on an exposed nerve. Soon we begin to climb through the Tanggula range, the mountains which separate the Tibetan Autonomous Region from Qinghai. Once again winter descends upon us. Snow and ice. Dramatic mountains and cliffs. Some cliff faces are eroded into deep red and yellow welts. In one place, the erosion has turned the cliffs and rocks into what look like Roman ruins, even the semblance of a Roman road rises high above. We drive through a narrow gorge, the high cliffs sheltering carvings of Egyptian-looking faces in various states of agony, sculpted by centuries of wind, snow and rain. In another place, strange brooding beings look down upon us from above dark caves. We pass glaciers which have been cut so sharply into the mountains, they leave a silver edge hanging in the sky. It begins to snow. We press on.

Flat tyre. Mohammed and Jigme repair it, taking the opportunity to tinker with the engine, while we freeze. They return to the cab in possession of two jars of preserved apples or pears; it's hard to tell which, they look and taste the same. Jigme opens one of the jars. Still holding a screwdriver thick with engine grease, he gives it a cursory wipe on a filthy rag, and spears a piece of fruit, first for Mohammed, then for himself. I'm eating last night's noodle mixture from a plastic container. Jigme offers me some fruit. I decline. Thinking I'm just being polite, and wanting to share the delicacy with me, he plops several pieces of fruit, pierced with grease, into my noodles and tomato sauce. I'm starving and eat the lot. If the rotten yak meat didn't do me in, I guess this won't either.

We come to the Tanggula Shankou pass, about 18,000 feet high, snowbound all year long. A blast of freezing wind whips through the pass as we enter Qinghai. Qinghai province, although taken over by China, is historically part of Tibet. Like Siberia, it is the dark land of labour camps where prisoners are never seen, never heard, exiled into a desolation of mountains and plateaus. It was closed to the rest of the world until 1980. We're not supposed to be seeing it now, or the men working on the roads, probably prisoners. Once through the pass we cross a stream which is the source of the Yangze, the third largest river in the world. There are several streams in the Qinghai plateau flowing from prehistoric glaciers, and almost every one is the source of one of the world's great rivers, like the Yangtze and the Mekong.

After a while the country flattens. It is no longer snowing. We continue over steppes, surrounded by rolling hills where only drokpa herdsmen live, their yak-hide tents set into the desolation. Then once again we come to a mountain range, the Kunlun mountains, and once again the scenery is spectacular. It begins to grow dark. At the foot of the Kunlun Shankou pass we see a wide stream with deer grazing nearby, ravens flying above them. The herd scatters into the twilight as we approach and the ravens disappear.

Once through the pass we begin the descent into the Quidam basin and into Golmud. It's early evening, still light. The road remains bad, but everything else changes. We haven't seen a tree in days. Our route has been a series of runs through long stretches of lifeless plateau relieved only by mountain passes. Now trees appear, thin, stunted, but still trees. I missed them. People appear as well, houses, small villages. The incredibly inhospitable, bleakest place on earth, becomes softer, warmer, as we descend from the plateau into the valley.

Not far outside Golmud we're stopped briefly at a checkpoint, which doesn't seem to do much checking, and we're waved on. We have passed several checkpoints along the way, but although we're not supposed to be here, a blind eye is turned. Our foreign presence is no disadvantage either to ourselves or to Mohammed. Once it is even used to advantage. All along the route, barriers are set up where all vehicles must leave the road to allow for repair work. Guards stand at the barriers to make sure no vehicle escapes. At several of these barriers, Mohammed recognises the guard and offers him a packet of cigarettes. Sometimes we're allowed through. Although the road is badly broken, it's preferable to the alternative. At one barrier, Mohammed is especially anxious. We can see trucks bogged down in a field of mud, desperately revving their engines, but only churning themselves deeper into ruts.

Mohammed stops the truck well before the barrier and performs an intriguing charade. Pressing his hands into his belly he grimaces painfully, doubling over in simulated agony. He repeats the charade pointing at me, then towards the barrier, until I understand what he wants. I'm to pretend a severe bellyache to help persuade the guard to let us through. He'll offer two packets of cigarettes as additional incentive. When we reach the guard, I go through my act so convincingly that Mohammed keeps the cigarettes. They guard takes one look at my tangled hair, twisted mouth and bizarre outfit and is convinced I'm having an attack of something. This foreign person needs all the help she can get. Graciously he waves us through. Actually a skin graft on my coccyx wouldn't go amiss.

At eight forty-five hearts filled with alleluias, we finally enter Golmud. Mohammed drives to a truckers' hostel. The man in charge examines our Western faces and says we can't stay. It's against the law to accept foreigners, although we've been accepted everywhere else. He suggests the tourist hotel. It seems peculiar that, despite Golmud being a closed city which doesn't allow tourists, there is a tourist hotel. Mohammed drops us at the hotel, saying he'll collect us at eleven o'clock tomorrow morning as he has repair work to do. The hotel is large, Russian looking, almost modern. With any luck we'll be able to shower. Best of all we don't have to get up at the crack of dawn. The luxury is overwhelming. Although tourists are not permitted in Golmud, we're asked to pay in FEC, tourist money. Tim breaks into his familiar Taiwanese-student-card-routine and emerges from it with two rooms at six RMB, local money, per person; one room for us and one for Ian and Jaye, who unlike us, are not studying in Taiwan.

'Good on you, Tim boy,' Ian says appreciatively and proceeds to make his own contribution to confronting bureaucracy by getting us beer after we've been assured that everything is closed. We must be back in China.

Our room is quite civilised, boasting a wash basin and an easy chair. The public shower is closed so we take turns at the basin. Golmud is lower than Lhasa and we've been returned to summer. It's a great relief to be warm and partially clean. I make a quick dinner for everyone, with boiled eggs supplementing the inevitable noodles, tinned fruit for dessert and beer for afters. Then we go in search of Texas Dave. We find him in his room in the midst of a mini-party, drinking beer and cracking nuts with several Westerners. Hugs all around. He tells us that train tickets to Xining are hard to come by and that we're lucky to have a ride there. We can't get any information about this ride except that it's about five hundred miles long. No one knows anyone who has done it by road. Not to worry. We're back in civilisation and feel our ordeal is over. But how wrong we are.

While the others are cracking nuts, exchanging notes, and

chatting, I slip back into our room to open Pascal's gift. It's the first moment I've had alone. The package contains a small blue box lined with red velvet. Lying in a groove against the velvet is an ancient silver Tibetan seal, and a tiny bristle brush with a silver handle, for cleaning it. I had spotted that seal in a stall one day when Pascal and I were in the Barkor and had looked at it for a long time, admiring the delicate carving of Tibetan symbols, the ornamental script the seal produced when stamped, and the shape of the seal, a small temple that fitted perfectly into my hand. I rarely yearn for something, feel I must have it. But I really wanted that seal. Alas, it was far too expensive. I couldn't afford it. However, whenever I was in the Barkor, I never failed to return to the stall. It gave me pleasure just to look at the seal and to hold it. The last day Doune and I were in the Barkor, I made a farewell pilgrimage to the seal. It was gone.

Tucked into the box is a note from Pascal:

To say farewell
Is to be sad
Be not sad, my love
For after every parting
Comes another meeting

Tsangyang Gyatso,
The Sixth Dalai Lama

The last thing I do before falling asleep is place the silver seal, together with the small brush, under my pillow. That night I dream with the angels.

Chapter Nineteen

Back in China

Next morning, Texas Dave, as the expert on Golmud (he's been here two days), takes us for breakfast in a scruffy market area with food stalls and small shops. We're excited by the soya milk, dumplings and fresh bread. The dusty streets are filled with a mixture of Muslims, Tibetans, Mongolians and Chinese. We don't have time to explore Golmud, but Texas Dave says we're not missing much. At eleven o'clock sharp we're in the hotel lobby waiting for Mohammed. He's not there. We wait. Hours go by. We take turns buying biscuits and raisins in a shop next door. I write in my journal. A yak standing in a yard behind the hotel observes me mournfully through the window. At one point we hear a rumpus and rush out to find the yak bleeding on the ground, slaughtered. Someone comes into the lobby waving his tail.

The incident inspires Ian to rent a bicycle and go off in search of our drivers. It's three o'clock. He returns at four, unsuccessful. At five o'clock he organises a hunt for the truck. I watch the bags. An hour later the search party brings the news that we're departing immediately. We say our goodbyes to Texas Dave and arrange to leave messages for each other in Beijing, where we'll all meet again. At six thirty Mohammed and Jigme arrive, smiling, and we slot into place. There's more room in the back as several people stayed in Golmud. As soon as I'm squeezed into the seat with its renegade springs poking tender bits, my backside erupts in pain, my tailbone screaming. It feels like I've never left this position. Sighing a chorus of 'Ah-yahs', we head for Xining.

It's daylight when we set out, but gradually the sun sinks into the horizon and it grows darker. Once again we climb onto a dry desert plateau, and once again its cold. I thought we had finished with the cold, but no such luck. At least the roads are good. Jigme drives, then Mohammed. They are both very tired. Jigme dozes off. Mohammed slaps his head to stay awake. I'm sleepy too, but daren't close my eyes. I must keep a close vigil on Mohammed, frightened he'll drowse. He opens the windows to revive himself and the wind hits out at me, whipping me wide awake. Finally at three-thirty am he gives up the struggle and pulls over. Mohammed's head collapses onto the steering wheel, Jigme puts his against the window. I have no place for mine.

Aching all over, resting my weight on one bum cheek to take the pressure off my tailbone, I pause to reflect, to see if I have any blessings to count. At least I feel unthreatened, in no danger. The last time I drove in a truck late at night, with men I didn't know, I was almost raped by the driver, a German, a man sharing my culture, my way of life. Now, pressed between Mohammed and Jigme, two strangers from a culture entirely foreign to me, there is no fear in my heart. I feel safe. They would never do me harm. I know them in a way I could not know the German. They are accessible to me, the German was not. I close my eyes counting one enormous blessing, a wondrous affinity, a shared humanity with these two strangers, and the pleasure in my soul outweighs the displeasure in my body.

Although I'm desperately sleepy, I can't sleep. Cold wind creeps through the floor. Wind forces its way through spaces where the windows don't fit. I'm wedged forward, immobilised under part of Mohammed's coat. Unable to sleep, I witness the moon grow fuller and brighter, asserting a final authority before it's obliterated by streaks of cold dawn. A mist rises from the land and the meeting point of sky and earth, just visible, is obliterated as well. I feel obliterated with them. At precisely six twenty-five – I know because I keep checking my watch – Mohammed wakes, his face drawn with exhaustion, and continues driving without the benefit of a single 'Ah-yah'. Around noon we stop in a small village tea house where Mohammed is on friendly terms with the owners. We drink Muslim tea and eat more biscuits and soggy noodles. On a wall of the tea house are two pictures, side by side, one of Mao Tse-tung, the other of the Dalai Lama, sticks of incense burning before both. 'An unholy matrimony,' Ian comments dryly. A family of Tibetans gather around us. The women have hair braided into elaborate hairdos, shining with large silver discs, coins, and strands of silk. Jewelled charm boxes hang from their necks. They are fascinated by our clothes, cameras and strange faces, but we're too tired to respond.

As we leave the tea house, Mohammed checks the sky and looks concerned. Up ahead are black angry clouds. His concern proves justified. Shortly after we begin driving, the heavens release a heavy shower of snow. Thick flakes blow into the back of the truck covering everyone with an unwelcome white blanket. We're plunged back into winter. The road continues straight and good but slippery with slush. We drive fast, making up for yesterday's delay. The relief of smooth rhythmic progression without tensing to meet jolts or cringing to avert catastrophe, releases my mind for easier considerations.

I begin by considering Mao Tse-tung and the Dalai Lama, not as unholy a matrimony as it first appears. These two men not only respected each other, but a genuine fondness existed between them. Mao admitted to the Dalai Lama, when they first met in 1954, that although religion was poison, Buddhism was different. He considered it a good religion because of the Buddha's deep concern for the common people and his desire to improve their conditions, even though he began life as a prince. And the Dalai Lama believed that there was an affinity between Marxism and Buddhism because they shared ideals, for example that of an egalitarian society, and therefore they could be integrated and work together. The Dalai Lama, not quite twenty at the time, found Mao to be sincere, honourable and kind, and was convinced that Mao himself would not use force to convert Tibet to Communism. Even much later, when the Chinese policies of oppression and persecution were in full swing, he believed that these policies could not have had Mao's approval. He was right. Mao had severely condemned the mistakes being made in Tibet.

My train of thought is suddenly shattered by a violent swerving of the truck. Mohammed flinches and for a moment pulls back from the wheel. He has seen a truck approaching and moves over to give it passing room. Applying the brakes to slow down, he turns the wheel, but instead of a gentle tapering, the truck skids so abruptly that Mohammed loses control. We're wrenched in the opposite direction, on the same side as the advancing vehicle, face-to-face, positioned for a head-on collision. Mohammed swerves, just missing the oncoming truck, and our truck reels insanely from side to side – bashing me against Jigme, then Mohammed, then Jigme – slithering sideways up the road and then lurching toward the edge. Mohammed pulls the steering wheel from right to left in a desperate attempt to regain control and straighten the wheels, but the truck behaves like a panicked animal and plunges over the edge, landing with a tremendous jolt. It tilts sharply and for a split second balances on two wheels, hovering between toppling over and righting itself. Luckily it chooses the latter. We've fallen about three feet into a barren field.

For a moment there is no movement, only stricken silence. Then Mohammed and Jigme leap from the front of the truck, just as the others jump from the back. I lower myself slowly from the cab surprised to be intact, and find that my hand is clutching the mani stone. We're all badly shaken, but by some major miracle no one is injured except for Jaye, who was slightly hurt by a petrol barrel almost tipping onto her. We're thankful to be alive. It could have happened on a road with sheer drops, or on one cut into rock walls, or there might have been other traffic. As soon as the Tibetans discover we are all unharmed, they begin to laugh. We are contemplating the near disaster and regard them with utter dismay. But they continue to laugh with such mirth, that although this isn't exactly our kind of joke, we find ourselves joining in. We laugh as well, probably with relief. In my mind, an irrelevant thought persists – at least I'll get to read Tashi's story.

Mohammed inspects the truck for damage. There is none. With spirits lifted by the sheer joy of survival, we begin a pushing and shoving session, moving the truck to where the incline is minimal, and heaving it onto the road. The engine starts up. Once in the cab, Mohammed smiles, sighs some serious 'Ah-yahs', and we take off, driving much slower, reluctant to press our luck.

After a few hours of driving we come to Lake Koko Nor, a long beautiful lake set against snow mountains, white ice gripping its turquoise waters, the still water mirroring a still sky. The photographers among us assess the view lovingly through camera lenses. Unexpectedly Mohammed pulls up beside the lake and we burst from the truck, the serious photographers looking for vantage points for photographs, even before looking for vantage points for bladder relief. Mohammed and Jigme disappear down the road and return with several friends and a bucket of fish. Like fishermen proud of their catch, they hold the fish to be photographed.

We follow the shore of the lake for about sixty two miles. Lake Koko Nor ('the Blue Lake') is about seventy-five miles from Takster, the village where Tenzin Gyatso, the Fourteenth Dalai Lama was born, although we can't find it on the detailed Chinese map Ian has; nor can we find Kumbum, the monastery town nearby. As we pass so close to his home, I feel a deep sadness twisting through my thoughts. I recall the Dalai Lama's deserted rooms in the Potala, his empty jade teacup with the gold lid, his people lost without their spiritual leader, bereft of their protector. For them the Dalai Lama is more than a ruler, he is a living Buddha, a deity on earth. When they pray to him it is as though they were praying to Chenrezig, Lord of Compassion, who the Buddha himself sent as his manifest form, to protect Tibet. Because the Dalai Lama is Chenrezig's incarnation, he is the Lord of Compassion, Patron Divinity of the Land, Protector of Tibet. Tibetans regard him with supreme reverence, just as they have always regarded Chenrezig, just as they regard the Lord Buddha. Because the Dalai Lama has a sacred duty to protect his people and his land, Tibetans could always rely upon him implicitly. The people and their king were closely bound to one another. In a life that was often unjust, they could appeal to the Dalai Lama as their ultimate source of justice. His very presence was beneficial, a blessing without which the country could never prosper. Now that blessing is no more. The Dalai Lama, so vital to the life of his people, is exiled from them. He cannot minister to the pain of his country.

Only two hours from Xining, a diversion forces us off the road. We should have reached Xining about four thirty, but the diversion is dreadful. Once more we climb mountains up into winter, with landscape much like the other side of Golmud: barren mountain walls, high peaks, ice and snow. We drive along steep cliffs on narrow trails hanging from their edges, like the mountain pass near Nagarze; only the road here is worse and our truck less nimble than the jeep. We cross streams, ditches, excruciating terrain. I'm on the edge of my seat, so nervous since the accident, that I'm unaware of my coccyx.

Jigme is driving. We are going down a steep incline with a

truck stopped ahead trying to negotiate a fast-moving stream, when, for some inexplicable reason, we don't slow down but continue advancing on the truck. I see it happening but don't believe it. Besides, what can I do? Mohammed is dozing but wakes suddenly, frantically pulling the emergency brake just as we smash into the truck. Although we weren't going fast, the impact is staggering. Mohammed examines the engine and utters a heart-rending 'Ah-yah', without a trace of comic relief. Both the radiator and the fan belt are badly damaged, the headlights crushed and the frame severely dented. He attempts to patch up the engine, but I know by the look of desolation on his face, when we finally return to the cab, that it's very bad news. Despite the damage we take off. Mohammed says nothing to Jigme, but I can tell he's angry by the dark obsessive manner and the frenzied speed with which he drives, as though the road is an enemy he wants to eliminate. Jigme doesn't utter a sound. I'm terrified. We hurtle down the mountains at breakneck speed, bad roads, hairpin bends and all. Perhaps I won't get to read Tashi's story after all. I wasn't this scared even in the jeep. Finally it's over. We're safe in the embrace of a green valley. It's summertime and the roads are easy.

After endless stops to replenish the steaming radiator, we reach Xining at seven-thirty and limp into town. Poor Mohammed, his fury spent, he smiles weakly, apologetically, as though asking forgiveness, not only from me, but also from Jigme. Now that our ordeal is over, I forgive him entirely. Poor bugger, his truck is so badly damaged, the cost of repairs will probably exceed any profit. He shrugs philosophically and insists on driving us to a hotel even though the truck stop is before the town centre and the Tibetans get off there.

At the hotel we say goodbye and force several packets of cigarettes on Mohammed and Jigme, who accept them reluctantly, probably feeling they shouldn't be rewarded for almost killing us. We shake hands and embrace and take a last look at the truck which has seen us through some pretty harrowing times. Mohammed's final 'Ay-yah' is a huge exhalation of warmth and affection. As I watch them climb into the cab, the familiarity of their movements creates in me a responsive surge of affection. The truck pulls away without us

We get two rooms for four and a half RMB, without any FEC argument. No wash basin, but there are showers down the hall. They aren't clean, only one works, but the water is steamy hot. Doune and I share the cubicle with several modest Chinese girls who shower in their underwear. The hot water is exquisite. My long-suffering body sucks in the warmth like the balm of Giliad that makes the wounded whole. Fields fragrant with spring flowers can't rival the perfume of my bargain basement shampoo. I inhale deeply, ecstatically, as the suds turn black with dirt and a stream of filth pours onto the floor, much to the dismay of the Chinese girls. I sing songs of praise as I scrub every nook and cranny pristine clean, feeling the tension, strain, aches and pains, dissolve into unmitigated pleasure. The hardships of the road, even the brush with death were well worth this glorious finale.

As I close my eyes that night I remember that the Dalai Lama travelled over three months to make the expedition we completed in five days. He, however, was entering Lhasa, beginning his journey; whereas we have just left Tibet, ending ours. But if the external journey is over, I know the inner one is not. Tibet has become part of my consciousness. In Tibet I have discovered a radiance which before had been darkness. I fall asleep knowing that Tibet has filled my heaven with new stars. A gentle conclusion to a fierce day.

Our hotel is close to the railway station and next morning we go there to arrange tickets for Xian. We're treated to a special foreigners' queue. Our fraudulent student cards work wonders and we're able to get a 'soft class' sleeper for nearly the same price Ian and Jaye pay for berths in a 'hard class' one. The train leaves in a few hours and arrives in Xian early the following afternoon. Walking to the station I had noticed a man in the doorway of a tiny shop, hammering jewellery, his walls hung with necklaces, earrings, beads and strands of wool and silk. A strand of purple caught my eye. On an impulse, returning to the hotel, I enter the shop. Producing my mani stone, I indicate I want a hole made in it, and wait as the man carefully drills the hole and threads it with the strand of purple silk I choose. I place the mani stone around my neck, under my clothes and leave the shop with Tashi's amulet, a Tibetan benediction, lying against my heart.

Since arriving in Golmud, we've been in a limbo between Tibet and China. But when we return to the station with our bags, the fact that we're back in China is undeniably confirmed. The staring is so intense, so unnerving, that we're ushered into a special waiting room by a guard. My fingers circle the mani stone, like a Greek worry-bead, and I feel calmed.

The 'soft-class' sleeper sleeps four, but the Chinese man assigned to share it with us, hears our voices, peeps in and never reappears. The compartment is unbelievable: lace-trimmed sheets, embroidered frilly pillowcases, a white linen table-cloth, porcelain teacups, hot water in a spouted hot-pot, shelves, reading lights, a lamp, a mirror, even hangers. The door closes to shut everyone out and we enjoy our privacy in spotless luxury, a luxury made even more divine by juxtaposition with our recent mode of transport. Our dining car serves Western food, and as soon as we're settled, the cook himself comes to discuss the menu, fortified by his own personal phrase book containing an elaborate food section. By the time we reach Xian I'm a 'soft-sleeper' addict.

The impact of the Remin Daxia Hotel is even more spectacular. We drive through its gates and enter a palace. The grounds are set with fountains, small bridges, garden walks, the driveway lined with trees and flowers, the buildings elegant with domes and turrets. With money saved from the truck ride, we indulge in yet greater luxury. Tim, Doune and I get an air-conditioned suite. It has a large sitting room furnished with sofas, easy chairs, a coffee table, desk, even a combined television and liquor cabinet. The bedroom is enormous with a walk-in closet and an adjoining tiled bathroom bigger than my room in Lhasa. Our windows face the fountains and gardens. It's as though we've struck gold.

Although my first impulse upon entering the Remin Daxia is to rush to the reception desk and ask for mail, I refrain. I feel too unsettled, too excited by events and impressions. I need a moment to catch my breath. It's like coming to a poetry reading breathless from running. You can't hear the poetry because of the blood pounding in your ears. I must be stilled, tranquil. All through Tibet, travelling in his landscape, Tashi was very much with me. But now, in this foreign place, I must pause a while. It's like being the medium for my own séance. I must be in harmony with myself before I can hear his voice.

The next afternoon I'm handed a large envelope addressed in a poignantly familiar script. I take it into the garden, by the fountain, near the pool. Walking slowly, I press the mani stone, imprinting its inscription like a Tibetan seal. For a moment I watch a bird bathing. Beads of water gather on its feathers, sparkling like tiny jewels against the perfect white. Slowly they join together in a rainbow of light. The bird dips its wing, the rainbow spreads into the pool and is gone. 'A thing of beauty that disappears even as it comes into being.' I open the envelope and read.

Chapter Twenty

The Brothers – A Tibetan Tale

Once long ago, in the land of snows, where the hills turn to the east, there lived two brothers: the older one a young man of twenty winters and the younger, a boy of ten summers. These brothers lived alone in a humble cottage, their parents having died of a terrible illness which befell their part of the country when the younger brother was born. And so it was left to the older brother to raise the younger and he tended him with great love. The younger brother received the love and returned it with great veneration, for his brother was the source of his sustenance, being not only his mother and father, but also his teacher and protector.

From the time they could remember, each brother held a great wish in his heart, and every morning and every evening and many times in between, they prayed, reciting mantras and chants, moving the worn beads of their rosaries through their fingers, each asking the deities to grant him his wish. The older brother prayed to become a healer so that he could save his countrymen from illness and disaster such as had befallen his mother and father, for he never forgot the suffering. The younger brother prayed to become a storyteller for he spent long hours listening to the travelling bards, the lama manis, telling tales full of wonderment and magic, and singing epic verses about gods, fierce demons and flying steeds, tales with special power, gained over the long years of telling. The tales of his land and his people and of the lives of the great holy men stirred his imagination with adventure and romance and made him proud. A great longing arose in his heart to learn these tales so that he could tell them to his brother during the long dark nights, and perhaps, if he learned them well, to the people throughout the land. But he knew that to become a storyteller he must have much knowledge and much skill.

It came to pass that a famous lama arrived in the village near the place where the brothers lived. 'I will go to the wise lama and ask to speak with him,' the older brother said. 'I will tell him of our wishes, and perhaps, in his wisdom, he will know how to help us.' So saying he went into the village and asked permission to see the lama. Although there were many people waiting to receive the lama's blessing, his wish was granted.

After he paid homage to the lama by offering an auspicious greeting scarf, the whitest and longest khata he could find, and prostrating at his feet, he spoke thus: 'I would like to become a healer so that I can help all living beings and heal the people of my land, and my younger brother wishes to become a storyteller and learn our great tales so that he may tell them to the people throughout the kingdom and bring them knowledge and joy. What shall we do?

The lama saw that the older brother's heart was sincere and that his motives were of the purest, and so he said to him: 'You and your brother must journey to the centre of learning in the great and holy city. There you will both learn the knowledge to complete your tasks from the wise and holy men who reside there. When you reach the sacred city, you must make a pilgrimage to the palace where the greatest lama resides and ask his blessings for your endeavours.'

Having said this, the lama took from his bag a small stone of an almost ice blue colour which had the characters of a prayer carved into it. The lama blessed the stone and then gave it to the brother saying, 'Receive this mani stone with my blessings. Your journey is a long and hazardous one and many have failed to complete it, but if you hold the mani stone in your hand and think upon it, it will keep you from fear and give you strength.' The older brother received the stone with deep gratitude, for it was a sign of the lama's love and compassion and his wish to help them.

And so, after sewing the mani stone into the sleeve of his chuba and stringing cubes of dried cheese into a loop for chewing, the older brother filled two travelling bags with provisions, took the younger brother by the hand, and together they set off to the holy city. The journey was indeed a difficult and hazardous one. They walked for many days and many months through harsh and desolate lands ruled by strange spirits, through rocky wilderness and barren plains. They crossed swirling rivers and were discouraged by the looming fierceness of the mountains as they struggled up their slopes. Often they were frozen with cold and starved with hunger for they had little to wear and their provisions soon ran out. They were forced to live on wild berries and sometimes a little hard cheese or roasted barley begged from the few travellers they chanced to meet. Often they thought they could go on no longer, so weary did they become and so many were their trials. But they held the mani stone and thought upon it and chanted the holy sounds of its prayer and they received the strength to continue.

Before they could reach the holy city they had to pass through the valley of the solitudes, a silent valley where many demons dwelt among the bleak rocks and danced silently upon the stony wastes. The ghostly glow of the moon chilled their hearts with fear, for they knew that few ever left the valley of the solitudes. Upon entering the valley, each brother, in turn, took hold of the small ice blue stone given to them by the lama and held it, thinking upon it, feeling its power and sending their prayer to its deity, and then they were no longer afraid. And with their fears thrown from them, they passed through the valley, unharmed.

Always the thought of the great palace moved them forward and the mani stone eased their fears and gave them strength, for in it was the lama's love and the deity's protection. And so they climbed and walked and stumbled, with prayers on their lips and courage in their souls. When they first saw the golden spires of the great palace in the far distance their hearts stopped in awe and reverence and their pace quickened. Thus they reached the holy city, and when at last they beheld its gate, they fell to their knees in prayers of thankfulness, for their hearts had been filled with deep longing to reach this city and were brimming with happiness to enter its great gate. When they had prostrated three times, and given thanks to the deities who had guided them on their journey and brought them safely into the holy city, they asked a beggar how they could find the great palace. The beggar pointed upwards to the heavens, and there in the sky, shining more purely than in any of their dreams, rose the palace. They gasped in wonderment.

They reached the palace with ease, for the palace itself seemed to lead them to its walls, beckoning to them like a blessing. However, since night was falling they thought it wise to wait until morning before seeking entrance. They made camp for the night on a hill close to the palace, finding shelter beside a rock, and lay down to rest with joy and contentment in their hearts.

But suddenly in the night their contentment was broken by a fierce storm such as they had never known. The sky became dark and angry, the winds howled and bent the trees to the earth, bolts of thunder crashed with a mighty roar and in the flashes of white light they could see the trees and the rocks trembling with fear and feel the earth shake beneath their feet. 'We must go to the palace and seek shelter,' said the older brother, 'for surely this storm shall destroy us.' They began running to the palace, the black sky fierce with white light, the earth rumbling and roaring until the mountains became loose and huge rocks crashed down from above.

But as they ran, hand in hand, the earth seemed to slide apart and the younger brother was wrenched from the older brother and swallowed by its force. He tried to shout for help but his mouth was frozen and could not form the words. Finally his mouth opened in a piercing scream that took moments to tear itself from his being. The older brother heard his scream but could not reach him. Earth and rocks hurtled from the mountains, falling in the dark hole where the younger brother was struggling. He tried again and again to climb the walls of the hole but was pushed back by the earth and rocks piling over him until he was weary with the struggle. He grew full of despair, gasping and choking as the earth filled his nostrils, driving the breath from him, until only a feeble whisper came from his lips.

With a sudden energy, the older brother jumped into the deep crevice and lifting the younger brother onto his shoulders, pushed him to safety. The rocks and earth tumbled into the hole with such speed and such force that the older brother could not fight them. Filled with terror, the younger brother stood helpless as the earth swallowed his brother who had saved him from that very fate. But before the hole was sealed and the darkness descended upon him, never to be relieved by dawn, the older brother shouted, 'Go to the palace and wait for me there, for the chaos will surely subside and one day I will come to you.' When the younger brother remained motionless, unable to move, he shouted again, 'Go now, go at once, go with my love.' Then there was a great flash of light and in the white light the younger brother ran to the palace, obeying the wishes of his older brother. But even as he ran, he could feel that his heart was truly broken.

When the holy men who dwelt in the palace heard what had befallen the younger brother, and beheld his sorrow, they were consumed with pity and asked him to remain among them and live in the palace. But although the younger brother was aware of the great honour bestowed upon him, and although the holy men in their compassion did their best to please him, and although he was blessed by the highest lama in his private chambers and served tea from the jade teacup, his heart could not be eased. His sorrow grew and multiplied, the weight of unhappiness fell heavy on his shoulders, for his brother, whom he deeply loved and who was all things to him, was now gone.

Sorrow sapped his strength and fear weakened his body. He never departed from the palace walls, for the fear of falling into the earth and being engulfed by it never left him, not by night and not by day. Visions of the earth and the rocks burying first himself and then his brother, invaded his sleep and woke him with sudden anguish, and when he was awake he pined for his brother and grieved for his loss.

The holy men grew worried and knew they had to help the younger brother for surely he would die with the sadness and the grief. They consulted healer upon healer, but no healer had the knowledge of a cure. Then word came that a young healer with special powers had appeared in the land and that this healer was seeking permission to see the younger brother for he had secret knowledge which could relieve him of his suffering. Immediately a messenger was sent to bring the healer to the palace.

When he arrived the younger brother was brought before him. The healer laid his hand on the younger brother in the place between his shoulders and felt the grief knotted in his flesh. Then he gazed deep into the eyes of the younger brother and saw the place where the fear lay hidden. When the younger brother felt the healer's touch and looked into his eyes, he was sure he could recognise something. Suddenly he felt a powerful stream of love enter his being and his heart grew light with love, the terrible fear was driven out, banished from his heart and with it the sadness and the suffering. His being was filled with great bliss. Then the healer took from the sleeve of his chuba a stone of an almost ice blue colour, which had the characters of a prayer inscribed upon it. 'Think upon this stone.' He said, 'and love will be with you and your fear shall never return.' So saying, he placed the stone in the younger brother's hands and departed from the palace.

The healer wandered far and wide, healing the people of his land, and the younger brother, the mani stone always on his heart, became famous as a storyteller. People from near and from far came to hear him tell tales and they received knowledge and joy. Although the two brothers lived in different parts of the kingdom, they remained united because their spirits were as one, for there was much love between them and there was much love for their land.

The older brother's name was Tashi, the younger brother was called Nyima.

Epilogue

The compulsion I had to visit Tibet did not diminish after I had been there. On the contrary, it seemed to increase. It was like discovering a new love; I was constantly preoccupied with thoughts of Tibet, thoughts of the people I had met there, thoughts of going back. I knew I had to return, and made plans to do so as soon as I could save the money. But alas, that was not to be.

October 7, 1987, marked the thirty-seventh anniversary of the Chinese invasion of Tibet. In anticipation of that date, Tibetans began a series of pro-independence demonstrations. The Dalai Lama had called for protests against Chinese rule to be conducted 'in a peaceful manner', and this is what the demonstrators set out to do. On September 27, twenty Tibetan monks, together with about three hundred ordinary citizens, began a peaceful demonstration in support of their exiled spiritual leader. Carrying the Tibetan flag, they circled the sacred Jokhang temple, chanting independence slogans. All the monks and about fifty other demonstrators were immediately arrested.

On October 1, 1987, a crowd of several thousand unarmed Tibetans carrying flags and chanting slogans, gathered to protest against the arrest of the monks and to call for greater political and religious freedom. Police fired into the crowd, killing and wounding at random. Angry and frustrated, a group of monks set fire to the police station, determined to rescue those arrested. A group of eighty novice monks coming from the Drepung monastery on their way to Lhasa, also to demand the release of the arrested lamas, were surrounded by hundreds of police in combat gear, brutally beaten and taken away in trucks.

Several days of bloody street fighting and rioting began, especially around the Jokhang temple. The Chinese government airlifted hundreds of armed police into Lhasa. There were killings, beatings and mass arrests. Police moved in to occupy the Jokhang, while heavily armed security forces patrolled the streets. Monasteries were sealed off. A cordon of roadblocks was thrown around the city and a curfew enforced.

There were about one hundred and seventy foreigners in Lhasa at the time, of whom twenty were journalists. They found themselves caught up in the bloodshed: treating Tibetans with bullet wounds, who were either afraid to go to hospital or who had been refused treatment; providing eye-witness accounts; and collating reports of shootings and arrests. It was through them that the world learned the truth about the events in Lhasa. As a result, all foreigners were expelled and no foreigner allowed to enter Tibet. My plan to return there was now impossible.

More unrest and demonstrations followed the October '87 riots, resulting in more arrests, killings and torture. But gradually, over a period of time, a strictly controlled trickle of foreigners was allowed back into Tibet. Such was my desire to return there, that I began to explore the possibility of becoming one of them.

On March 5, 1989, 20,000 unarmed Tibetans demonstrated in the Jokhang Square to commemorate the thirtieth anniversary of the Lhasa uprising against the Chinese invasion. Again tourists, although this time very few in number, provided eye-witness accounts. Chinese police savagely beat Tibetans in the street, then began firing into the crowd. But despite bullets and teargas, they were unable to clear the square. Groups of young Tibetans, hurling stones and chanting pro-democracy slogans, kept returning to the square, challenging the soldiers who were armed with sub-machine guns. Many of them were beaten to death or shot, thousands were arrested. Rioting spread throughout the Tibetan quarter and police engaged in widespread shooting, following a shoot-to-kill policy. Scores of trucks entered the area carrying troops armed with pistols, rifles and sub-machine guns. They shot wildly at rooftops and into Tibetan homes, spraying bursts of automatic gunfire indiscriminately – a security force out of control. Two days of horrifying violence followed – the worst since the cultural revolution over twenty years earlier.

In a fury of revenge, Tibetans retaliated by stoning innocent Chinese, raiding their shops and burning their belongings. The Dalai Lama pleaded throughout for an end to the violence, and said in a statement: 'I have always tried to find a peaceful solution to the tragic situation in my country.'

On March 7, the Chinese declared martial law. Thousands of armed troops entered the Tibetan quarters. By evening the entire city was ringed with troops. Truckloads of soldiers, armed with Kalashnikovs patrolled the streets, headlights blazing. Everyone had to carry identification at all times, and all meetings, petitions and public gatherings were banned. Once again foreigners were expelled. Lhasa became a garrison town.

The riots of 1987 and 1989 made two things dramatically clear: firstly, that despite almost forty years of Chinese rule, Tibetan nationalism was an active, living force; secondly, that the discontent wasn't the work of a small group of troublemakers, as the Chinese claimed, but a mass response to their policy of brutality and denial. Tibetans view the Chinese as not merely wishing to conquer them, but as wishing to annihilate them.

If there was any doubt that the Chinese were capable of carrying out acts of terrible brutality in Tibet, and were impervious to human rights considerations there, the handling of the pro-democracy demonstrations in Tiananmen Square is convincing evidence. Until then the Chinese had enjoyed the privilege of unofficial immunity from international accountability for their human rights abuses. However, if the Chinese were able to display such brutality towards their own people before international television cameras, what horrors were they capable of perpetuating in the privacy afforded them by martial law, towards a people whom, in any case, they considered backward, barbarous and badly in need of Chinese civilising?

But although I was unable to return to Tibet, I was granted a massive compensation. I discovered that the Dalai Lama was coming to England in April 1988, and that I would be able to see him. This was wonderful news. All through my time in Tibet, I was fascinated by the Dalai Lama. He was a mystery, a phenomenon, who constantly occupied my thoughts. Although exiled in India, he was present everywhere in Tibet. His presence was more real, more alive than if he had actually been there. Tibetans lived and breathed the Dalai Lama. The mere mention of his name evoked in them a great reverence, an adoration, a visible bliss. I could think of no other leader who was so personally, so unequivocally loved. But experiencing first-hand the response he elicited from Tibetans still did not prepare me for the impact he was to have on me.

The Dalai Lama's teaching was held in Westminster Central Hall, a large formal venue, with a stage distancing those seated in ascending rows from those seated on the platform below. But when the Dalai Lama stepped onto that stage, the separation vanished, the formality was suddenly transformed into intimacy. The Dalai Lama's manner was so easy, so unassuming, so warm, that it felt as though everyone had disappeared and he was talking just to me.

The British government, bowing to Chinese pressure, had forbidden him to discuss anything political (and would not formally receive him), but what he did discuss was almost irrelevant. The Dalai Lama himself was his most powerful message. He projected an almost visible personal purity, compounded by simplicity and humility. He himself was compassion and love – the pillars of his Buddhist beliefs. He himself was the serenity and peace he wished for all mankind. I could almost touch it, hold it. And I felt in the presence of a great spirit, a truly special being, the jewel in the heart of the lotus.

But if he projected a sense of divinity – and there was no doubt that he did – he was also profoundly human. When he spoke he moved from English, to Tibetan, and back to English almost without effort, laughing easily, infectiously, speaking with his hands, his body, his heart, often laughing at himself in bursts of humour. He smiled a great deal, wonderful wide smiles, and even when he wasn't smiling I could sense a smile waiting to explode.

It seemed incredible to me that this man, who was forced to flee his country and live in exile, who was forced to witness the terrible cruelties inflicted on his people, impotent to help them, could still radiate such gentleness, such humanity, such joy. Meeting him was not only a great privilege but, for me, an especially significant one. Although I hadn't been able to go to Tibet, Tibet had been able to come to me. Once again I was touching Tibet.

A leaflet given to everyone at the gathering began with a 'Tibetan Prayer for the Long Life of His Holiness the Dalai Lama'. I left the hall with the wish that the wind horse would carry that prayer into the universe:

'In the Heavenly Realm of Tibet
(surrounded by a chain of snow mountains)

The source of all Happiness and Help for beings
Is Tenzin Gyatso – Chenrezig in person.'

And to that prayer I added my blessings for the people of Tibet: that they may be reunited with their spiritual leader and live in peace and happiness. And the Dalai Lama's own prayer:

'I pray for a more friendly
More caring, and more understanding
Human family on this planet.'

Om Mani Padme Hum.

Future titles by the author

Travels With My Daughter

Niema Ash

A word from the author:
One of the inspirations behind "Travels with My Daughter" was the desire to show that motherhood need not be the end to travel and adventure.
The central journey of the book is a trip to Morocco with my daughter, however, I wanted to include the formative experiences which shaped my desire for adventure. The foremost of these experiences was my involvement with the music scene, which led to my coming to know such talented poets and musicians as Bob Dylan, Leonard Cohen, Irving Layton and Seamus Heaney. Being exposed to such exceptional people developed in me a thirst for the exceptional, a thirst which eventually found fulfilment in the wonder of travel.
I wanted "Travels With My Daughter" to be not only an insight into Morocco, not only a celebration of travel and motherhood but an inspiration for all travellers.
"Whatever you can do, or dream you can do – begin it. For boldness has power and magic and genius in it." (Goethe)

Publication date: October 2000

Other titles from TravellersEye

Discoveries

The Jungle Beat – fighting terrorists in Malaya

Author		Roy Follows
Editor		Dan Hiscocks
ISBN:	0 953 0575 77	R.R.P £7.99

This book describes, in his own words, the experiences of a British officer in the Malayan Police during the extended Emergency of the 1950's. It is the story of a ruthless battle for survival against an environment and an enemy which were equally deadly, and it ranks with the toughest and grimmest of the latter-day SAS adventures.

Fever Trees of Borneo

Author		Mark Eveleigh
Editor		Gordon Medcalf
ISBN:	0 953 0575 69	R.R.P £7.99

This is the story of how two Englishmen crossed the remotest heights of central Borneo, using trails no western eye had seen before, to visit Borneo's last remaining independent jungle dwellers. On the way they encounter shipwreck, malaria, amoebic dysentery, near starvation, leeches, exhaustion, enforced alcohol abuse, barbecued mouse-deer foetusn and a ferocious craving for chocolate!

"Mark has the kind of itchy feet which will take more than a bucket of Johnson's baby talc to cure... he has not only stared death in the face, he has poked him in the ribs and insulted his mother."

The Independent

Dreams

Discovery Road

Authors		Tim Garratt & Andy Brown
Editor		Dan Hiscocks
ISBN:	0953 0575 34	R.R.P £7.99

Their mission and dream was to cycle around the southern hemisphere of the planet, with just two conditions. Firstly the journey must be completed within 12 months, and secondly, the cycling duo would have no support team or backup vehicle, just their determination, friendship and pedal power.

Frigid Women

Authors		Sue & Victoria Riches
Editor		Gordon Medcalf
ISBN	0953 0575 26	R.R.P £7.99

In 1997 a group of twenty women set out to become the world's first all female expedition to the North Pole. Mother and daughter, Sue and Victoria Riches were amongst them. Follow the expedition's adventures in this true life epic of their struggle to reach one of Earth's most inhospitable places, suffering both physical and mental hardships in order to reach their goal, to make their dream come true.

Heaven & Hell

An eclectic collection of anecdotal travel stories – the best from thousands of competition entries.

Traveller's Tales from Heaven & Hell

Author		Various
Editor		Dan Hiscocks
ISBN:	0 953 0575 18	R.R.P £6.99

More Traveller's Tales from Heaven & Hell

Author		Various
Editor		Dan Hiscocks
ISBN:	1 903070 023	R.R.P £6.99

"...an inspirational experience. I couldn't wait to leave the country and encounter the next inevitable disaster." The Independent.

A Trail of Visions

Guide books tell you where to go, what to do and how to do it. A Trail of Visions shows and tells you how it feels.

Route 1: India, Sri Lanka, Thailand, Sumatra

Photographer & Author		Vicki Couchman
Editor		Dan Hiscocks
ISBN:	1 871349 338	R.R.P £14.99

"A Trail of Visions tells with clarity what it is like to follow a trail, both the places you see and the people you meet."
Independent on Sunday

Route 2: Peru, Bolivia, Ecuador, Columbia

Photographer & Author		Vicki Couchman
Editor		Dan Hiscocks
ISBN	0 935 0575 0X	R.R.P £16.99

"The illustrated guide." The Times

TravellersEye Club Membership

Each month we receive hundreds of enquiries from people who've read our books or entered our competitions. All of these people have one thing in common: an aching to achieve something extraordinary, outside the bounds of our everyday lives. Not everyone can undertake the more extreme challenges, but we all value learning about other people's experiences.

Membership is free because we want to unite people of similar interests. Via our website, members will be able to liase with each other about everything from the kit they've taken, to the places they've been to and the things they've done. Our authors will also be available to answer any of your questions if you're planning a trip or if you simply have a question about their books.

As well as regularly up-dating members with news about our forthcoming titles, we will also offer you the following benefits:

Free entry to author talks / signings
Direct author correspondence
Discounts off new & past titles
Free entry to TravellersEye events
Discounts on a variety of travel products & services

To register your membership, simply write or e-mail us, telling us your name and address (postal and e-mail).

TravellersEye Ltd
30 St Mary's Street
Bridgnorth
Shropshire
WV16 4DW
Tel: (01746) 766447
Fax: (01746) 766665
website: www.travellerseye.com
email: books@travellerseye.com